FUNDING RELIGIOUS HERITAGE

The views expressed during the execution of the RELIGARE project, in whatever form and or by whatever medium, are the sole responsibility of the authors. The European Union is not liable for any use that may be made of the information contained therein.

Cultural Diversity and Law in Association with RELIGARE

Series Editor: Prakash Shah, Queen Mary, University of London, UK

RELIGARE was a project on Religious Diversity and Secular Models in Europe funded by the European Commission under the Seventh Framework Programme. The project brought together an interdisciplinary team of high profile researchers and 13 academic institutions to collaborate on examining how existing policy and practice is suited to the demands of religious diversity within Europe and what legal models can be recommended to accommodate such diversity in future. More details on the project can be seen at its website: http://www.religareproject.eu/. Cultural Diversity and Law in Association with RELIGARE provided an outlet for the results of specific research undertaken within the RELIGARE project.

Other titles in this series:

Public Funding of Religions in Europe
Edited by Francis Messner

Belief, Law and Politics
What Future for a Secular Europe?
Edited by Marie-Claire Foblets, Katayoun Alidadi, Jørgen S. Nielsen and Zeynep Yanasmayan

Family, Religion and Law
Cultural Encounters in Europe
Edited by Prakash Shah with Marie-Claire Foblets and Mathias Rohe

The Burqa Affair Across Europe
Between Public and Private Space
Edited by Alessandro Ferrari and Sabrina Pastorelli

Religion in Public Spaces
A European Perspective
Edited by Silvio Ferrari and Sabrina Pastorelli

A Test of Faith?
Religious Diversity and Accommodation in the European Workplace
Edited by Katayoun Alidadi, Marie-Claire Foblets and Jogchum Vrielink

Funding Religious Heritage

Edited by

ANNE FORNEROD
National Centre for Scientific Research, University of Strasbourg, France

Routledge
Taylor & Francis Group
LONDON AND NEW YORK

First published 2015 by Ashgate Publishing

2 Park Square, Milton Park, Abingdon, Oxfordshire OX14 4RN
52 Vanderbilt Avenue, New York, NY 10017

Routledge is an imprint of the Taylor & Francis Group, an informa business

First issued in paperback 2020

Copyright © Anne Fornerod 2015

Anne Fornerod has asserted her right under the Copyright, Designs and Patents Act, 1988, to be identified as the editor of this work.

All rights reserved. No part of this book may be reprinted or reproduced or utilised in any form or by any electronic, mechanical, or other means, now known or hereafter invented, including photocopying and recording, or in any information storage or retrieval system, without permission in writing from the publishers.

Notice:
Product or corporate names may be trademarks or registered trademarks, and are used only for identification and explanation without intent to infringe.

British Library Cataloguing in Publication Data
A catalogue record for this book is available from the British Library.

The Library of Congress has cataloged the printed edition as follows:
Funding religious heritage / by Anne Fornerod.
pages cm. -- (Cultural diversity and law in association with RELIGARE)
Includes bibliographical references and index.
ISBN 978-1-4724-2019-0 (hardback)
1. Cultural property--Protection--Law and legislation--European Union countries. 2. Church and state--European Union countries. I. Fornerod, Anne, 1975-
KJE6405.F83 2015
363.6'90681--dc23

2014030188

ISBN 978-1-4724-2019-0 (hbk)
ISBN 978-0-367-59956-0 (pbk)

Contents

Notes on Contributors

Lisbet Christoffersen is professor of law, religion and society at the Department of Society and Globalisation, Roskilde University and adjunct professor of ecclesiastical law and law on religion, Faculty of Theology, University of Copenhagen. She was leader of the Nord Forsk-funded Nordic Network on Law, Religion and Ethics 2003–2008 and in the same period research coordinator of the University of Copenhagen research initiative *Religion in the 21st Century*. She was a member of the RELIGARE project. She has published widely in Danish and English on law and religion. In 2013–2014, she was appointed a member of a committee entrusted by the Danish government with the task analyzing possible changes in the legal and economic structure of the Danish *folkekirke* and its relations to the state.

Frank Cranmer is a director of Central Lobby Consultants, secretary of the Churches' Legislation Advisory Service and a fellow of St Chad's College, Durham. He specializes in legislation as it affects the churches, charity law, and religion and human rights. Previously Clerk of Bills at the House of Commons, he is an honorary research fellow at the Centre for Law and Religion at Cardiff Law School. He has been a member of the editorial committees of the *Ecclesiastical Law Journal* since 2002 and of *Law and Justice* since 2006.

Alessandro Ferrari is associate professor in the Department of Law, Economy and Cultures of the University of Insubria (Como-Varese) and director of the research centre REDESM (Religion, Law and Economy in the Mediterranean Area) established in this department. He completed his PhD at the University of Milan (1999) and at the University of Paris XI (2003). His main research interests are: church and state issues in Italy and West Europe; Islam in Italy; and in Europe and comparative religious freedom in the two sides of Mediterranean.

Anne Fornerod is researcher at the CNRS-University of Strasbourg Centre of Research *DRES*. She completed her PhD in public law at the University of Paris XI (2006). Her works address several issues in law and religion: religious heritage, principle of *laïcité*, state support for religions, chaplaincies, cemeteries and ECHR freedom of religion. She edited a book on chaplaincies in 2012 and has published one book and several papers on cultural and religious heritage. She was a member of the RELIGARE project.

Carmen Garcimartín is professor of law at the University La Coruña and Vice-Dean for International and Institutional Relations. She is an associate member of the Royal Academy of Jurisprudence and Legislation in Spain and executive secretary of the International Academy for the Study of the Jurisprudence of the Family. She is also a member of the boards of several law journals.

Hans Guggenbühl is honorary delegate of the National Foundation for Cultural Heritage. He has held various positions in the private sector (industry and social housing, honorary head of the *Banque Populaire* in Alsace) and is the honorary president of the Protestant Foundation Sonnenhof.

Françoise Jeanmougin is co-executive of the Heritage Conservation Office at the French Ministry of Culture and Communication.

Solange Lefebvre is a professor in the Faculty of Theology and Religious Sciences at the University of Montreal. Since 2003 Ms. Lefebvre has held the Research Chair in religion, culture and society which is dedicated to the study of religion in the public sphere. She is also a member of the Centre of research in public law (University of Montréal). In addition, she was the founding director of the Centre for the Study of Religions at the University of Montreal (2000–2008). Most notably she was a member of the committee of experts, as part of the Consultation Commission on Accommodation Practices Related to Cultural Differences, chaired by Gérard Bouchard and Charles Taylor (2007–2008). Her current research deals with religion in the public sphere.

Francis Messner is Emeritus Director of Research at CNRS (University of Strasbourg/CNRS). He is involved in the editorial board of several reviews of law and sociology of religion. He was a member of the *Commission* for legal consideration of the relations between *religions* and *public authorities*, appointed by the Minister of Interior in 2005. He co-edited the *Traité de droit français des religions* (2003 and 2013). He was a member of the RELIGARE project and as such managed the research group working on state support for religions.

Adriaan Overbeeke is assistant professor/researcher at the Faculty of Law, Free University Amsterdam (VU), participating in a research group on *Fundamental rights, regulation and responsible government* and participated in the interdisciplinary research institute VISOR (VU Institute for the Study of Religion, Culture and Society, 2008–2012). He is a member of NISIS (*Netherlands Interuniversity School for Islamic Studies*). He is also a part-time researcher at the University of Antwerp, Law Department, where he is involved in a research programme on religion, life stances and law. His research topics are mainly education law and law relating to church–state issues. He was a member of the RELIGARE project.

Pierre-Henri Prélot is professor of public law at the University of Cergy-Pontoise, where he teaches, among other subjects, constitutional law and human rights. He was a member of the *Commission* for legal consideration of the relations between *religions* and *public authorities,* appointed by the Minister of the Interior in 2005. In addition to numerous publications on law and religion, he edited a handbook of the law of human rights (2010) and co-edited the *Traité de droit français des religions* (2003 and 2013).

Ringo Ringvee is advisor at the Religious Affairs Department at the Estonian Ministry of the Interior, and a member of the board of the State Development Plan for Historical Sacred Places in Nature and member of the expert group of the same development plan. He graduated from the University of Helsinki in 1998 and received his PhD from the University of Tartu in 2011. He is also a member of the research group in religious studies at the Centre of Excellence in Cultural Theory at the University of Tartu.

Tuğba Tanyeri-Erdemir is the director of the Science and Technology Museum, lecturer at the Graduate Program of Architectural History and a member of the executive board of the Centre for Society and Science at Middle East Technical University (Turkey). She has directed comparative projects on competitive sharing of religious sites and regulation and management of religious sites. She was a member of the RELIGARE project.

Stéphanie Wattier is currently a PhD candidate, studying at the Belgian *Fonds de la Recherche Scientifique (F.R.S.-FNRS)*. Her main area of study is constitutional law relating to the funding of religious and non-religious groups at the Faculty of Law and Criminology in the Centre of Research on State and Constitution and in the *Chaire de droit des religions* at the Catholic University of Louvain. She was an associate on the RELIGARE project.

Introduction

Anne Fornerod

In many European countries, places of worship and the movable goods they contain traditionally constitute a significant part of cultural heritage,[1] as well as being familiar landmarks reflecting the role of religions in national histories. As they embody public interest, we might hope that religious buildings and cultural heritage do not succumb to economical considerations. Be it for the sake of religious freedom or in the name of common good, both should be protected and are expected to be funded accordingly, hopefully from public resources. A more realistic approach entails taking into account the challenges facing both religious assets and cultural heritage, in the knowledge that the specificity of religious heritage stems from its dual dimension – religious and cultural. In both cases, these valuable assets have undergone in-depth changes that call into question the long-established schemes.

Funding Cultural Heritage: A Shared Concern

As regards the challenges faced by cultural heritage in general, in all the countries surveyed here one observes a consensus about the necessity to preserve cultural heritage. The purpose of heritage protection and the legal frameworks designed for it consist in essence in supporting a specific national or public interest. This has been variously managed, according to the importance granted to private property in domestic legislation and traditions. Moreover, the financial parameter very often underpins projects related to heritage, in that the care and maintenance of historic buildings is quite systematically and narrowly linked to its cost. Be it for upkeep or even enhancement, it is almost unavoidably dealt with in financial terms. In this regard, discussions focused solely on defending the public interest in preserving cultural heritage can scarcely be heard nowadays, being overshadowed by the 'recognized limits on state budgets to support the built heritage' (Pickard 2009: 12). This common agreement on the need to maintain cultural heritage very often cannot resist a certain financial reality. Public authorities responsible for the selection and preservation of heritage can scarcely support an all-encompassing approach to cultural assets worthy of protection, as this is no longer financially

1 Though significant does not systematically mean 'numerous' as prove the Dutch and English cases.

sustainable. Insufficient resources, the repeated lack of funding to achieve satisfactory maintenance of valuable buildings and assets could well amount to a major feature of the issue of heritage management and this seems unlikely to weaken in the light of the phenomenon of 'heritage inflation' and in times of financial crisis. Herein lies perhaps the reason why over several years – and even decades – cultural heritage has been focused on in terms of economy.[2] The result is that cultural heritage cannot escape market logic and the need to resort to private funds, as 'public funding alone is increasingly inadequate'.[3] The issue is no longer whether it sounds appropriate to involve private actors, but rather to explore the most efficient ways to compensate for the lack of public resources by combining public sector initiatives and private involvement and investment. The traditional scheme for funding heritage closely linked to widespread public support – if it ever existed as such – has had its day. One consequence of this situation is the necessary involvement of private stakeholders. The positive aspect of this involvement comes from the 'democratization' of heritage management. Civil society has long since developed an ability to make cultural heritage its own especially through the creation of an impressive network of associations. This phenomenon has strengthened in the face of increasing needs in this area.

On these points, religious heritage does not differ from cultural heritage in general. Whether in the countryside or major cities, religious buildings might be subject to the same challenges.[4] Although at first sight religious heritage is logically exposed to the evolutions of cultural heritage itself, the question remains over the specificity of valuable religious buildings within the general debate on funding heritage. Does special treatment of the buildings derive from their religious dimension?

State Support for Religions: Manifold Influence on Religious Heritage

The Influence of State Support Systems

Although listed religious buildings benefit from widespread consensus around the need for their conservation, their religious nature makes it necessary to investigate

2 See, among others, Fazi and Furt (2012).

3 Parliamentary Assembly of the Council of Europe, *Tax incentives for cultural heritage conservation*, Document 9913, 13 November 2003.

4 The delimitation of the category of heritage rests on criteria designed according to cultural and historical considerations. Although it leaves aside many valuable properties, it was decided within this volume to focus on listed assets only, in that it indicates an unambiguous acknowledgement of their heritage value through the implementing of the relevant legislation. Furthermore, priority is given to places of worship that embody the religious purpose of these buildings. This does not exclude here and there consideration for the specificities of national frameworks.

the topic in the light of questions raised by the issue of state support for religious groups in general. Domestic legal frameworks applicable to religious practices could influence the way funding for religious heritage is managed. Religious monuments and their numerous related assets fall within the combination of two legal regimes and hence two sources of funding: as religious buildings on the one hand, as listed buildings on the other. For dealing with *religious* heritage does not only mean focusing on monuments with a specific use. It also implies looking at the law pertaining to buildings that are – or were – primarily places of worship. In consequence, their funding is likely to be based on two different objectives: maintaining places of worship to ensure religious practice and the upkeep of buildings considered as listed monuments. In other words, besides funding religious heritage as part of cultural heritage, religious buildings potentially benefit from the state support system for religious groups. Moreover, the issue of state support for religions is one – if not the main – way of characterizing the place granted to religion in public affairs and might be reflecting the impact of state–church relationships on the implementing of heritage legislation. State support systems very often put in place in the nineteenth century still influence the current regulations.[5] In this regard, funding mechanisms allowing such state support vary significantly from one country to another and provide an amazing stability. Hence, does a shared concern for preserving religious heritage result in a funding commitment (on cultural grounds)? Or do the domestic specificities of state–church relationships prevail? Moreover, it might be argued that, whether or not intended for the building (monument), funds directly or indirectly benefit the religious group which owns or uses it. To what extent can a religious building be funded solely as a listed monument? In consequence, the first challenge consists in providing some clarity about how funds are assigned, through mapping the funding sources available and bearing in mind the need to assess the exact proportion of funding within the global process of heritage management.

As said before, protection costs are very often – if not systematically – higher than what can be borne by public, but also private, means, implying multi-source funding. Moreover, the parts played respectively by central government, local authorities, religious authorities and private organizations can vary from one country to another. Apart from funding religious monuments as part of cultural heritage, there is a need to better identify the various origins of funding due to these buildings potentially benefiting from the state support system for religious groups. As a result of history, listed places of worship may benefit from a support system which provides for building maintenance.

More generally, the aim is to identify the limit of what relates to the exercise of worship and what belongs to cultural policy, in the knowledge that the societal and cultural character of religious activities and property is becoming an ever more frequently invoked argument in favour of state support for religious institutions. How do both sources of funding – religious and cultural – combine? Is funding

---

5 On this issue, see Messner (2015).

religious heritage equivalent to funding religions? Do religious authorities receive funding that they would not receive strictly on religious grounds?

In addition, besides the amount of funding, the question arises about the use of such funding, which calls for coordination between partners. The interest in mapping out this funding also lies in the overall question of possible improvement. One perspective of this research consists in identifying efficient funding tools, likely to meet the task of preserving an important part of European heritage[6] in such a changed context, but with legal frameworks still shaped by national histories and thus offering irreducible specificities.

Another trend characterizing the state support issue, and likely to influence the funding of religious heritage, lies in the legitimacy of such public funding.

What Legitimacy to Funding Religious Heritage?

Religious heritage illustrates the potential tensions between secular and religious values, and therefore constitutes a relevant tool for investigating the question of the legitimacy of state support for religions in secularized societies. No one can ignore the deep process of secularization that has been taking place for some decades in the European context, although varying according to the country. The impact on religious heritage is visible and acknowledged. If only from a material point of view, the decreasing number of faithful deprives the building of regular care and maintenance, while regular attendance proves to be helpful in preventing or delaying the building's degradation. The specificity of religious heritage has long relied on it mainly being used for worship. Unlike many other listed buildings, churches are supposed to have kept their original function. This potentially competes with their cultural heritage dimension on a dual level, since heritage is usually considered as a twofold concept: material preservation and enhancement or promoting its artistic and historical value to citizens. Hence, the preservation of the monument embodying an historical or artistic interest, which is different from the original use of the buildings, gives rise to a commitment by the state to ensure this preservation. The legislation places limits on full use of the monument insofar as they might constitute a threat to satisfactory preservation. Most, if not all, countries under survey here – and beyond – share this legislative pattern. The primary use of religious monuments carries greater weight compared to other categories of listed buildings and the challenge comes from combining religious use with attendance stemming from the listing and characterized by a cultural purpose. On this point, and although maintaining such use is proven to contribute to the conservation of the building, it is likely to constitute a limitation on the willingness of private actors to invest in the maintenance.[7] The

6 This has been a concern of the Council of Europe for many years, with it providing numerous documents on this endless task.

7 For private investment in the rehabilitation process of cultural heritage in general, see Pickard (2009: 11).

requirements of religious practices automatically put limitations on implementing heritage legislation.

As regards the cultural uses resulting from a monument's enhancement, it should be considered that, for some decades now and as a consequence of the heritage being touched by the cultural democratization process, religious practices find themselves competing with mass tourism. This should be put into perspective alongside the argument in favour of funding, which lies in religious groups contributing to social life through activities of common interest that they carry out. Does this argument apply to religious heritage and, if so, how? Indeed, the funding of some places of worship might draw its legitimacy from their being used for activities other than worship, particularly as they provide venues for cultural events. In this latter case, there would be a shift in the legitimacy of the funding as well. Now, what if the religious use disappears? In consequence, the question of use is central here in that it notably reveals the change in perception of religious heritage that has occurred over recent decades.

While focusing on this issue of use, it rapidly comes to light that the main challenge for the future lies not only in managing the dual purpose of religious monuments, but also in re-using those buildings which have definitively lost their original purpose. The Council of Europe already expressed its concern about this situation in 1989 in a resolution on *Redundant religious buildings*.[8] In some cases, be it for the most renowned and frequented buildings or smaller isolated rural places of worship, the faithful are disappearing, to be replaced by visitors interested mainly in buildings' cultural significance. It follows that religious monuments might be considered first and foremost as cultural heritage, shedding their spiritual function.

Once the religious use has disappeared, because it has been terminated, the question arises of this heritage falling within the debate on alternative use and the rehabilitation process. Does such a shift in use, from religious to – mainly – cultural, lead to a renewed understanding of religious buildings and a change to the legitimacy of stakeholders' financial involvement? The process of secularization has brought about the closure of church buildings and raises the question of the legitimacy and the meaning of this heritage. It was stated that 'people want new buildings, good new architecture and access to modern lifestyle with cars and computers, but there is a general assumption now in most countries that people also, equally, want connections, tangible and associative, with the past within their landscapes' (Fairclough 2009: 126). The 'connection' provided by religious heritage is beyond discussion. However, it also means a secularized approach to religion and the 'heritagization' of religious buildings, which goes hand in hand with new claims and ways of considering them. This potentially implies shared responsibilities and the acceptance of new opinions on what to decide about the future of unattended and redundant religious monuments. Benefiting from

8 Parliamentary Assembly of Council of Europe, *Redundant Religious Buildings*, Resolution 916, 9 May 1989.

increased funding, the destiny of religious buildings should be decided beyond the limits of the religious community. Who is then entitled to arbitrate?

The exact influence of this secularization of religious heritage nevertheless calls for accurate assessment. Does the loss of religious use put an end to the particular features of this heritage and make it part of cultural heritage no longer with its distinctive character? Do the religious origin and status of monuments win over in other ways? Here it is important to consider that religious and public cultural authorities do not have the same approach or philosophical background when they tackle this question. Religious bodies care about declining church attendance, while cultural authorities pay attention to the cultural and/or historical significance of the building. However, they share the same concern about having – where possible – a future use for this heritage, namely an alternative use that would be respectful of the image attached to it. It should not be by chance that the Council of Europe's resolution on redundant religious buildings quotes Article 9 of the European Convention of Human Rights and encourages 'appropriate' new uses.

A Comparative Approach

State support varies according to the national system of state–religion relationships. Consequently, this volume draws on legal perspectives on religious heritage in various European countries, chosen according to the system of state–church relationships that they embody. State support for religious groups in general reflects the particularity of each domestic system of state–religion relationships. When dealing with religious heritage, does one encounter the heterogeneity that defines state support for religious groups in Europe? Or does the shared concern for preserving religious heritage lead to a common pattern of funding in Europe?

The chapters presented in this book are the fruit of the proceedings of a conference which took place within the European Commission funded *RELIGARE Project: Religious Diversity and Secular Models in Europe* (2010–2013).[9] One of the research fields in this project dealt with state support for religions and focused, among others, on the issue of religious heritage. Indeed, with a view to analysing the main evolutions in public support models, religious heritage potentially proves to be a place to assess the impact of secularization on these models.

The focus is on the following countries: Belgium, Denmark, France, Italy, the Netherlands, Spain, Turkey and the United Kingdom. They constitute a sample of various systems of state support. Moreover, the opportunity has been seized to have French scholars and administrative authorities come together to provide an in-depth analysis of the situation in France. This explains why one whole

9 The chapters were delivered at an international symposium on *Funding Religious Heritage*, Strasbourg, France, 14–15 November 2012, organized under the umbrella of the EU-funded FP7 RELIGARE (Religious Diversity and Secular Models in Europe – Innovative Approaches to Law and Policy): http://www.religareproject.eu/

chapter is dedicated to France. Moreover, although Quebec was not part of the RELIGARE project, the dynamism of cultural politics pertaining to religious heritage there mean that this country should also be taken into account. The same applies to Estonia, which offers a view of how this issue is being dealt with after the end of the Soviet Union. The interest and challenge of a comparative approach result from this variety, with the aim of identifying the most appropriate funding tools for managing the future of religious heritage in a secularized context. This variety, which might either impair or facilitate a solution that is applicable on a European Union scale, entails adopting a broad approach to the issue of funding valuable religious buildings by setting out all the main legal elements constituting the framework applicable to religious heritage. The conclusion will provide a comparative approach by highlighting common points and lingering divergences between the national systems studied here.

References

Fairclough, G. (2009), 'The cultural context of sustainability – Heritage and living', in Council of Europe, *Heritage and Beyond* (Strasbourg: Council of Europe Publishing).

Fazi, A. and Furt, J.M. (eds) (2012), *Vivre du patrimoine, un nouveau modèle de développement?* (Paris: L'Harmattan).

Messner, F. (ed.) (2015), *Public Funding of Religions in Europe* (Farnham: Ashgate).

PART I
Funding Religious Heritage in France: Theory and Practice

Chapter 1
Funding Religious Cultural Heritage: Administrative Texts and Practices

Françoise Jeanmougin

Even if numerous religious buildings and their contents are protected as historic monuments,[1] in law they do not differ from other assets making up cultural heritage. No legislation exists specifically for religious heritage in the texts relating to historic monuments. Religious buildings fulfilling the legal criteria for protection are therefore eligible. Just as when applying heritage policy, funding provisions – public and private – are extended to all protected religious property likely to benefit from them. The peculiarity of religious heritage doubtless becomes more tangible when it comes to enhancing and promoting it, which can be achieved by using it for cultural purposes. In addition to reconciling religious practice and tourist attendance in this context, non-religious events result in consultation between administrative and religious authorities.

Legislation Applicable to Religious Heritage

The Administrative Doctrine of Protection

Decisions about whether movable or immovable goods should be listed as historic monuments stem from several elements that form the *doctrine* in protection terms. The foundations of heritage policy are determined by the measures in the Heritage Code in respect to two protection provisions – classification and registration.[2] As regards the listing of immovable goods, Article L. 621-1 states that:

> When the conservation of properties is in the public interest, as seen from a historical or artistic perspective, then buildings are classified in whole or in part as historic monuments by the administrative authority. Among the buildings likely to be classified as historic monuments are:

1 In French law on historic monuments, the term 'protection' refers to two measures: classification and registration.

2 Registration replaces 'inscription in the Supplementary Inventory of Historic Monuments' [*inventaire supplémentaire des monuments historiques*], in force until the publication of the Heritage Code in 2004.

> a) megalithic monuments and lands that contain prehistoric sites or remains;
> b) buildings requiring classification in order to isolate, free up, clean up or enhance a building listed as a historical monument.

Article L. 621–5 on registration provides that:

> Buildings or parts of public or private buildings which, while not justifying immediate classification as historical monuments, are of sufficient historical or artistic interest to make them worthy of protection, can at any time be registered as historic monuments upon the decision of the administrative authority.
> The same applies to any finished or unfinished construction built within line of sight of a building already registered as a historical monument.

On this basis, several facts result in a monument becoming protected. They are essentially founded on two elements: the interest of the monument and the risks that it incurs. The interest of the monument, which is the legal primary criterion, is evaluated in the light of national or regional history, archaeology, the rarity of the evidence formed by the remains, the architectural, scientific or technical quality, the quality and rarity of its adornments, the aesthetics of the historic monument, the tourist interest, the environment … As to the risks incurred by the monument, they relate to threats resulting from human activity (destruction, modification) or else to lack of maintenance, to the poor condition of the building or to the failure of the owner.

It is, however, important to stress that neither the restoration costs, nor the owner's status nor the type of heritage – religious, military, private, public – play a role when considering and deciding what to protect. The ownership of religious heritage is not then considered when determining registration or classification. In France, for mainly historical reasons, religious buildings belong overwhelmingly either to the state (cathedrals) or to the *communes* (churches and former cathedrals) or to public authorities or, more rarely, to individuals (abbeys, convents, old rectories …), or else to associations, for example, buildings belonging to non-Catholic denominations.[3] The type of ownership has no impact either on the works to be undertaken.[4] This indifference as regards the type of heritage has resulted in ancient cultural, medieval and modern assets being widely represented today (new protection in the contemporary era applies to parks and gardens as twentieth century heritage). Any religious heritage – churches, mosques, synagogues or temples – can be protected as historic monument, if it meets the criteria defined by the Heritage Code. Religious heritage is not protected for its religious character, but for its historical, artistic, architectural or technical interest.[5] It follows that it

---

3 On this point, see Chapter 2 of this volume.

4 See below, the funding of heritage protected as historic monuments.

5 Hence, the church of Notre-Dame in Royan (Poitou-Charentes Region), built in 1958, owes its classification as a historic monument to the feat of the concrete work that it embodies.

covers the majority of protected buildings, considering that this includes, not only cathedrals and churches, but also convents, monasteries, abbeys, Gallo-Roman temples ... and movable goods.

Similarly to immovables, criteria for the classification and the registration of movable assets as historic monuments are defined by Articles L. 622-1 and L. 622-20 of the Heritage Code.[6] These criteria today apply more to objects of industrial, railway and aviation heritage and to heritage linked to occupations (weavers, cabinet-makers, goldsmiths, photographers ...). These are less well protected than older objects that have already been widely referenced and have been granted protection. Over more than 20 years, an active and sustained policy has helped to restore most of the great cathedral organs and has led to new protection with a view to performing major works on organs that are most of the time the property of the *communes*.

Selecting Buildings or Objects Likely to Be Protected

Lawmakers have given the administrative authority significant room for manoeuvre when defining notions of historical or artistic interest, as well as the public interest of the monument. This freedom has meant that there are no rigid criteria for classifying or registering a monument, which has allowed the doctrine relating to historic monuments to evolve without limiting the administrative authority's freedom of decision. Everything can be the subject of a classification, the 'nature' and age of the object is not specified, nor the legal status of the owner, since properties or objects may be classified whether they belong to the state, to a public institution, to a local authority or one of its institutions or to any person other than those mentioned.

The very general nature of the articles determining the scope of the law and the notions of public interest and sufficient interest, as defined in the Heritage Code, leave a large margin of discretion for the administrative authority to take decisions, yet structured by procedures guaranteeing the rights of third parties and the relevance of the decision. But, to avoid arbitrariness, the Heritage Code has organized the procedures that precede the decision, which notably involve

---

6 Article L. 622-1: 'movable objects, either movables in the strict sense or fixtures, conservation of which, from a historical, artistic, scientific or technical perspective, is in the public interest, may be classified in whole or in part as historic monuments by decision of the administrative authority. The effects of classification provided for in this section apply to goods which have become movables as a result of their detachment from buildings classified pursuant to article L. 621-1, as well as to fixtures that have reverted to being movables.' Article L. 622-20: 'movable objects, either movables in the proper sense or fixtures, which, without justifying immediate classification as historic monuments, are of sufficient historical, artistic, scientific or technical interest to make them worthy of protection can, at any time, be listed as historical monuments. Movable objects belonging to a private person can be registered only with the person's consent.'

consulting commissions: the national commission of historic monuments (protection department), regional commissions on heritage and sites, *département* commissions for movable objects. These commissions are made up of *ex officio* members, elected national or local officials, experts, qualified individuals and representatives from heritage associations.

Ministerial policy has consisted over several years in greater selectivity, considering that the conventional areas of protection (ancient, medieval and modern periods), as well as the majority of buildings worthy of protection, had already been classified or registered. In fact, the separation of church and state brought about by the Act of 9 December 1905 upset this framework and the pace of classification that had been started in 1840 in the form of lists; this followed the creation of the first national commission of historic monuments in 1837 by Mérimée, then in 1887 of buildings and movable objects, after the adoption of the first act on historic monuments. There was a rise from 4,000 assets listed prior to 1905 to more than 30,000 in 1905. This urgency to classify involved above all religious objects, overshadowing civil heritage that is more complex to protect.

As to buildings, the 1913 Act considered as officially classified buildings those already on the lists of 1840 and 1887, by including them among historic monuments (alongside many religious buildings). If the monument classification orders were somewhat reduced before 1905, they increased significantly after the Act of Separation.[7] By way of comparison, the average rose to 260 classifications per year between 1905 and 1914, while subsequently the figure varied between 80 and 200 annually.[8] The peak occurred between 1985 and 1995, for classifications as well as for registrations, while clearing a significant backlog at the time. Currently, decisions of protection (classification and registration) are progressing at a more moderate pace. As of 31 December 2011, the total number of buildings protected as historic monuments amounted to 43,969 (including 14,499 classified and 29,470 registered). Today, classifications can also result from thematic studies, such as recent ones on lighthouses.

Half the protected buildings belong to public owners, mainly the *communes*, and the other half to private owners. But one must distinguish classified buildings, mainly belonging to public owners (over two-thirds), and registered buildings, 60 per cent of which belong to private persons (individuals, associations, companies). Of the types of listed buildings, 39.5 per cent relate to domestic architecture, 34.6 per cent are religious buildings and, of these, 44 per cent are churches belonging to the *communes*. The state owns 87 cathedrals, including the Basilica of Saint-Denis and two churches – Saint-Julien in Tours and Saint-Nazaire in Carcassonne.

With regard to movable objects, 132,000 assets are classified, about 80 per cent are religious objects. It is worth mentioning here instrumental and bell-ringing

---

7 On protective measures in respect of historic monuments contained in the Act of 9 December 1905, see Kagan (2006) and Fornerod (2013). See also Chapter 2 of this volume.

8 In 1957, 9,824 buildings were classified and 14,160 registered. In 1973, there were 11,214 classified and 17,481 registered.

heritage, made up of 997 classified and 111 registered organs and a total of 5,454 bells protected as historic monuments. Today, protection tends to apply to civil objects or industrial, scientific and technical heritage. Over 150,000 objects are registered locally, although before 2007 this protective measure applied solely to assets belonging to public entities. This probably explains why 80 per cent of movable assets belong to public authorities (including 3.6 per cent to the state or to public establishments, 1 per cent to the *départements* and 95.4 per cent to the *communes*) and why private owners possess 20 per cent of the objects, 71 per cent of which are in the hands of private individuals.

Funding Heritage Protected as Historic Monuments

All listed historic monuments, irrespective of their nature or their owners, are likely to benefit from public funding. The menhir, the prehistoric cave, the village church, the wayside cross, the Renaissance castle, the Le Corbusier house and the hospital, are all concerned, once they are protected. But it remains that religious monuments in France account for more than 30 per cent of heritage and that 48 per cent of the funds reserved for historic monuments and put at the disposal of decentralized state services have been destined for restoration, that is more than 100 million euros. The restoration of stained-glass windows, for example, is essentially an operation to protect the enclosed space within a building. Spectacular operations to create stained glass are either part of a special programme within the context of a specific, long-term regional project (contemporary stained glass of Nevers Cathedral) or part of a patronage operation. In such cases, public authorities fund the necessary works for installing the stained glass (for example restoring the windows) and patronage funds the restoration of the stained glass and possibly their installation. The state may have to fund the masonry work that accompanies their creation in buildings that do not belong to it.

Public funding for heritage is broken down into direct and indirect aid and relates first and foremost to various maintenance and restoration work. One should also consider the issue of the use made of religious heritage, which is not without impact on its funding.

Direct Aid to Maintenance and Restoration Work

Direct contributions to funding heritage obey a number of principles. First, financial aid provided by the state through the Ministry of Culture and Communication for historic monuments applies to maintenance and restoration work: the state funds 100 per cent of the work on its own monuments, which means that it is supporting work on 87 cathedrals, including the two churches of Saint-Julien in Tours and Saint-Nazaire in Carcassonne. Then, it provides the main funding for work on buildings endowed to its public establishments by paying annual subsidies to have them opened to the public. Lastly, the Ministry of Culture and Communication supports, at differing rates and according to differing criteria, restoration work to buildings belonging to regional or local authorities and private owners. It is to be noted that the Ministry of Culture does not fund restoration work to buildings belonging to other ministries, each being in this respect responsible for their own monuments, following a decision in 1975 by the Special Architecture Board advising the President of the Republic. However, there are exceptions such as the Defence-Culture protocol,[9] or one-off initiatives such as assisting the Ministry of Justice to restore the decor after a fire at the Rennes Parliament.

Each year, the Ministry of Culture delegates to the regional directorates of cultural affairs (*Directions régionales des affaires culturelles*, DRAC) a funding envelope based on a schedule of works to be performed in the regions both on state historic monuments and historic monuments not belonging to it. For the latter, the funding of projects generally includes funds from the state, public authorities, *départements* or *communes* and, if it is a private historic monument, the owner. There again, funding decisions do not take into account the nature of the building, but its state of conservation.

However, as regards religious heritage, the state initiated a major project from 2009–2010 to stimulate funding for restoration works to its cathedrals: with the help of an additional 100 million euros, this allowed work to be undertaken on 44 cathedrals. Reflecting the division previously mentioned, some regions have focused their monument restoration policy on cathedrals. For example, the state has undertaken the restoration of five cathedrals in the Centre Region, up to an annual amount of more than 3 million euros, which is set to continue until 2014 for three of them (Tour, Orléans and Chartres). Most of the cathedrals (Rouen, Saint-Claude in Franche-Comté, Nîmes, Montpellier) were the subject of major restoration programmes. The average annual budget allocated to the cathedrals represents an investment of approximately 36 million euros, to which should be added 6 million euros for ongoing maintenance.

In addition, funds from local authorities, including the *communes* that own protected churches, are used to finance restoration and repair work with the help of the state and the *départements*.

Indirect State Aid

Indirect tax incentives, which should also be considered as a state contribution to the enhancement of heritage, complement direct state aid, which is used to perform repair work. This financial support also concerns private owners, who may also own religious heritage – although this is a rare scenario for places of

9 This agreement has existed since 1983 and aims to preserve and promote the cultural heritage of the armies through a partnership between the ministries of defence and culture, who each provide equal funding for it.

worship. The fiscal regime of historic monuments is not considered as a means to optimize tax, but as compensation for the obligation private owners are under to conserve and enhance historic monuments, as they own more than 40 per cent of protected monuments.

Several types of measures are applicable under the General Tax Code:

- Income tax-related deductions: if owners open a monument to the public for 50 days a year, including 25 non-business days between April and September, or for 45 days from July until September inclusive (business days or not), they can receive tax benefits that will be calculated differently depending on whether the historic monument generates any revenue or not.
- VAT-related deductions: owners can deduct VAT in full on sums collected as admission fees to historic monuments, as well as commercial products, such as postcards, brochures, photos … They can also waive their VAT exemption on admission fees and ancillary products and benefit in return from exemptions on work to historic monuments for their buildings once these become accessible to the public (except for the private areas). The rate varies between 5.5 per cent and 20.60 per cent, depending on each case.
- Exemption from transfer rights: this is an exemption from the rights of succession on the building, as well as on movable assets and fixtures which are part of its artistic or historic character, in return for opening it up to the public.

Finally, it is worth mentioning the role of patronage by foundations and businesses in favour of built monumental heritage. Act no. 2009–709 of 1 August 2003 on patronage, associations and foundations and Decree no. 2009–158 of 11 February 2009 on endowment funds and their creation have increased genuine awareness among companies and facilitated contact with them (as they are open to incentives, particularly tax-related). Patronage takes place within the context of specific agreements on certain types of religious heritage, such as stained-glass windows. Over 18 years, the corporate foundation of the GDF SUEZ Group has provided remarkable support for the restoration and creation of stained-glass windows throughout France. Most recently, Van Cleef, for example, has been committed to restoring the treasury in the Cathedral Notre-Dame in Paris.

Use(s) of Religious Heritage and Funding

As has been said above, the funding of heritage is indifferent to its nature. We might also think *a priori* that maintaining usage conforming to the original function of the monument makes no difference. Yet, some monuments of religious origin now have a cultural purpose that ensures their sustainability. So it is with the Convent of the Bernardins in Paris, owned by a diocesan association, that was completely restored between 2004 and 2008 with 40 per cent state aid. Similarly,

Fontevraud Abbey, now a cultural centre, is constantly undergoing restoration work in collaboration with the regional council, which manages it and takes care of its enhancement, promotion and cultural activities. In general, the re-allocation or reuse of redundant religious heritage is not very common. Examples of cultural meeting centres located in former abbeys (such as Ardenne Abbey in St Germain la Blanche Herbe in Lower Normandy,[10] the aforementioned Fontevraud Abbey, Noirlac Abbey or former convents, abbeys, monasteries … that have become private properties) do not reflect the reality of a huge religious heritage which sometimes struggles to find a second vocation when religious use has disappeared.

However, it is a fact that the use of buildings of worship has funding repercussions in that it contributes to their physical conservation. Therefore, the question of buildings that are little frequented, more often than not away from town centres, becomes an issue. Restoring them places a heavy burden on the *commune*, while the asset is a marker of its identity. Dwindling attendance becomes a worry, because it goes hand in hand with a lack of heating and ventilation of these churches in rural areas, which, for many, harbour artistic treasures. The Heritage Foundation[11] is working to save these buildings and associations are being formed, enabling communities and residents to be mobilized to fund repair work.

A cultural purpose can complement religious attendance in church buildings.[12] Visiting historic places of worship is free, unless special arrangements are made to allow the visit (displaying the treasures, special tour circuits that may require guarding, security or specific safety arrangements). This use may constitute a source of income for the state, as is the case with some historic, religious and emblematic monuments, such as the towers of Notre Dame in Paris, for example, but these revenues remain very marginal. Such paid visits can be organized by the state (Centre for National Monuments), the clergy itself, the tourism office in the *commune*, an association of friends of the religious building, and are subject to management agreements put in place mainly for cathedrals. In respect of the latter, important work has been undertaken by the Ministry of Culture, the Ministry of the Interior and the clergy (Conference of Bishops of France) on the compatibility of religious use with cultural events, in a context of church–state dialogue. In general, the conservation and enhancement of religious heritage creates contact between the owner (the state or the *communes*) and the religious beneficiary: the historic monument status of these buildings requires the religious beneficiary using the building to ensure compliance with the requirements of the Heritage Code. However, it falls within the prerogatives of religious authorities to give their agreement for non-religious events and they have to be informed of proposed works, so that these do not disturb the practice of worship.

---

10 On this abbey, see: http://www.imec-archives.com/l-abbaye-d-ardenne/ (accessed 14 November 2014).

11 On this topic, see Chapter 3 of this volume.

12 On this issue, see Chapter 2 of this volume.

References

Bady, J.P., Cornu, M., Fromageau, J., Leniaud, J.M. and Negri, V. (eds) (2013), *1913. Genèse d'une loi sur les monuments historiques* (Paris: La documentation française).

Desmoulins-Hemery, S. and Palouzié, H. (eds) (2006), *Regards sur les églises de France* (Arles: Actes Sud).

Fornerod, A. (2013), 'Les prémices d'une réforme de la protection des monuments historiques: la loi du 9 décembre 1905', in Bady, J.P., Cornu, M., Fromageau, J., Leniaud, J.M. and Negri, V. (eds), 70–78.

Kagan, J. (2006), 'La loi du 9 décembre 1905 et la conservation du patrimoine mobilier protégé "au titre des monuments historiques". Une genèse', in Desmoulins-Hemery, S. and Palouzié, H. (eds), 19–46.

Chapter 2
Funding Religious Heritage in France

Pierre-Henri Prélot

The Heritage Code, which was adopted in 2004 and brings together all legislative and regulatory provisions accumulated since the nineteenth century, defines the notion of heritage as 'all property, immovable or movable, falling within public or private ownership, which is of historical, artistic, archaeological, aesthetic, scientific or technical interest' (Article L. 1). At the outset, it seems that, if a major part of French heritage is of religious origin, religious interest is not mentioned as such in the list. It is not in the list, but it is not excluded from it, insofar as the listing implicitly includes religious assets of – in some cases invaluable – historical, artistic or aesthetic interest. The religious heritage of France, for example, Notre-Dame in Paris, Reims Cathedral or Mont Saint-Michel, is one of its great riches, but in terms of Article L. 1 mentioned above, it is not its religious nature that qualifies it as heritage. This 'silence' surrounding heritage legislation makes it worthwhile dwelling first on the concept of religious heritage. For the sake of the clarity of this presentation, we will then examine the legal rules applicable to maintaining and conserving buildings of worship in a second part, as well as those relating to their enhancement (cultural, artistic, tourism ...), the purpose of which is equally to fund their maintenance in a third part.

The Extent of Religious Heritage

The notion of religious heritage can be comprehended by considering where it comes from. For example, the seat of a region's president housed in a former episcopal palace or else the buildings of an old abbey converted into a hotel or residence for the elderly are part of this historic religious heritage. But, from the heritage protection or funding perspective, these premises do not differ from others devoid of religious origin. There is no justification for differentiating between an ancient abbey and a castle fort built at the same period which are both subject in principle to the same legal provisions on heritage and the same funding regime.

In a narrower sense, religious heritage encompasses all assets which present an interest in the sense of Article L. 1 of the Heritage Code (historical, artistic ...) and which are currently used for worship. Such a definition excludes all the items of religious heritage that the ups and downs of human history have at any given time diverted away from their primary role. It should be noted here that if classification is generally associated with age, it is not always the case. For example, the Chapel of Ronchamp built by Le Corbusier in the 1950s, together with its surroundings, are now classified as a historic monument. Provisions of the same Article L. 1 add to the difficulty of defining the concept of religious heritage. In accordance with Article L. 1, the notion of heritage actually includes the entirety of assets 'under public or private ownership', which has led to a distinction between religious heritage which is on the one hand part of the public or private domain of public entities and that owned by private individuals, in particular (but not only) the property of religious communities (especially denominational associations and congregations).

For well-known historical reasons, namely the nationalization of the property of the clergy decided upon at the start of the Revolution, it happens that a significant part of religious heritage in France is public property. It is a paradox that cannot be highlighted enough: if France is the country in Europe that has organized the most successful separation of church and state, it has done so using a fusional approach, in which a large part of the religious heritage assigned to worship remains the public property of the *communes*, *départements* (more rarely) or the state (for cathedrals), as the result of the nationalization of the property of the clergy in 1789.

During discussions about the Act of 9 December 1905, Socialist Minister Victor Augagneur,[1] Mayor of Lyon and Freemason,[2] had proposed to return church buildings to Catholics in a well-understood logic of separation[3] – each to his home. This proposal was contained in an amendment discussed at the Chamber of Deputies the 8 June 1905 and formulated thus:

> The State, *départements* and *communes* donate to church institutions and associations substituting them, such as they are designated and established by Title IV of the present Act, institutions used exclusively for the practice of religion: cathedrals, churches, relief chapels, temples and synagogues, properties of the state, *départements* and *communes*, either before promulgation of the Concordat or subsequent to its enactment;
> Residences of archbishops and bishops, rectories, seminaries and their outbuildings are put into the possession of the state, *départements* or *communes* whose property they are;
> The movable dependencies of religious institutions devoted or not to worship are assigned, in sole ownership, to the aforementioned associations.

1 He was to resign on 30 October 1905 to become Governor of Madagascar, leaving his position to Édouard Herriot (who did not give it back upon his return).

2 His biographical notes refer to him as the 'Vénérable' of the Lyon Lodge *Les amis de la Vérité*.

3 On this point, the reverse argument was put forward in Quebec – still relating to Catholic buildings, defending the idea of a transfer of these buildings to public heritage: see Chapter 12 of this volume.

However, for his friends it was out of the question of course to restore the Catholic Church's patrimony and the proposal was rejected.[4]

Maintaining and Conserving Religious Assets as Historic Monuments

The Act of 1905 is famous for the separation regime that it introduces; it is lesser known as a great act on heritage.[5] Article 16 sets out the 'additional classification of buildings used for public worship (cathedrals, churches, chapels, temples, synagogues, residences of archbishops and bishops, rectories, seminaries), which must include all buildings representing, in whole or in part, artistic or historical value'. Article 16 also provides for classification of movable objects and fixtures, 'conservation of which would be of sufficient interest from a historical or artistic perspective'. Article 17, meanwhile, declares classified fixtures to be inalienable and imprescriptible and gives a pre-emptive right on movable objects '1. to denominational associations; 2. to *communes*; 3. to *départements*; 4. to museums and societies of art and archaeology'. The same Article 17 enables buildings used for worship, as well as the listed assets they contain, to open free of charge to the public. With the 1905 Act, we move, regarding criterion of classification, from the national interest requirement to one of simple public interest; it is the whole of local religious heritage (the village bell-tower!) which is henceforth intended to be part of French heritage. From the viewpoint of protecting heritage, the 1905 Act somehow makes the link between the two great acts – the Act of 30 March 1887 on the conservation of historic monuments and the Act of 31 December 1913 on historic monuments – to the passing of which Maurice Barrès[6] contributed so powerfully.

This heritage dimension to the 1905 Act is fundamental when considering the issue of funding heritage. Indeed, legislation on historic monuments has this

---

4 Augagneur notably argued that it was not 'giving much', because 'in theory, if legally buildings of worship belong to the *communes*, it is ownership of little value – theoretical ownership. Being a bare owner with the presence of an eternal usufructuary is a foolish situation; this is the reality of the situation for all *communes* with regard to churches. The *commune* is the bare owner, the usufructuary never dies and ownership of this kind brings only costs. Nobody would have the idea of buying property for a life annuity from a gentleman who would never die. Therefore, it is property of zero value at the present time. I go further. I say that tomorrow, if you want to dispose of it, it would be a property of completely relative value. The churches are only suitable for the use for which they were intended. It is said that we wanted to make some into museums: the most beautiful are Gothic churches, in which the absence of light will always prevent the installation of some or other museum'.

5 On this point, see Fornerod (2013).

6 Maurice Barrès (1862–1923) was a French novelist, journalist and politician. At the time of the separation between church and state, he called for an extended protection of all the churches as historic monuments.

characteristic of transcending the two major taboos that exist in France in terms of public funding, namely the ban on public funding for religious groups, in the name of *laïcité*, and the ban on funding private activities and property, in the name of the principle of specialization of public entities and equality of all citizens before the law. Article 2 of the Act of 9 December 1905 states that 'the Republic neither recognizes, nor salaries, nor subsidizes any religion'. But, as it happens, the rules for funding listed heritage have always been considered as an exception, ever since the very beginning, to the strict rule of Article 2.

Originally, the provisions of the Act of Separation relating to religious assets as historic monuments were aimed as much at drawing the attention of the fine arts administration on the monumental qualities of a collection of parish churches so far ignored by the Act of 1887, as at ensuring financial support, which is anyway neither compulsory nor automatic. Moreover, at that time, the 1905 Act provided the transfer of places of worship to private law denominational associations (*associations cultuelles*) designed for replacing the former public religious institutions of the four recognized religious denominations. The parliamentarians then deemed that these denominational associations, deprived of public funding by the same 1905 Act, were likely to neglect the listed buildings maintenance. Accordingly, Article 19 of the 1905 Act on denominational associations states that 'Not considered as subsidies are amounts provided for repairs to listed monuments'. As for private religious heritage, and in particular that which belongs to denominational associations established on the basis of the Act of 1905, it too is destined to benefit from public subsidies provided it is classified or registered, although it is used for worship and although it belongs to private bodies. As the Catholic Church refused to establish such denominational associations, its patrimony entered into the public domain.

In any case, the public owner is authorized to take on the costs of repair and maintenance to listed buildings assigned to religious denominations in application of the 1905 Act. For the *commune* which is owner of a listed church, for example, its character as a historic monument has the additional advantage of permitting financial contributions from the state and, where applicable, other public authorities, the *département* or *région*, to help with restoration work.[7] Registration as Historic Monument also allows, even if the amount is generally less, for state contributions to fund work to religious buildings of which it is not the owner.[8]

Basically, the secular character of French republican legislation has never erased the fact that it is first and foremost heritage legislation, in charge of a

---

7 See Chapter 1 of this volume.

8 Article L. 621-5 *et seq.* of the Heritage Code: 'Buildings or parts of public or private buildings which, without justifying immediate classification as historic monuments, are of sufficient historical or artistic interest to make them desirable of protection can, at any time, be registered as historic monuments upon decision of the administrative authority.'

heritage that carries with it all the memories – past but very much alive – of our national community.[9]

The 1905 Act deals not only with listed buildings. The new common law of separation initially envisaged religious denominations benefiting from the buildings legally allocated to worship to be 'held responsible for repairs of any kind, as well as insurance fees and other costs relating to buildings and the furnishings lining them'. In other words, for the Catholic Church, which is essentially the one concerned here, lawmakers allowed it free use of churches that had become part of public patrimony at the time of the Revolution and for which it was now to assume fully the financial cost. But a new act passed in the days following separation, dated 13 April 1908, added a new subsection to Article 13 according to which: 'The state, the *départements* and *communes* (and public agencies of inter-municipal cooperation) will be able to assume the expenditure necessary for the maintenance and conservation of buildings of worship, their ownership of which is recognized in the present act.' If this new solution has been discussed and debated from a perspective of strict financial separation, the fact remains that it is much more relevant to the ownership regime than that adopted in 1905. By focusing on the responsibility of the owner in the event of a lack of maintenance of the building, administrative case law very quickly confirmed the consistency of this solution.[10]

Today, the involvement of municipal authorities in funding maintenance and conservation work for the buildings of worship they own has become common practice. More often than not, the difficulty is not so much the support generally acquired from the *commune*, but rather the lack of *commune* resources for the necessary investments, which are sometimes considerable. The faithful remain of course able to intervene via support funds, which may contribute partly or wholly to the costs of works. These support funds can be a way of encouraging municipal owners to undertake work which they would not otherwise have ventured upon. Case law has also enshrined the principle that the public owner is required to undertake the necessary repair and maintenance work when the offer of support allows for full funding to be assured.[11]

This right of public owners to assume the expenses of maintaining and conserving their buildings has been extended in parallel to buildings owned by denominational associations. The Decree-Act of 25 December 1942, modifying Article 19 of the Act of 1905 on denominational associations, authorizes public subsidies for repair work to buildings assigned to public worship, whether listed

9 See, in this sense, Delannoy (2009).

10 Council of State, 20 June 1921, *Commune de Monségur*, *Recueil Lebon*, 573.

11 Council of State, ass., 28 October 1945, *Chanoine Vaucanu*, *Recueil Lebon*, 212. Solution confirmed by Council of State, 29 June 1957, *Commune de Saint-Martial-le-Mont*, *Recueil Lebon*, 408.

as historic monuments or not.[12] At the time this provision was particularly aimed at Protestant temples, which, unlike churches, mostly do not belong to *communes*, but to denominational associations, and thus receive no financial support. But this provision was largely lost sight of after 1945 and has seemingly hardly been used by the *communes*. Here, it should be noted about denominational associations that they are included among the organizations capable of receiving donations made to bodies of general interest (two-thirds of the sums paid give an entitlement to tax deduction up to a limit of 20 per cent of taxable income), meaning that public aid for maintaining cultural heritage is also indirect, from supporting patronage. Beyond the specific case of denominational associations, individuals are regularly asked to pay their share for restoration of heritage assets, whether religious or not. Indeed, even if religious communities are generally the first concerned when it comes to preserving buildings of worship, nowadays it is most probably associations for the protection of heritage that mobilize to collect all or part of the sums necessary. Consequently, they do not hesitate to rely on promoting religious heritage to raise public awareness.

Enhancement as a Method of Funding Buildings of Worship

The traditional rules just described are characterized by the fact that they do not take into account the enhancement and promotion of religious heritage. The 1905 Act considers buildings of worship mainly in their religious dimension that it intends to preserve. The only exception to using the building exclusively for worship that the Act of 1905 expressly authorizes is visits to the buildings (Article 17). Moreover, the financial aspect of non-religious uses taking place in church buildings has remained unsettled for several decades.

Combining Religious and Non-Religious Uses

If the Act of 1905 raises the question of visiting, in contrast it is silent about other uses that may be made of the building, for example, organizing cultural events like concerts. It was deduced from this silence that use for worship had an 'exclusive' character and that any use not allowed by the law was absolutely prohibited. This strict interpretation was reinforced by the Republican legislator, who had intended to guarantee the Catholic Church full use of its buildings in the new regime of separation, provided that it would abide by the legal conditions, in particular that it would not make other use of the churches than for celebrating worship. The owner, just as the clergy, were somehow bound by having to use the buildings for religious purposes.

---

12 'Not considered as subsidies are amounts provided for repairs to buildings used for public worship, whether or not they are listed as historic monuments.'

The gradual decline in churchgoing, increased interest in heritage and culture, but also the more considerable financial burden weighing on *communes* having to maintain religious heritage, have gradually led to a softening of the situation created by the separation, allowing us to envisage the use of religious buildings for events such as concerts, exhibitions or performances. This secular enhancement of religious buildings has equally been facilitated by easing relations between public authorities and religious denominations. Playing on the accessory theory, religious authorities have themselves sometimes organized concerts of sacred music which, if they do not meet the definition of worship *stricto sensu*, are part of its continuation and constitute its accessory. They have also received requests from the public owners with a view to organizing events. Instructions have been drafted for parish priests to assist them in responding in line with Canon Law.[13] Only, in line with the *Abbé Chalumey* case law from 1994,[14] issued pursuant to Article 25 of the Act of 31 December 1913,[15] the mayor cannot organize visits of a listed church without the agreement of the religious assignee of the building (the parish priest), whose right of veto is intended to protect religious freedom. What is unique about the case law is pointing the finger at conflicting assumptions, but it is clear that they are rather rare, and that religious authorities do not preclude visiting, generally speaking.

On this issue of diversified secular uses, the judge of the Council of State later considered that the owner may not himself use a legally assigned building, even though it may no longer be used for worship, without the authorization of the religious authority. The solution that emerges from the ruling *Commune de Massat*[16] extends the rule applicable to visits to all non-religious uses of the building. The priest's recognized power of opposition in this sensitive case where the celebration of worship was not an issue, could be denounced as an unfair privilege, but in reality this one-off conflict reveals the transition that is taking place towards more shared use of places of worship. The decline in religious practice makes such developments inevitable.

13 Canon 1210 of the Code of Canon Law on sacred places provides that 'Only those things which serve the exercise or promotion of worship, piety, or religion are permitted in a sacred place; anything not consonant with the holiness of the place is forbidden. In an individual case, however, the ordinary can permit other uses which are not contrary to the holiness of the place'. The Episcopal Commission for Liturgy, which is attached to the Conference of Bishops of France, had also produced a note on concerts in churches, in May 1999.

14 Council of State, 4 November 1994, *Abbé Chalumey*, no. 135842.

15 Article 25 of the Act was repealed with the adoption of the Code of Ownership by Public Entities (Article L. 2124-31). See below.

16 Council of State, 25 August 2005, *Commune de Massat*, no. 284307.

Enhancement as a Financial Resource?

Article 17 of the 1905 Act states that 'visits to the buildings and the exhibition of listed movable objects will be public: they cannot give rise to any tax or charge'. In other words, secular visits are hardly conducive to the accumulation of resources to the extent that the law prescribes that they are free with a view to providing wide public access to cultural heritage. The Act of 31 December 1913 on historic monuments (Article 25) tempers this general obligation to be free. It allowed charging for visits to listed movable goods, due to the costs borne by the owner *communes* and *départements* for implementing security and conservation measures.[17] This is a source of profit that is intended to be reassigned to the preservation of the building or at least to the listed assets it houses. But the provision applies only to places of worship belonging to *communes* and *départements*. As for buildings belonging to the state, if the Finance Act of 31 December 1921 (Article 118) authorizes the administration of fine arts to collect an entrance fee for visiting museums, collections and monuments, permission is not extended to cathedrals, which in principle remain free to visit. Having visitors pay implies making a distinction between the faithful, for whom the visit must remain free, and tourists on whom a visit fee may be imposed, which proves difficult in concrete terms. On the other hand, the principle of free entry has long been bypassed in a number of buildings assigned to worship, in which certain parts are not used for religious practice, but are accessible by paying a fee, for example the towers of a cathedral, a crypt … Such practices were obviously questionable under applicable laws until 2006, but found their justification in the need to fund the upkeep of heritage, which is extremely expensive.

The adoption in 2006 of a new Code of Ownership by Public Entities was an opportunity to consolidate the above-mentioned case law and complement it with financial arrangements, because cultural and patrimonial enhancement of buildings of worship is of course also a matter of money. Article L. 2124-31 of the Code provides that:

> When visits to parts of buildings assigned to worship, including those where registered or listed movable objects are exhibited, justifies specific organizational conditions, their access is subject to authorization by the assignee. The same applies to the use of these buildings for activities compatible with their religious assignment.
> The agreement specifies the terms and conditions of this access or use. Such access or use gives rise, where appropriate, to payment of a fee, the revenue from which can be shared between the public owner and the assignee.

17 However, these provisions were deleted when Article L 2124-31 of the Code of Ownership by Public Entities was adopted in 2006.

These new provisions now validate all forms of secular use of legally assigned buildings of worship and remain 'compatible with assignment for worship', subject to the agreement of the assignee. Possibly sharing the rental fee may, in certain cases, enable common ground to be found.

In a case delivered in 2012 relating to the Church of Saintes-Maries-de-la-Mer,[18] the Council of State provided a number of useful details. The dispute related to the roof terrace of the church which provided a panoramic view over the city and beyond, over the sea and the plain of Camargue; the *commune* had since the 1960s charged for this access. In its judgement, the Council of State recalls the traditional rule that using a building assigned to worship in accordance with the Acts of 1905 and 1907 'applies to the whole of a religious building, including necessary outbuildings that are operationally inseparable from the building of worship'. As a result, 'the roof of a religious building, as long as it is necessary for the proper conduct of religious celebrations organized in the building that it protects, is assigned to worship under these same provisions'. But the Council of State adds: 'However, that it is different for facilities which, even though they are located on the roof of the religious building, must be considered – in view of their specific characteristics and the possibility of accessing them without entering the religious building – as functionally separable from this building.' In other words, facilities that are functionally separable from the building remain at the disposal of the owner who can enhance them by organizing visits. This notion of functional separability can be appreciated in relation to two criteria: first, the very characteristics of the facilities in question and, secondly, the fact that they are accessible without entering the religious building. We may think here about visiting a tower or a church tower or even adjoining premises accessible from the outside and which are not used for worship. Seen from this angle, case law opens up interesting prospects for public entities that organize the enhancement of religious heritage, at least for buildings the layout of which lends itself to this type of development. In the parts that the Council of State determines as functionally inseparable from the building of worship, visits are of course allowed in accordance with Article L. 2124-31 of the General Code of Ownership by Public Entities,[19] they may even be charged for.

In line with these new provisions, the practical implementation of which is proving difficult, it is interesting to highlight that recent case law from the Council of State in terms of funding buildings of worship also tends more and more to juxtapose the religious interest and local public interest, whether for

18 Council of State, 20 June 2012, *Communes des Saintes-Maries-de-la-Mer*, no. 340648.

19 This article continues, by extending it, the right to visit provided for in Article 25 of the Act of 31 December 1913, which allowed charging a fee intended exclusively to fund the security and conservation of movable objects on exhibit.

promoting tourism,[20] culture[21] or artistic activities.[22] This case law has been abundantly discussed from the perspective of prohibiting subsidies for religions in Article 2 of the Act of 1905, but it cannot be understood in isolation from the transformations that are influencing law on religious heritage. These transformations which law on public religious heritage is undergoing today are disrupting the original economy of the 1905 Act. They accompany a process of enhancement and promotion of cultural and artistic religious heritage which is today still a work in progress, but sure to grow stronger over time.

References

Basdevant-Gaudemet, B. and Jankowiak, F. (eds) (2009), *Le droit ecclésiastique en Europe et à ses marges (XVIIIe–XXe siècles)* (Leuven: Peeters).

Delannoy, J.P. (2009), 'Cultuel et culturel dans les travaux parlementaires relatifs à la protection des monuments historiques (1880–1914)', in Basdevant-Gaudemet, B. and Jankowiak, F. (eds), 267–84.

Fornerod, A. (2013), *Le régime juridique du patrimoine religieux* (Paris: L'Harmattan).

Messner, F., Prélot, P.H. and Woehrling, J.M. (eds) (2013), *Traité de droit français des religions* (Paris: LexisNexis).

20 Council of State, 19 July 2011, *Fédération de la libre pensée et de l'action sociale du Rhône*, no. 308817. The French highest administrative court validates the town's funding of a lift facilitating access to the Basilica of Fourvière, on the grounds that if the equipment is likely to benefit the faithful, the facility is of local public interest, 'linked to the importance of cultural reach or developing tourism and the local economy …'.

21 See Council of State, 3 October 2011, *Communauté d'agglomération Saint-Étienne Métropole*, no. 326460, in which the Council of State approved the decision by said urban community to complete the construction of the Church of Firminy-Vert in accordance with the plans of Le Corbusier, on the grounds that in the deliberation it was envisaged that two-thirds of the future construction would be assigned to cultural activities, corresponding to the unfinished foundation of the building, with only the remaining third being assigned to worship.

22 Council of State, 19 July 2011, *Commune de Trélazé*, no. 308544. The Council of State approved the installation in a church of an organ paid for by the *commune* with the assignee's permission, provided that the organ could also be used by the *commune* 'so as to develop teaching of the arts and to organise cultural events targeting a communal public interest'.

Chapter 3
Funding Religious Heritage: The Role of the French *Fondation du Patrimoine*

Hans Guggenbühl

The boundaries of the category 'religious heritage' cannot be definitively fixed and depend on the point of view from which it is approached (use, ownership, legal or sociological approach ...). A correct, albeit somewhat restrictive, notion would limit religious heritage to assets that have been the subject of protection measures for historic monuments. Yet, it is precisely outside this boundary that the Heritage Foundation steps in, its role largely being concerned with unprotected heritage. Its specific character requires us first to introduce the Heritage Foundation (*la Fondation du Patrimoine*). This will be followed by a detailed analysis of its achievements in support of religious heritage. Finally, the actions of the Foundation will, if briefly, be placed within the French context of *laïcité.*

Introducing the Heritage Foundation

According to Article L. 143-1 of the Heritage Code, the Heritage Foundation 'is a private, non-profit legal entity, subject to the rules on recognized foundations of public utility, respecting the provisions of this chapter'. The Heritage Foundation was created on 2 July 1996 by an act passed in a frenzy of enthusiasm, thus according its statutes a legislative basis, something which is extremely rare. The recognition of its public utility was to follow on 18 April 1997. According to Article 1 of the annex to the Decree of 18 April 1997 on the recognition of public utility and approval of the statutes of the Foundation:

> The Heritage Foundation is set up to promote knowledge, conservation and development of national heritage.
> It is committed to the identification, preservation and development of unprotected heritage.
> It contributes to safeguarding monuments, buildings, groups of movables or remarkable elements of natural or landscaped areas threatened with degradation, disappearance or dispersal. It thereby contributes to employment, recruitment, training and transmission of expertise in the areas of restoration and enhancement of heritage and sites. It supports public or private persons, notably via subsidies, in the acquisition, maintenance, management and presentation to the public of

> these assets, whether or not they are the subject of protection measures provided for in law.
> It may also acquire assets referenced in the third paragraph, where such acquisition is a necessary part of its actions to safeguard what it is putting in place.[1]
> It can assign a label to unprotected heritage and sites. This label is likely to be taken into account when granting approval under 1.3 of part II of Article 156 of the General Tax Code. […]

It was founded by 14 large groups (industrial, banking, professional federations, foundations), reunited and led by Édouard de Royère, captain of industry and first President of the Foundation. The initial capital contribution was 40 million francs (the equivalent of slightly more than six million euros).

A private body, the Foundation also welcomes representatives from national public institutions onto its Board of Directors, such as from the Ministry of the Interior, Culture, the Environment, the Senate or the National Assembly. The advisory boards for Jewish and Protestant heritage, which I have had the honour of forming and presiding over, include highly qualified figures, as well as representatives from heritage associations who contribute to the actions of the Foundation. The boards are internal bodies that provide an opinion to the Directorate-General of the Foundation on the appropriateness of an intervention. In practice, such advice is generally followed. They equally decide on the amount of any grant awarded.

If the initial inspiration was certainly the formula of the British 'Trust', here we are dealing with 'a foundation of a new kind that does not fit into the usual legal categories, aimed at acquiring private support for its mission' (Court of Auditors[2] 2013: 525). With regard to tradition and the French institutional landscape, the Foundation embodies a very original public-private mix,[3] with an operating structure that is appropriately decentralized, not devoid of a certain pragmatism, a rather Anglo-Saxon concept, globally oriented towards efficiency as well as to strengthening good citizenship.[4] The Foundation now has a territorial structure,

---

1 In practice, this option is not really used.

2 *Cour des comptes*.

3 See, more generally on this issue, Cornu and Fromageau (1999).

4 It was also decided in case law that the Foundation should provide a public service 'having regard to the general interest of its activity, the conditions of its creation, organization or its operation, the obligations which are imposed upon it, as well as the measures taken to verify that the objectives assigned to it are achieved'. Furthermore, 'with regard to missions assigned to the Heritage Foundation and the fiscal consequences linked to the granting of an authorization, the administrative court is competent to deal with the legality of the Foundation's acts in granting and withdrawing the label', Administrative Court of Clermont-Ferrand, 3 February 2009, no. 080834.

insofar as delegations in the regions and *départements* were set up soon after its creation.[5]

The tasks entrusted to the Heritage Foundation are of varying order. The first objective consists in identifying, safeguarding and developing the immense – not to say immeasurable – local heritage. At least 400,000 sites make up this category. Local heritage consists of unsung treasures or those whose conservation is threatened, unprotected by the state as historic monuments (through classification or registration), yet worthy of being handed down to posterity. Its ambition is then to mobilize both private, individual and collective energies and foster partnerships. Within such an approach, the Foundation encourages and develops both corporate patronage and the large pool of people's patronage, both often lacking, or seeking relevant uses. Finally, the Foundation aims to promote the transmission of knowledge for the preservation of heritage as well as employment, thus becoming an actor in sustainable development, including in the natural environment.

The Role of the Heritage Foundation in the Domain of Religious Cultural Heritage

The Spiritualities in Question

To introduce this section, it may be meaningful to quote an extract from the letter of engagement sent to me by Édouard de Royère the President of the Foundation, when he entrusted me with a specific mandate for Protestant and Jewish faiths in 2005. These lines could have been written at the birth of the Foundation:

> Beyond our duty to transmit to future generations the legacies of those who preceded us, the Heritage Foundation has the burning obligation to reinforce the cohesion of our country, to strengthen the social bond and, to this end, defend and promote our cultural and spiritual heritage, while respecting its entire diversity.

The tone was set and, thanks to the efficiency of its internal organization and decentralized deployment, satisfactory results have been achieved with progress ongoing.

It is true to say that, quite logically, Catholic religious heritage in France almost exclusively benefited from the actions of the Heritage Foundation in the early years. What is more, its artistic richness and symbolism in general make it a field of investigation over the long term.

Then, from 2005–2006, Protestant and Jewish cultural religious heritage in France was added to the Foundation's numerous targets for action. Not only is the influence of these two spiritualities inversely proportional to their numbers of followers, but they still also have a remarkable cultural heritage, even though,

5 On this point, see Decré (1999: 29).

when it comes to Protestants, their temples were all razed to the ground in the aftermath of the Revocation of the Edict of Nantes by King Louis XIV in 1685. The two communities – which willingly declare their mutual 'tenderness'– also have in common (except for in Alsace-Moselle) a relatively rural dispersion in diaspora and a concentration in the cities. It should be added that the national representative bodies of the various faiths engage strongly in collaboration with the Heritage Foundation, including through their presence in the aforementioned advisory boards. They contribute effectively, making use of resources in their spheres of influence to communicate with their audiences, whether via newspapers (*Tribune juive*, *La Croix*, *Réforme* …) or other channels of communication. We may emphasize above all the involvement of local religious structures (mainly religious associations) in the submission of funding requests; as project managers, they play a pivotal role in raising money.

As a result, the measures implemented by the Heritage Foundation to the three aforementioned spiritualities regularly account for roughly 74 per cent of the total amount of the Foundation's annual commitments.

As to other spiritualities present on the national territory, their heritage with regard to the Foundation may be considered, to date, to be 'in the making', in the sense that one should expect that these assets are part of heritage and the need for their protection finds expression as such.

Criteria for Intervention

The Foundation's intervention criteria with respect to religious cultural assets do not differ from those applied to the great diversity of its commitments. The first of these criteria is quite logically that of the heritage interest of the asset, which is based on the architecture itself, the memorial and historic dimension.[6] Also to be taken into account is assignment of the project management (with some exceptions) to a local authority (*commune*), to an association (including religious associations, such as dioceses and consistories) and the heritage strictly speaking, a criterion for which architectural characteristics play a crucial role. Logically, buildings such as churches, temples, synagogues, places of remembrance, sanctuaries, chapels, cemeteries, enclosures and presbyteries are taken into consideration. In the same spirit, religious movables, including organs and related works of art, are also considered. The Foundation's intervention provides for restoration work only, excluding replacement by anything new, even if perfectly identical. Regarding work to buildings (interior and exterior), those involving heating, electricity and

---

6 The opinion of the architect of *Bâtiments de France* is taken into consideration for property belonging to individuals, but not for that owned by local authorities. The architects of *Bâtiments de France* are civil servants in charge of the implementing of legislation on cultural heritage in each *département*.

security are excluded. On the other hand, intervening on façades, windows, roofs, stained glass,[7] floors and paintings is permitted.

Finally, the criteria for the Foundation's intervention are of course financial, which works as follows.[8] The funding plan must be watertight in its entirety. There is also a requirement *sine qua non* for public fundraising, in the sense that 'popular' patronage is required, amounting to 5 per cent of the cost of eligible works. This 5 per cent limit is certainly not exhaustive and a higher sum can obviously be obtained or, in the best of cases, the total amount for the proposed work. This obligation is the keystone of the system, which is based on the proximity of the site and its interest from a heritage standpoint. There will therefore be no grant from the Foundation in the absence or failure of 'popular' fundraising. It is worth noting that the label, issued by the body to private owners whose property fulfils the conditions (heritage interest and non-protected as historic monuments), allows them to benefit from tax deductions for protection or restoration work.

However, the overall financial volume to be incurred by the Foundation in respect of Catholic heritage is not specifically prescribed every year. Such is not the case for Protestant and Jewish heritage, which benefits from annual donations laid down since 2006, amounting to 150,000 euros per year (or 900,000 euros up to 2011 inclusive). The sum was raised to 200,000 euros per annum from 2012, in principle for three years.

The percentage of subsidy in relation to the amount of works eligible can vary, with the average being around 11 per cent, and the rate is often higher for very small operations. It very exceptionally attains a maximum of 40 per cent. One satisfactory observation can be made in this regard, namely that in many cases the active, intermediary presence of the Heritage Foundation is the factor triggering the interest – and therefore the financial contribution – both from the public (in terms of the local population or further afield) and various local bodies. But it cannot be denied that, in this context, the idea of the binding premise of popular patronage has proven itself to be formidable, its effectiveness having exceeded all expectations.

The Financial Means Put in Place

One must distinguish here between two categories that sometimes interlink – Foundation's own funds and external funds.

The former includes the initial endowment (long since granted), contributions from members of the Foundation (individuals, *communes*, businesses), gifts and bequests, as well as financial investments.

---

7 Only their restoration is funded, not their replacement.

8 Emphasis will be placed here on the heritage of local authorities, as most religious heritage is public property. For actions by the Heritage Foundation to assist private persons, see the Foundation's website: http://www.fondation-patrimoine.org/ (accessed 29 January 2014).

External funds include those from popular patronage via public participation, therefore local, like the sites concerned. Indeed, the Foundation undertakes operations to 'mobilize popular patronage': 'residents, traders and local contractors, tourists and all those attached to the site, may donate to the project, to raise the money required for its completion.' Donors benefit on that basis from tax reductions. This popular dimension – in the noble sense of the term – singularly echoes remarks made regarding the adoption of the FARO Convention within the Council of Europe and according to which: 'Heritage atrophies in the absence of public involvement and public support. This is why heritage processes must move beyond the preoccupations of the experts in government ministries and the managers of public institutions, and include the different public who inhabit our cities, towns and villages' (Palmer 2009: 8). In addition, there are funds from companies, including from large corporate patrons (rarely religion-oriented) and small or medium-sized companies often grouped into 'patronage clubs'. For these two types of external funds, 'generosity' flew through the roof as a result of the revision to taxation in Act no. 2009–709 of 1 August 2003 on patronage, associations and foundations, known as the Aillagon Act. The principle introduced by this act is as follows: 'The tax credit granted to companies is henceforth 60% of the amount of their payments, up to a limit of five per thousand of their turnover, with the possibility of spreading the tax deduction over five consecutive years, should the threshold for deductibility be exceeded.'[9] In fact, France was lagging miles behind other countries in matters of tax deductibility, both for individuals and businesses. The positive effect was quickly felt.

Still in respect of external funds, it is advisable to mention those arising from partnerships with local authorities, often conscious of the favourable effects from economic and social viewpoints, in addition to the strictly cultural and heritage aspects. Finally, external funds come directly from the state and consist of an allocation of a portion of unclaimed estates. This new contribution was established by the Finance Act 2003 (Article 13),[10] resulting from an initiative by Senator Yann Gaillard, who argued in this regard that there would be consistency 'in devoting to heritage what the state received as a legacy from the French people' (Court of Auditors 2013: 527). This 'windfall' increased the overall contribution from the sums collected by the state from 30 per cent to 50 per cent, in other words an annual allocation ranging from 8 to 11 million euros for the exclusive benefit of the Heritage Foundation. Three remarks should be made in this regard. On the one hand, one can see a recognition by public authorities of the quality of the Foundation's work. On the other hand, thanks to its relative regularity and magnitude, this endowment helps the Foundation to argue on many issues from a year-on-year perspective. Lastly, the endowment largely funds religious

9 Reply to Parliamentary question no. 100268, *Journal officiel*, *Assemblée nationale*, 31 October 2006.

10 Finance Act no. 2002–1575 of 30 December 2002 for 2003. See also Decree no. 2004–868 dated 26 August 2004.

cultural heritage. May it long continue, because it counts for much in achieving the ambitions of the Heritage Foundation.

The 'Religious' at the Heart of the Heritage Foundation

What was described as an 'adventure' (including its 'religious' element) at the outset by its President, Édouard de Royère has turned out be a real success story. The confidence of public authorities has strengthened over the years: from their point of view, the rigorous governance of the Heritage Foundation brings a kind of national surety to interventions. It even ensures the traceability of funds and, more generally, a greater transparency, all important considerations when, in part, management of public funds is at stake.

Regarding religious cultural heritage, one cannot exclude fears expressed here and there, as to alleged communitarianism, all the more as public authorities – the guarantors of *laïcité* – have the duty of best managing national cohesion in the diversity of its elements. Here, the figures speak for themselves, illustrating the practical implementation of the rules examined above. Thus, of the project holders who can be labelled 'religious', 80 per cent are from the *communes*, 17 per cent associations and 1 per cent joint *communes*. With regard to the proportion of religious buildings belonging to *communes*, the first of these percentages will come as no surprise. Then, as regards the proportion of religious sites, there are 60 per cent Catholic churches, 13 per cent chapels, 13 per cent movables, 1.5 per cent Protestant temples and 0.4 per cent synagogues. Furthermore, in the area of religious heritage, since 2002, 2,782 public fundraising initiatives were successful, of which 1,420 have been completed. Such contributions have provided, on average, 11 per cent of the costs of the works. In 2011, there were 789 new fundraising initiatives, including 580 for solely religious heritage. Over 10 years, public fundraising has accounted for about 8 million euros, including 6 million from individuals. Work carried out in this context has been of the order of 120 million euros in relation to 1,420 completed fundraising initiatives, as mentioned above.

To this could be added, in general, that in the light of the realities uncovered on the ground, that is a certain spontaneity in the collaboration between public and private parties, based on mutual respect and concordant visions of heritage, one can safely say that French *laïcité*, deeply rooted in mentalities, is fortunately not free from intelligent flexibility, especially when it is associated, as here, with the issue of safeguarding the heritage that belongs to us all.

Similarly, one can easily imagine that there would be few citizens rejoicing in a decline in religiosity, such as desacralization, re-qualification or re-appropriation of famous religious sites, therefore in a lack of interest in safeguarding them. Quite the contrary, because religious cultural heritage, like so many other monuments, is more than a witness to the past and traditions, more than a preserver of memory: it is, in our opinion, the receptacle (not to say the setting) of one of the most worthy cross-denominational, cross-generational and, hopefully, cross-temporal messages which humanity needs in its destiny and our national society in its dignity.

With this in mind, it appears that, for many 'workers' of any rank in the Heritage Foundation, for the majority of donors and hundreds of volunteers involved in these achievements, serving such a noble cause is not only a privilege, but a discreet offering to our country.

References

Cornu, M. and Fromageau, J. (eds) (1999), *Fondation et trust dans la protection du patrimoine* (Paris: L'Harmattan).

Cour des Comptes (2013), *Rapport public annuel. La Fondation du patrimoine: un modèle singulier* (Paris: La Documentation française), 521–47. Available at: http://www.ccomptes.fr/Publications/Publications/Rapport-public-annuel-2013 (accessed 29 January 2014).

Decré, M. (1999), 'La Fondation du patrimoine, philosophie et pratique d'une institution nouvelle', in Cornu, M. and Fromageau, J. (eds), 27–33.

Palmer, R. (2009), Preface to *Heritage and Beyond* (Strasbourg: Council of Europe Publishing), 7–9.

Chapter 4
Funding Religious Heritage in Local Law in Alsace-Moselle

Francis Messner

Introduction

If we start by assuming the specific nature of funding for religious heritage in local law in Alsace and Moselle, we would first need to seek it out in the principle behind the existence of this law and in relation to the historical circumstances which governed its constitution. This applies as much to the law on historic monuments as to that prevailing for religious assets: the specific nature of the latter responds to the absence of the former. Indeed, if there is no local law on historic monuments, specific rules apply, however, to the restoration and maintenance of buildings used by the four recognized religious denominations for public worship, conferring a specificity on management of religious inheritance in the three *départements* (counties) of the East of France (the Lower Rhine, Upper Rhine and Moselle). Assets that make up this historical and cultural heritage are both numerous and diverse as to their status. Mandatory and voluntary subsidies from local authorities and the state, as well as contributions from public and private organizations, have enabled an important and well-maintained religious heritage to be preserved in these three *départements*. Indeed, in conjunction with public religious institutions (établissements publics du culte) responsible for managing material and financial interests of recognized religious groups, in Alsace and Moselle there are foundations, registered associations and jointly owned property managed by public institutions whose purpose is to preserve religious heritage. We will begin by considering the latter in greater detail.

The Composition of Religious Heritage in Alsace-Moselle

Religious heritage in Alsace-Moselle consists very largely, or even exclusively, of immovables and movables belonging to the four recognized religious denominations (see *infra*) and reflects different architectural trends.

It includes jewels of Romanesque art, such as the Church of St Foy in Guebwiller, the octagonal Church of St Peter and Paul in Ottmarsheim and the Church of St Peter and Paul in Rosheim. Gothic art is mainly represented by the church, which is the seat of the Archbishop of Strasbourg, Notre-Dame Cathedral.

The classical period gave rise to numerous constructions, particularly under the impetus of the Jesuit artisans of the Counter-Reformation, such as the Church of the Trinity and St Georges in Molsheim or the Parish Church of St Étienne in Rosheim. Baroque art finds expression in Ebersmunster with its remarkable Benedictine abbey church, now a parish church. The construction of buildings of worship restarted with intensity in the nineteenth century. During the Second German Reich, the absorption of churches assigned to the two Christian faiths (Catholic and Protestant), called '*simultanea*', led to a series of neo-Gothic constructions, witnesses of a period marked by romanticism and nostalgia for an idealized Middle Ages. The neo-Baroque style developed during the period in some localities, as evidenced by the Church of St Fridolin in Mulhouse, modelled on the Abbey Church of St Fridolin in Bad Saeckingen (Baden-Württemberg). It should also be recalled that numerous renowned spiritual centres, such as Mont St Odile or Mariental and Thierenbach, which are both places of pilgrimage and parishes. Grand seminaries, episcopal palaces and a multitude of clergy houses used for the public service of worship and protected as historic monuments also form part of this religious heritage.

To complete the picture, we should highlight Jewish heritage in the region.[1] More generally, the property portfolio of the Jewish faith stands out from that in the rest of France by its dwindling religious use.[2] On the other hand, the heritage approach to Jewish cultural assets is characterized by its richness. Some *European routes of Jewish heritage* have been created in France, one of which passes through Alsace and Lorraine. These routes include different testimonies of the life of local Jewish communities, involving synagogues, ritual bathing and cemeteries or even a *matzah* bread factory dating back to 1870 (Wasselonne, Bas-Rhin).

Law Applicable to Religious Heritage in Alsace-Moselle: Between Generalism and Particularity

The Applicability of the General Law on Historic Monuments

The Heritage Code, adopted in 2004 and including a Book VI devoted to historic monuments, protected sites and spaces, applies throughout French territory. In Alsace and Moselle, local law is still in force in several areas – including the

1 See the heritage conservation project run by the Heritage Foundation: http://www.fondation-patrimoine.org/fr/alsace-1/tous-les-projets-128/detail-fonds-pour-la-sauvegarde-du-patrimoine-juif-du-bas-rhin-14610 (accessed 7 May 2014).

2 See Jarassé (1991: 164): out of 88 buildings in Alsace-Moselle, 'there are barely 36 that have not been transformed; some, moreover, do not offer more than one service a year', while in the rest of France, 38 out of 48 buildings are still in use. The former Strasbourg synagogue, built in 1896, belonged to the neo-Romanesque style. Burned and razed to the ground by the Nazis, it was rebuilt in 1954 in a resolutely modern style.

system of the four recognized religions (see *infra*) – which are governed by specific provisions.[3] There is no local law, however, on the conservation of historic monuments. Indeed, at the time when the French Act of 30 March 1887 was passed, which established for the first time in a legal text the criteria and procedure for the classification of historic monuments, Alsace-Lorraine was part of the Second German Reich. Member states exercising their jurisdiction in this area did not have any *ad hoc* legal tools. The Germans – and specifically the Confederation of Learned and Archaeological Societies and the National Confederation of German Architects – considered the French system put in place by the Act of 1887 with interest and expressed their desire for a law that would apply to all the states of the Reich (Michler 2013). More modestly, the French model inspired the first Act on historic monuments by a federal, that of the Grand Duchy of Hesse-Darmstadt, which entered into force on 1 October 1902. Felix Wolff, Curator for Historic Monuments in Strasbourg at that time, regretted not being able to achieve the same results in Alsace and Lorraine as in France and Hesse-Darmstadt. It was only in the aftermath of the First World War that the entirety of German federal states adopted laws protecting historic monuments. Once returned to France, the *départements* of the Rhine and Moselle were to be placed under the regime of the French Act of 31 December 1913, which replaced that of 1887 (Michler 2013).

It should be mentioned that the 1913 Act was only introduced much later in the three *départements* of the Lower Rhine, Upper Rhine and Moselle. It was made applicable to immovables by the Act of 20 March 1929, introducing legislative and regulatory provisions relating to historic monuments and immovables in these *départements*. The reintegration of the department of architecture in Alsace into the administrative organization of historic monuments would itself be gradual (Auduc 2008: 464 *et seq.*). But it was not until the Act of 30 December 1963 that this regime was applied to movables in the three *départements*. Article 2 of the Act of 1963 provides for 'repeal of all provisions contrary to this Act and, in particular, Article 5 of the Act of 20 March 1929, introducing legislative and regulatory provisions relating to historic monuments and immovables in the *départements* of the Lower Rhine, Upper Rhine and Moselle'.[4] This delay could be explained by the concern of the legislator in 1929 to avoid, by excluding movable objects from the scope of the Act, 'colliding with a clergy fearful of seeing the classification amend the legal status of the objects used for worship, most often property of the public religious institutions' (Jung 1962: 2).

The regime of historic monuments in these *départements* is therefore more or less the same. Thus, 'the transcription of classification and registration decisions does not take place in the mortgage office, as in other French *départements*, but in the form of a marginal mention on the land register' (Perrin 1962). Above all, conservation and maintenance of buildings is a matter for institutions of recognized religions (parish *fabriques*, episcopal mensa, presbyteral councils and

3 On the local law of Alsace-Moselle in general, see Glenn (1974).

4 On this issue, see Fornerod (2013).

Protestant consistories, consistories for the Jewish faith in the *départements*), in collaboration with departments of historic monuments. Indeed, the understanding of the funding mechanisms for religious heritage in Alsace-Moselle depends closely on the influence of the local law on religions.

The Influence of Local Law on Religions

Generally speaking, local law, territorially applicable only to the *départements* of the Lower Rhine, Upper Rhine and Moselle, is made up of three elements: 'the French texts prior to 1870, the so-called laws of Alsace-Lorraine of a local nature and, finally, the so-called laws of the Empire applicable throughout Germany' (Woehrling 2012). Local law on religions currently in force was established by the Act of 18 Germinal year X (Concordat and Organic Articles of the Catholic religion and Protestant faiths) and by two decrees of 17 March 1808 concerning the Jewish faith. Preserved in the Imperial Territory of Alsace-Lorraine *(Reichsland Elsass-Lothringen)* following the annexation of the three *départements* of the East by the Second German Reich, local law on religions was maintained by the Act of 17 October 1919 and later by that of 1 June 1924. Its legality was enshrined in an opinion of the Council of State of 24 January 1925. Abolished by the Nazis in 1940, it was revived by an Order of 13 September 1944, in the context of the restoration of republican law.[5]

In local law on religions in Alsace-Moselle, the Catholic dioceses of Strasbourg and Metz, the Protestant Reformed Church of Alsace and Lorraine and the Protestant Church of the Confession of Augsburg in Alsace and Lorraine (both combined into a federation), the Union of Protestantism in Alsace and Lorraine and the Jewish faith are organized by the state within the framework of local districts and public religious institutions. The religious leaders of these four religions paid by the Ministry of the Interior are appointed either directly by the head of state or the prime minister, or subsequent to a governmental agreement endorsing the nomination made by religious authorities, or else freely appointed by religious authorities. Protestant and Catholic parishes and Jewish consistories that are self-funded are managed by public religious institutions (*établissements publics du culte*). The latter take care of all expenditure linked to worship, except that of providing lodgings for religious leaders or, failing that, paying a housing allowance, which is a direct obligation of the *communes*. *Communes* and their clusters are responsible for balancing the budgets of local or parish public religious institutions when they are in deficit.[6]

---

5 A decision by the Constitutional Council of 21 February 2013 (no. 2012-297 QPC) confirmed that local law on religions and in particular the remuneration of ministers of recognized religions was consistent with the French Constitution.

6 The state also bears the costs of religious education taught to students of the four recognized religions in state primary and secondary schools, as well as maintenance of two faculties of Catholic theology (Strasbourg and Metz) and a faculty of Protestant theology.

Non-recognized religions organize themselves within the framework of private law and may receive voluntary subsidies from local authorities.

Religious Heritage in Alsace-Moselle: Differing Statutes

Buildings Used for Local or Parochial Worship

Local law on recognized religions protects and guarantees the use for worship of all buildings legally assigned to the locality or the parish providing a public service for the Catholic, Protestant and Jewish faiths. It includes legally owned church buildings that are necessary for the proper functioning of the recognized religions. Protestant and Catholic parish churches, consistorial synagogues in the *départements* and the synagogues in rabbinical districts form part of these.

Buildings used for lodging ministers and properties of *communes* are part of the public, municipal domain. As such, they are inalienable and imprescriptible. Buildings of worship under legal ownership are exclusively used for worship. In principle, they cannot be used, even temporarily, for another purpose. *Ad hoc* derogations from use for worship for cultural events compatible with the specific nature of the place must be authorized by the religious leader in charge of the parish or rabbinical district of the place of worship concerned. Church buildings and municipal clergy houses are made redundant by order of the *préfet* where there is the agreement of the religious authority, in accordance with Article 1 of the Decree of 23 November 1994.[7]

The obligation to repair and embellish these buildings falls to public religious institutions: the *fabriques* for the Catholic Church, presbyteral councils for Protestant parishes, consistories in the *départements* for the Jewish faith. They are funded through donations, bequests and gifts bestowed at weddings and funerals, from the income of the assets of these institutions and, lastly, by voluntary grants from local authorities. Unlike Catholics and Protestants, members of the Jewish community are obliged to pay a contribution to consistories. In the absence of such payment, they do not appear on the electoral register of their rabbinical district.

Available revenue covers operating and investment costs of these public religious institutions, including the costs necessary for worship, insuring goods and people and covering public liability risks, salaries and costs of personnel employed by the institution (sacristan, cleaning staff) and, lastly, improvement, maintenance and repair work and reconstruction of buildings of recognized religions (temples, churches, synagogues) and lodgings for ministers of religion appointed at the head of a parish (clergy houses) or a rabbinical district.

Religious buildings used for the public service of local or parish worship, whether or not classified or registered as historic monuments and whether owned by the *communes* or public religious institutions, are necessarily maintained and

7 *Journal officiel* no. 279, 2 December 1994, p. 17022.

repaired by the aforementioned public religious institutions. But the resources of public religious institutions are often inadequate, especially when major work must be carried out on these buildings. In case of insufficient income from the *fabriques*, presbyteral councils and consistories, as justified by their accounts and budgets, the costs of worship – and importantly for our study – those related to the maintenance of religious buildings, are required to be included in the budget of the *communes*.[8] Communities of *communes* and urban area communities may exercise such authority in lieu of member *communes*.[9]

Project management is provided by the *commune* or the public religious institution concerned. Public religious institutions very rarely take on project management due to their non-eligibility for recovering value-added tax. On the other hand, work carried out by the *communes* on a building of worship or a clergy house owned by the *commune* confers a right to compensation from the *Fonds de compensation de la TVA*, as long as it constitutes a compulsory charge.

Local and Parochial Buildings of Worship of Recognized Religions Without Legal Title

This category of buildings includes relief chapels (Catholic faith), subsidiary churches (Protestant faiths) and subsidiary synagogues (Jewish faith). These places of worship, where the celebrations of the parish or local faith are permitted by the administration, were built at the request of parishes or individuals, with the agreement of the religious authority, due to the vast area of the religious district and difficulties of communication. Necessary for religious practice in the nineteenth century, when the distance travelled by the faithful to the parish place of worship was an obstacle to attending religious services, they no longer have the same utility today; parishes have been regrouped and religious celebrations are in sharp decline due to the drop in religious practice and the decrease in the number of religious leaders in the Catholic Church. Those buildings without legal title are assigned for worship using administrative regulations, at the end of the procedure authorizing them to open, which is in reality an assignment – to religious use – procedure and thus a measure of protection. They are made redundant using the same procedure as for buildings with legal title. Thus, the relief chapel of Vieux Thann (Church of St Odile), built in 1960, was the subject of a risk order in 2011 and was transferred to the *commune* by the *fabrique* council (its owner) for one symbolic euro. The redundant and desacralized building will be transformed into a cultural and sports centre.

Subsidiary churches and synagogues, as well as relief chapels, which are included in a parish or rabbinical district, are exclusively maintained by their

8 Article L. 5812-1 and L. 5814-1 of the local government Code (*Code général des collectivités territoriales*).

9 Local government Code, Art. L. 2543-3, 3°.

owners: *communes* or public religious institutions.[10] The *commune* does not intervene under the principle of subsidiarity.

Maintenance of a building of worship or a clergy house can be funded at local or parish level by many public and private institutions: mandatory or voluntary local subsidies from *communes*, voluntary grants from general councils and the regional council, donations from the faithful, subsidies from associations established to maintain a church building, grants from the public religious institution and Heritage Foundation grants.

When these places of worship, with legal title or not, are historic monuments – classified or registered – work is undertaken under the supervision of the administration of cultural affairs, which pays the subsidy granted by the Ministry of Culture to the recipient religious denomination.

Diocesan Buildings

Cathedral churches

Cathedral churches are represented by cathedral *fabriques*, at the head of which the diocesan bishop plays a dominant role in accordance with standard regulations approved by the administration in 1822. The Ministry of Culture bears the costs of maintaining these buildings in the name of national cultural heritage, as for all cathedrals in France built before the Act of 18 Germinal year X (8 April 1802). Metz Cathedral, which has no parish, is one such case.

When the parish is merged with the chapter, as in Strasbourg where the cathedral is also a parish church, the *commune* is required in principle to fulfil its subsidiary role for everything relating to the costs of parish worship. Furthermore, restoration and maintenance of Strasbourg Cathedral are dependent on a special statute, which naturally involves the state, but above all the *Fondation de l'Œuvre Notre-Dame*, which is a foundation in local law created in the Middle Ages and administered by the City of Strasbourg by Consular Order of 23 November 1803.[11] The budget of the *Fondation de l'Œuvre Notre-Dame* amounts on average to 2 or even 2.5 million euros per year. Half is made up from revenue from its land and real estate assets. The rest comes from a balancing subsidy paid by the City of Strasbourg. An agreement signed on 26 June 1999 determines the relations between the state and the *Fondation de l'Œuvre Notre-Dame*. It assigns the foundation the status of Delegate Project Manager for certain operations on Strasbourg Cathedral. According to this same convention, the management of works is ensured by a chief

---

10 See the ruling: Strasbourg Administrative Court, 9 February 1988, *Conseil de fabrique de la paroisse de Bazoncourt-Sanry-Sur-Nied*.

11 In its recommendation on management of cathedrals and other major religious buildings in use, the Council of Europe refers to this foundation and considers it, among others, a possible 'arrangement' to be 'reached between the religious authorities and those concerned (at local and national levels) with the conservation of the cultural heritage'. See Parliamentary Assembly, Council of Europe (2000).

architect who combines the titles of Chief Architect of Historic Monuments and Architect of the *Fondation de l'Œuvre Notre-Dame*. Other local authorities do not participate as a rule in restoring this building. The Ministry of Culture participates in funding the works. For example, it contributed 4,445,000 euros between 2000 and 2005 for ancillary work to the spire and octagon. The cathedral's Society of Friends, which was established in 1902 to safeguard the cathedral, is a local law association the utility of whose public purpose mission was recognized in 2001 by prefectoral order. It recently contributed 350,000 euros to the restoration of the stained-glass windows. Finally, the *fabrique* of the Cathedral of Strasbourg is responsible for maintaining the astronomical clock.

The buildings assigned for training the clergy and lodging bishops
Contrary to other recognized religions, the Ministry of the Interior (and its internal department of religious affairs) maintains the diocesan buildings of the Catholic Church: episcopal palaces and grand seminaries. Pursuant to Article 106 of the Decree of 30 December 1809, the *départements* within a diocese were held to the same obligations towards the cathedral *fabrique* as the *communes* were towards their parochial *fabriques*. Since the Act of 10 May 1823, the state was to perform this subsidiary role. In practice, credits are voted annually onto the state budget in relation to estimated needs. Maintenance of the diocesan buildings of the bishoprics of Metz and Strasbourg amounted to 0.05 million euros in 2005. The episcopal palace in Strasbourg, which was the residence of the dean of the great chapter under the *Ancien Régime*, was built in 1727 and registered on the list of historic monuments by the Decree of 25 June 1929, which does not however alter its funding, obligatorily provided by the state.

Maintaining a Historic Monument which is the Property of the Public Establishment of the Episcopal Mensa

The diocese, in local law on religions, is a district that does not have legal personality. The bishops circumvent this difficulty by using the episcopal mensa – representing the interests of the episcopal title – to manage and acquire diocesan property with the agreement of the administration. The mensa, which is managed by the bishop, administers the assets necessary for diocesan pastoral activity. The episcopal mensa notably owns Mont St Odile, bought by the bishopric in 1853 and which is a place of pilgrimage and a renowned tourist site, welcoming throughout the year tens of thousands of tourists and pilgrims. The 'convent' of Mont St Odile is maintained by the episcopal mensa and public subsidies. The first stage of major renovation work undertaken in 2006 amounted to 8,799,800 euros. The state contributed 632,000 euros, the Alsace regional council 2,144,000 euros, the county general council 2,000,000 euros, individuals and various donors contributed 279,000 euros and the archbishopric 3,743,000 euros. The management of Mont St Odile illustrates the possibilities offered by local law for collaboration between religious authorities and public authorities with regard to (mainly) public buildings hosting activities of general or local interest.

The Specificities of the Lutheran Church

The recognized Lutheran denomination, whose goods were not secularized during the French Revolution, benefits from jointly owned property belonging to several parishes, but managed by the consistories and foundations that contribute to the restoration of religious heritage.

The assets of the Protestant Church of the Confession of Augsburg (EPCAAL) and the Reformed Protestant Church (EPRAL) were not secularized during the Revolution. The Decree of 1 December 1790 forbids possessions from the public religious institutions of the two Augsburg and Helvetic denominations in Alsace from being nationalized and from clergy property being sold, as decided on 2 November 1789. The Lutheran Church (EPCAAL) has an important real estate from which part of the revenue is assigned to maintaining religious buildings.

A first category of these assets is the property of parishes, parish annexes or consistories. These jointly owned assets called *fabriques (schaffnei)* still number seven. They are managed by the consistories, intermediary institutions between the parishes and the upper consistory, which is the deliberative assembly of EPCAAL. When these *fabriques* are required to maintain religious buildings, the managing consistory pays the sums available and the rest comes from the presbyteral council. In cases of insufficient revenues, the *commune* balances the budget.

The second category of assets consists of a set of foundations administered by the St Thomas Foundation, which is a foundation of local law, created by a local Act of 29 November 1873. The higher authorities of EPCAAL exercise a right of control over this institution, which funds, among others, places of worship. Thus, the clergy houses of the Protestant parishes of St Thomas, St Aurélie and St Nicolas in Strasbourg are properties of the St Thomas Foundation and maintained by it. It is also required to maintain the Church of St Thomas, seat of the authorities of the Lutheran Church (EPCAAL), a much frequented place dating from the late Romanesque period and part of the historical heritage of Alsace. Lutheran *fabriques*, as well as the St Thomas Foundation, facilitate the implementation of the principle of obligation to maintain religious buildings in local law through their revenue and the skills of the technical team employed by the St Thomas Foundation.

Conclusion

Modes of funding and protecting religious heritage tend to converge in local law and general law (applying throughout French territory). The Heritage Code applies to the whole of French territory and, in fact, maintaining church buildings and protecting their use do not diverge in general and local law.[12] The vast majority of buildings legally assigned to worship in general law (Act of 9 December 1905) are part of the public domain of the state and the *communes*. They are maintained by their owners with, if applicable, support from the Ministry of Culture. In the same way, in local law, public religious institutions or, subsidiarily, the *communes* are obliged to maintain and rebuild places of worship with legal title.

Taking charge of religious heritage is, however, much broader than that implemented in general law and this is for two main reasons.

The first relates to the diversity of the buildings that must be maintained by public authorities. It not only involves parish churches and cathedrals, but also housing for local ministers of religion, episcopal residences and grand seminaries. Diversity of course, but also streamlining – only buildings deemed necessary for worship are necessarily maintained by public authorities, although all places of worship of recognized religions, with legal title or not and the opening of which has been authorized by regulation, are exclusively assigned to religious practice. From this point of view, the disappearance of the religious use of a building and church redundancy puts heritage in Alsace-Moselle in the same problematic situation as the rest of French religious heritage, which is that of its reconversion and assignment to another use – social or cultural.

The second is related to the heritage importance of several public and private institutions whose revenues are allocated to maintain religious buildings and which contribute to creating healthy competition between the various groups required to maintain these buildings. In the end, this favourable context has generated expertise in this domain and a culture conducive to the maintenance and protection of religious heritage.

References

Auduc, A. (2008), *Quand les monuments construisaient la Nation: le Service des monuments historiques de 1830 à 1940* (Paris: La Documentation française).

Bady, J.B., Cornu, M., Fromageau, J., Leniaud, J.M. and Negri, V. (eds) (2013), *1913, Genèse d'une loi sur les monuments historiques* (Paris: La Documentation française).

Flores-Lonjou, M. and Messner, F. (eds) (2007), *Les lieux de culte en France et en Europe: statuts, pratiques, fonctions* (Leuven: Peeters).

Fornerod, A. (2013), *Le régime juridique du patrimoine religieux* (Paris: L'Harmattan).

Glenn, P. (1974), 'The local law of Alsace-Lorraine: A half century of survival', *The International and Comparative Law Quarterly*, 3: 4, 769–90.

Jarassé, D. (1991), *L'âge d'or des synagogues* (Paris: Herscher).

12 On general law on this matter, see Chapter 2 of this volume.

Jung, L. (1962–1963), *Rapport au nom de la commission des affaires culturelles du Sénat* (France: Journal Officiel Sénat), 1962–1963, Appendix no. 12.

Messner, F. (2005), 'Régime des cultes. Financement et patrimoine des cultes', *JurisClasseur Alsace-Moselle*, fascicule 232.

Messner, F. (2007), 'Les lieux de culte en Europe', in Flores-Lonjou, M. and Messner, F. (eds), 57–79.

Michler, F. (2013), 'La loi du 30 mars 1887 et son influence en Allemagne', in Bady, J.B, Cornu, M., Fromageau, J., Leniaud, J.M. and Negri, V. (eds), 48–59.

Parliamentary Assembly, Council of Europe (2000), *Recommendation 1484 (2000), Management of cathedrals and other major religious buildings in use*, available at: http://www.assembly.coe.int//Main.asp?link=http://www.assembly.coe.int/Documents/AdoptedText/ta00/erec1484.htm#1 (accessed 7 May 2014).

Perrin J. (1962), *Rapport relatif à l'extension aux départements concordataires de la loi du 31 décembre 1913 concernant les biens mobiliers* (France: Journal Officiel Assemblée Nationale), Appendix no. 1831.

Woehrling, J.M. (2012), 'Perspectives sur le droit local', *JurisClasseur Alsace-Moselle*, fascicule 30.

PART II
Funding Religious Heritage in Dominant Church Systems

Chapter 5
Living Hand-to-mouth: Regulating and Funding Religious Heritage in the United Kingdom

Frank Cranmer[1]

The United Kingdom consists of four jurisdictions – England, Scotland, Northern Ireland and Wales – and two of them have Churches 'established by law': the Church of England and the Church of Scotland. Responsibility for historic buildings is a devolved matter, with the result that there are four territorial executive agencies responsible for historic buildings: English Heritage, Historic Scotland, the Northern Ireland Environment Agency and, in Wales, Cadw.[2]

Funding for religious heritage across the United Kingdom is much more subject to the prevailing political and economic climate than in some of the other countries of Western Europe. The United Kingdom is not like France, where church buildings in existence at the time of the act separating church and state[3] are maintained largely at public expense. Nor, in modern times, has it had anything remotely resembling the church tax of the kind which seems to be causing so much controversy in Germany (and which, it should be said, has also enabled several of the Nordic countries to keep their churches in such good repair). In the United Kingdom, religious communities are largely expected to fund themselves.

Nor is the United Kingdom any longer a 'dominant Church system' – if, indeed, it has been so since the mid-nineteenth century when religious toleration was finally settled. Though the Church of England and the Church of Scotland each has a particular legal status within its own territory, there is no establishment of religion in Wales or Northern Ireland; moreover, the religious demography of the United Kingdom has long since ceased to be monochrome. So far as England and Wales are concerned, results from the 2011 United Kingdom Census (Office of National Statistics 2012) revealed that, though Christianity remains the major religious presence with 33.2 million adherents (59.3 per cent of the population:

1 Some of the material in this chapter is a revision and update of part of an earlier article written jointly with Javier García Oliva of Manchester University Law Department (Cranmer and García Oliva 2010).

2 Pronounced 'Cà-doo', which means 'to keep'.

3 Act of 9 December 1905 on separation between church and state. On this point, see Chapter 2 of this volume.

down from 41 million in 2001), about 9 per cent of the population belongs to a non-Christian religious community and roughly one in four professes no religion whatsoever.

Religious Heritage and the Legislative Framework[4]

Overall, built heritage generally has been subject to three types of control: planning consent, conservation area controls and listed building consent. Planning controls apply to development generally; conservation area controls apply only to buildings within specific, designated areas scheduled as being of townscape merit, while listed building consent applies specifically to buildings considered to be of architectural or historical importance, wherever situated.

Planning Control

From a historical point of view the original motivation of planning legislation was public health rather than building conservation. In England, especially, the result of the Industrial Revolution was massive migration from the countryside to the towns; and the urban population often lived in overcrowded housing without proper sanitation or clean drinking water. Sir Edwin Chadwick's report on the living conditions of the working class (Chadwick 1842) sparked a raft of legislation aimed at improving the living conditions and the health of the working population. Local authorities gradually assumed responsibility for providing clean water and removing sewage and refuse. It was made obligatory for new and rebuilt housing to have adequate drainage and basic sanitary facilities and builders had to demonstrate compliance to the local authority before starting work. By 1875, legislation had been passed to tackle the problem of overcrowded housing; but though the earliest modern planning legislation dates from the early twentieth century, starting with the Housing, Town Planning &c. Act 1919, the foundations of modern planning law in the United Kingdom were laid after the Second World War with the passing of the Town and Country Planning Act 1947 and the Town and Country Planning (Scotland) Act 1947.

Planning in England and Wales is governed by the Planning Act 2008 and the National Planning Policy Framework 2012 and Schedules 16 and 17 to the Enterprise and Regulatory Reform Act 2013 (in England) and by Planning Policy Wales 2012. In Scotland the basic legislation is Chapter 8 of the Town and Country Planning (Scotland) Act 1997 as amended by the Planning etc. (Scotland) Act 2006. In Northern Ireland the basic planning law is contained in the Planning

4 For a more detailed summary of the relevant legislation see Tsivolas (2014: 168 *et seq.*). I should like to thank Diana Evans and the legal officers of English Heritage for their very helpful elucidation of the effects of Schedule 17 to the Enterprise and Regulatory Reform Act 2013.

(Northern Ireland) Order 1991. It should be emphasized that planning control is about *buildings and infrastructure*, not about their contents. Moreover, *places of worship are subject to planning control like any other building.* Therefore, if a faith-community wishes to erect a new place of worship or substantially extend or alter an existing one it will not be able to do so without planning permission from the local authority. This is usually dealt with by submitting a planning application for the local authority's approval, though for certain types of work planning permission can be "deemed" to have been granted under the terms of the Town and Country Planning (General Permitted Development) Order 1995.

Conservation Area Control

Conservation areas are neighbourhoods designated by the local planning authority as being of special architectural or historic interest, not necessarily because of the architectural merit of the individual buildings in the area in question, but because of their overall value as townscape: the way in which the individual buildings relate to one another. Bearing that in mind, the policy is that the character of conservation areas should be preserved or enhanced.

Until recently, prior conservation area consent was required from the local planning authority for the demolition of an *unlisted* building in a conservation area, as well as for a listed one.[5] However, conservation area consent has been superseded by the provisions of Schedule 17 (*Heritage Planning Regulation*) to the Enterprise and Regulatory Reform Act 2013, which reformed the system by inserting a new section 196D into the Town and Country Planning Act 1990. That section requires *planning permission* for 'relevant demolition', defined as the demolition of an unlisted building in a conservation area in England, and makes it clear that it is a criminal offence to demolish such a building without such permission. However, under section 75(1)(b) of the Planning (Listed Buildings and Conservation Areas) Act 1990 that requirement does *not* apply to 'ecclesiastical buildings which are for the time being used for ecclesiastical purposes'.

Listed Building Control

Under the Planning (Listed Buildings and Conservation Areas) Act 1990, as amended, and the parallel legislation for Scotland and Northern Ireland, certain buildings may be 'listed' by central government as being of particular architectural or heritage importance, which means that their structure, fixtures and fittings are subject to local government control in respect of alterations. Rather confusingly, buildings are listed as Grade I, Grade II* and Grade II in England and Wales, Grade A, Grade B or Grade C in Scotland and Grade A, Grade B+, Grade B1 and B2 in Northern Ireland. The principles, however, are the same for all three

---

5 See English Heritage (2013).

jurisdictions: the highest grade is reserved in all cases for buildings of exceptional interest, some of which are of international importance.

The Churches collectively are responsible for a huge number of listed buildings in the United Kingdom. For example, 45 per cent of all Grade I buildings in England are churches and, in total, the Church of England owns about 12,500 listed buildings.[6] In Wales, 29 per cent of Grade I listed buildings are churches belonging to the Church in Wales.[7]

Listed building consent is normally required for the demolition or partial demolition of any listed building or for its alteration or extension in any manner that would affect its character as a building of special architectural or historic interest. Examples of changes that would normally require listed building consent are any extension whatsoever,[8] alterations such as replacement of doors and windows and changes to the interior fabric. However, as we shall see, consent is not necessarily required if the building in question is a place of worship and the denomination in question comes under the 'ecclesiastical exemption'.

Ecclesiastical exemption: England and Wales

Generally speaking, faith communities are subject to listed building controls like any other owner; however, in England and Wales the 'listed denominations' under the Ecclesiastical Exemption (Listed Buildings and Conservation Areas) Order 2010 are exempt from listed building controls on their churches. Currently, the listed denominations are the Church of England, the Church in Wales, the Roman Catholic Church, the Methodist Church, the Baptist Union of Great Britain, the Baptist Union of Wales and the United Reformed Church. In addition, the Church of Scotland is exempt in respect of its (very few) churches in England.

The basis of the exemption is a requirement that the exempt denominations operate robust controls of their own which the UK Government is prepared to recognize as equal in rigour to secular listed building control. In reality, the internal controls on alterations to church property operated by the Church of England and the Church in Wales – known as 'faculty jurisdiction' and administered by the ecclesiastical courts – are much tougher than secular listed building controls. It should also be noted that faculty jurisdiction extends much further than secular control, because it applies to *all* churches of the two denominations, irrespective of their heritage status.[9] Moreover, as Jonathan Goodchild (1995) has pointed out, the Church of England's system of five-yearly building inspections has been taken up as a model by other Churches and by the National Trust – and there is no comparable regime of regular general inspections of *secular* historic buildings.

---

6 Figures from the Church of England's Cathedrals and Church Buildings Division.

7 Figure supplied by the Provincial Secretary of the Church in Wales.

8 In addition, an extension might also require planning permission.

9 A faculty is a licence authorising work in a church or churchyard; and no alterations, additions, removals or repairs may be carried out to the fabric, ornaments or furniture of a church without one.

Ecclesiastical exemption: Northern Ireland

Ecclesiastical buildings in Northern Ireland are (in effect) exempt from the normal controls as they apply to demolition, alteration or extension of a listed building. The future of the ecclesiastical exemption has long been under consideration but, at the time of writing, was still in place (Northern Ireland Environment Agency 2009).

Ecclesiastical exemption: Scotland

In Scotland, *all* churches in ecclesiastical use of whatever denomination are currently exempt from listed building control (but not from planning control) under section 54 of the Planning (Listed Buildings and Conservation Areas) (Scotland) Act 1997. There is, however, a 'voluntary' (that is, non-statutory) arrangement under the aegis of Historic Scotland for dealing with proposals for works to the *external* fabric of buildings in ecclesiastical use which, were it not for the exemption, would require listed building consent.

Under the voluntary arrangement, proposals affecting the exterior which would usually require consent are dealt with under the planning system by the local authority. In case of disagreement, under the exemption the planning authority will refer the application to the appropriate decision-making body of the denomination concerned, along with any written observations from Historic Scotland, the planning authority and others such as amenity societies. The final decision rests with the denominational authority, not with the secular planners, but both are required to abide by the *Scottish Historic Environment Policy* (Historic Scotland 2011 and Taylor 2010). The voluntary arrangement does *not*, however, apply to interiors which (unlike in England and Wales) continue to be exempt from listed building controls altogether.

Listing and Religious Minorities

Much of the foregoing has been about Christian places of worship and, in relation to listing, much of the impact of the policy relates to buildings in the ownership of the four historic territorial denominations – the Church of England, the Church of Ireland, the Church of Scotland and the Church in Wales – simply because between them they own the vast majority of the religious buildings erected before 1800. But there are also large numbers of buildings belonging to other denominations and faith-communities. Many non-Anglican places of worship in England and Wales are of considerable heritage value: for example the Bevis Marks Synagogue in London of 1701 and the Princes Road Synagogue in Liverpool, built in the Moorish Revival style in 1874, both of which are listed Grade I, the Shah Jehan Mosque in Woking, completed in 1889 and listed Grade II*, and the vast Grade I Tabernacle Chapel of 1872 in Morriston, Swansea.

However, what constitutes 'heritage value' is at least to some extent a matter of opinion and aesthetic judgement; and the tendency has been automatically to list the majority of places of worship built before 1800 and to be much more selective in listing newer ones. This policy has borne particularly harshly on the

Roman Catholic Church which, as a result, has proportionately far fewer listed buildings than do the Church of England, the Church in Wales or the Church of Scotland and, in consequence, receives proportionately less from the Listed Places of Worship Grant Scheme[10] – a phenomenon which the Vice-Chairman of the Patrimony Committee of the Bishops' Conference of England and Wales has described (Andreae 2009) as 'under-listing':

> [T]he Catholic heritage in this country is under-recognised and under-appreciated largely because so much of it is comparatively recent. The majority of Catholic churches were built during the Victorian period and during the twentieth century. Unlike their Anglican counterparts, which frequently define the centres of towns and villages, Catholic churches usually occupy secondary sites and are less visible, and many have very plain exteriors. They are thus easily overlooked … and as a result are significantly under-represented in the statutory lists. Plain exteriors often hide an interior of grandeur, magnificence and colour.

What is true for non-Anglican churches is equally true for non-Christian places of worship – and, where they *have* been listed, that has sometimes caused as many problems as it was intended to solve. Changing settlement patterns in the Jewish community, for example, have meant that listed synagogues in smaller towns have been left with ageing and dwindling congregations as the younger members of the community have moved to major centres like London, Manchester and Leeds.

Public Funding for Cultural Heritage

Public funding for cultural heritage *generally* comes from a variety of sources, of which the largest is the National Lottery. The Heritage Lottery Fund, a non-departmental public body linked with the Department of Culture, Media and Sport and administered by the National Heritage Memorial Fund (NHMF), distributes around 375 million pounds (469 million euros) annually for new projects. Since 1994 the Fund has supported over 36,000 heritage projects of all kinds and given grants of almost 6 billion pounds (7.5 billion euros) across the United Kingdom.[11] In addition, the territorial executive agencies responsible for historic buildings – English Heritage, Historic Scotland, the Northern Ireland Environment Agency and Cadw – provide limited amounts of direct funding. So far as religious buildings are concerned, the funding situation is more complex; and the major source of finance has come in various distinct streams:

10 For which see below.

11 Figures from the Heritage Lottery Fund. Currency conversions are at the fairly notional rate of 1.25 euros to 1.00 pound sterling.

1. Listed buildings generally are given a limited amount of direct grant-aided funding *as buildings* from the Heritage Lottery Fund and the four territorial executive agencies;
2. Listed places of worship are given a limited amount of direct grant-aided funding *as places of worship* from the Heritage Lottery Fund and the four territorial executive agencies, though this tends to be concentrated on the largest and most important buildings from a heritage point of view, such as the Church of England cathedrals;
3. Because 'the advancement of religion' for the public benefit is included in the statutory list of activities that are regarded as charitable,[12] religious organizations are given a degree of state support and preferential tax treatment by Her Majesty's Treasury and HM Revenue & Customs (HMRC) *as charities* – along with all other charities, secular as well as religious – particularly in relation to their treatment for VAT;
4. There has been direct reimbursement of VAT on repairs to listed churches, synagogues and the like via the Listed Places of Worship Grant Scheme; and
5. Under the Places of Worship Registration Act 1855 registered places of worship in England and Wales are exempt from the requirement to pay property taxes ('non-domestic rates').

It is to these that we now turn.

Direct Grant

There has been a very limited amount of direct grant from the four government heritage bodies: between 1990 and 2009, for example, English Heritage gave some 52 million pounds (65 million euros) to fund conservation work at English cathedrals – but that funding-stream came to an end five years ago.[13] In recent years Cadw has provided 500,000 pounds (625,000) annually for places of worship – but only to 'outstanding' buildings (Glanville 2011). In addition, the Heritage Lottery Fund (HLF) operates a specific scheme of Grants for Places of Worship – of individual grants between 10,000 pounds (12,500 euros) to 250,000 pounds (312,500 euros) to listed places of worship *only* – principally for urgent, high-level repair work but also for improvements to facilities. The condition for such a grant is that the place of worship must subsequently be opened to the public for at least 40 days outside normal worshipping hours. The scheme is operated jointly with English Heritage and Historic Scotland. The HLF also has links with Cadw and the Northern Ireland Environment Agency.

12 S 7(2)(c) Charities and Trustee Investment (Scotland) Act 2005, s 3(1)(c) Charities Act 2011 (which consolidated the earlier legislation for England and Wales) and s 2(2)(c) Charities Act (Northern Ireland) 2008. Many Irish Churches and charities are all-Ireland institutions; and in the Republic, 3(1)(b) of the Charities Act 2009 makes similar provision.

13 Information from the Secretary of the Association of English Cathedrals.

More generally, the HLF's main programmes of heritage grants are aimed at all types of national, regional and local heritage across the whole of the United Kingdom and are open to requests for grants for places of worship: but they do not have a special fund earmarked for them (National Churches Trust 2012).

In addition to general funding through the various heritage bodies, in his March 2014 Budget the Chancellor of the Exchequer, George Osborne, announced that he was allocating 20 million pounds (25 million euros) to a time-limited and targeted scheme of grants for necessary repairs to the fabric of the listed Anglican and Roman Catholic cathedrals in England (but not in the other three jurisdictions) in order to ensure that the buildings were in a good and safe state of repair prior to hosting events commemorating the First World War.[14]

The Listed Places of Worship Grant Scheme, VAT and Buildings for 'Charitable Purposes'

A major general source of funding for the ecclesiastical built heritage has been the Listed Places of Worship Grant Scheme,[15] introduced by the then Chancellor of the Exchequer, Gordon Brown, in March 2001, initially as an interim scheme until 31 March 2011. Under the scheme, listed places of worship are refunded the difference between 5 per cent and the actual amount spent on VAT on eligible repairs and maintenance; and between its inception in 2001 and March 2011 it had reimbursed 106.5 million pounds (133.1 million euros).[16]

Work done by Paul Walker (Walker 2006) suggests that there are about 14,500 listed places of worship in the United Kingdom, of which about 85 per cent are in the care of the Church of England. Moreover, almost half of all listed buildings in the highest categories across the UK – Grade I in England and Wales and Grade A in Scotland and Northern Ireland – are places of worship (Taylor 2012). The scope of the rebate was extended in March 2004 to cover the full amount of VAT levied on eligible works carried out on and after 1 April 2004.

The scheme as devised was in accordance with EU law because it provided matching grants, rather than applying an unauthorized reduced rate of VAT – which would have been contrary to the Sixth VAT Directive.[17] Gordon Brown's government wanted to make the scheme permanent and proposed to the European

---

14 HC Deb 19 Mar 2014 c 786. For further details about the First World War Centenary Cathedral Repairs Fund, see the website: http://www.churchcare.co.uk/images/First_World_War_Centenary_Cathedrals_Repair_Fund_detailed_application_criteria.pdf (accessed 6 November 2014).

15 See the website: http://www.lpwscheme.org.uk/index.htm (accessed 29 January 2014).

16 HC Deb 25 Jun 2012 c 25W.

17 Council Directive 77/388/EEC of 17 May 1977 on the harmonization of the laws of the member states relating to turnover taxes – Common system of value-added tax: uniform basis of assessment.

Commission that the Directive should be extended to permit a reduced rate specifically for repairs to listed places of worship; but in spite of strong pressure from HM Treasury, the proposal was rejected at the meeting of the EU Finance Ministers (ECOFIN) in March 2009.

In addition to the rebuff from ECOFIN, the continuation of the scheme was called into question as a result of the Comprehensive Spending Review undertaken by the Coalition Government in the wake of the international financial crisis of 2007–2008; and from January 2011 repairs to organs, pews, bells and clocks and – crucially – professional fees became ineligible for grant under the scheme. However, after considerable pressure from the Churches and heritage bodies, the government agreed to continue the scheme in its revised form until 31 March 2015 and to refund VAT at the increased rate of 20 per cent that came into effect from 1 January 2011 – but with quarterly fixed budgets rather than a rolling matching grant and subject to an annual ceiling on the total grant of some 12 million pounds (15 million euros). In the transition between the old eligibility criteria and the new, it was likely that around 24 million pounds (30 million euros) would eventually be paid in relation to claims for the 2010–11 financial year: around 10 million pounds more than was expected (Department for Culture, Media and Sport 2010). However, as we shall see, this was not the end of the story.

Where a charity (whether religious or not) constructs or acquires by sale or by long lease a building that is to be used for a 'relevant charitable purpose' (that is, a village hall, a building occupied by a charity otherwise than in the course of business, or a building used to provide social or recreational facilities for a local community), the construction or acquisition of the building is zero-rated for VAT (HM Revenue & Customs 2011). In order to qualify, the building must be wholly used for charitable purposes though, in practice, a *de minimis* non-charitable use of 5 per cent of the building's floor-area is permitted without contaminating the relief. A church would be zero-rated in almost all conceivable circumstances; but the *de minimis* threshold might come into play where the building was mixed-use: for example, a worship space with a café or book-shop attached.

In addition, until 31 October 2012 alterations to *all* listed buildings, sacred or secular, and whether owned by charities or in private hands, were zero-rated for VAT – while repairs were not. With VAT at 20 per cent the zero rate on alterations was extremely important where, for example, the congregation of a large church decided to turn one of its transepts into a community meeting-place and install a kitchen area and lavatories. However, in the 2012 Budget the Chancellor of the Exchequer announced the abolition of the zero rate on alterations. His ostensible reasoning was twofold: that the zero rate created a perverse incentive to alter a building rather than repair it and that it gave wealthy private owners of secular listed buildings what amounted to an unfair tax break. The perverse incentive argument was – and remains – extremely tenuous because it assumes that 'repairs' and 'alterations' are interchangeable alternatives; however, making alterations to accommodate disabled access is simply not an alternative to repairing a leaking roof. As to the fairness argument, whatever one thinks of private owners installing basement swimming pools without paying VAT on the installation, the knock-on effect on charities and churches was simply discounted.

After negotiations with the Church of England, it was agreed that the Listed Places of Worship Grant Scheme would be extended to include alterations as well as repairs and that the Treasury would make available an extra 30 million pounds (37.5 million euros) to the scheme in each financial year for the remainder of the present Parliament (Department of Culture, Media and Sport 2012). It was thought that the extra sum represented fair compensation for the additional VAT. Currently, therefore, the total available annual budget for the scheme, including the administration costs of grant assessment and processing is 42 million pounds (52.5 million euros) until 31 March 2016.[18] From 1 April 2013 to 30 September 2014 the total sum refunded was 24.6 million pounds (30.8 million euros).[19]

That remains the situation at the time of writing; but not everyone has been happy with the outcome, for three reasons. First, the concession applies only to listed *places of worship* – not to other listed buildings in the care of religious organizations such as schools, colleges and parsonage houses. Secondly, the commitment is only for one financial year beyond the end of the present parliament:[20] nor could it be otherwise, since it is impossible for the present government to bind its successor. Finally, the decision to abolish the zero rate on alterations is irreversible because, once a member state has surrendered an existing reduced or zero rate of VAT under EU VAT law, it cannot be resurrected without the unanimous agreement of all the other members – which would never be forthcoming.

Gift Aid

One of the most important sources of state support for charities generally is the Gift Aid scheme, under which a charity can reclaim from government the standard rate income tax paid by donors on the money that they have donated: 25 pence in the pound. Total Gift Aid repayments to all charities in 2013–14 were roughly 1,040 million pounds (1.3 million euros).[21] Almost all faith groups are constituted as charities and it is thought that some 20 per cent of the total Gift Aid repayments went to religious charities – in an average year about 10 per cent of Gift Aid repayments go to the Church of England alone. So far as maintenance of the religious built heritage is concerned, from the point of view of

---

18 HL Deb 12 Jun 2014 column 575.

19 Listed Places of Worship Grant Scheme: Value of Claims Received: http://www.lpwscheme.org.uk/value_of_claims_received.html (accessed 10 November 2014).

20 Which will be dissolved on Monday 30 March 2015, pursuant to s 14 of the Electoral Registration and Administration Act 2013.

21 See the HM Revenue and Customs statistics at: https://www.gov.uk/government/uploads/system/uploads/attachment_data/file/324080/Table_10_1.pdf (accessed 12 November 2014).

the recipients, income is income – and a considerable part of the receipts from Gift Aid repayments go to the upkeep and maintenance of buildings.

Gift Aid Small Donations Scheme

Linked with Gift Aid proper is the Gift Aid Small Donations Scheme under the Small Charitable Donations Act 2012, which came into operation on 6 April 2013. It provides for repayments to charities already operating Gift Aid of income tax at the standard rate in respect of individual cash donations (but not donations by cheque or electronic transfer) of 20 pounds (25 euros) or below, up to an annual limit of 5,000 pounds (6,250 euros) – so that a charity claiming against the maximum allowable figure would receive a repayment of 1,250 pounds (HMRC 2012). The scheme, which is analogous to Gift Aid and administered in the same way, does not require an individual donor to complete a Gift Aid Declaration or the charity to provide the donor's details with its repayment claim as required under the general Gift Aid regulations. However, the Scheme is complex and take-up has been disappointing, with only 6 million pounds (7.5 million euros) reimbursed in 2013–14 (HMRC 2014).

Exemption from Property Tax or 'Non-Domestic Rates'

Exemption from non-domestic rates, though it is revenue foregone rather than positive income, is the other major limb of state support for places of worship.

As noted above, under the terms of the Places of Worship Registration Act 1855, as amended, places of public worship in England and Wales registered under that Act are wholly exempt from payment of property tax ('non-domestic rates').[22] Places of worship belonging to the Church of England and the Church

22 In order to qualify, the place of worship has to be *public* – which means that a private chapel does not qualify – and what goes on inside it has to be *worship*. As to the first, the Court of Appeal decided *R v Registrar General ex parte Segerdal & Anor* [1970] 3 WLR 479 CA that what happened in a chapel belonging to the Church of Scientology was not 'worship' and that the chapel could not, therefore, be registered. The judgement in *Segerdal* was likely to be challenged in an appeal against a refusal to permit a religious marriage in a Church of Scientology chapel: see *R (Hodkin & Ors) v Registrar General of Births, Deaths and Marriages* [2012] EWHC 3635 (Admin). Eventually, 'in *R (Hodkin & Anor) v Registrar General of Births, Deaths and Marriages* [2013] UKSC 77 the Supreme Court unanimously allowed the appeal of Ms Louisa Hodkin against the refusal of the Registrar General of Births, Deaths and Marriages to record the Church of Scientology's chapel in central London under section 2 of the Places of Worship Registration Act 1855'. See http://www.lawandreligionuk.com/2013/12/11/uksc-holds-that-the-activities-of-the-church-of-scientology-are-religious/ (accessed 29 January 2014). As to the second, in *Gallagher (Valuation Officer) v Church of Jesus Christ of Latter-day Saints* [2008] UKHL 56 the House of Lords held that worship in the Mormon Temple in Preston was not 'public' because non-Mormons were not admitted.

in Wales are also exempt – but in those cases the exemption is automatic and they are not required to register under the Act in order to benefit from its provisions.[23] In Scotland, under section 22 of the Valuation and Rating (Scotland) Act 1956, as amended, churches, church halls and other places of worship are entered in the Valuation Roll for property tax but are wholly exempt from payment. Likewise in Northern Ireland, places of public worship and ancillary buildings are exempt.

The total value of the exemption is impossible to quantify – but it must be enormous. Peter Brierley calculates that there are some 50,000 places of worship in the UK (Brierley 2011). Even at a very conservative average annual rateable value of 2,000 pounds, the global amount of revenue foregone would be some 100 million pounds (125 million euros). In reality, however, the figure must be considerably higher than that. In Scotland, unlike England and Wales, places of worship are entered on the Valuation Roll,[24] even though they are exempt from payment; and the rateable value of some of the larger churches is considerable: for example, 76,200 pounds (95,250 euros) for the High Kirk of St Giles and 62,800 pounds (78,500 euros) for St Mary's Cathedral, Palmerston Place – both in Edinburgh – and 20,000 pounds (25,000 euros) for St Andrew's Cathedral, Inverness. Even a very small, simple church such as St Donnan's Episcopal Church in rural Wester Ross has a rateable value of 1,025 pounds (1,280 euros). The standard business rate poundage for Scotland for 2014–15 is 47.1 pence – which means that a church with a rateable value of 1,000 pounds (1,250 euros) is excused payment of 471 pounds.

The total value of the exemption is impossible to quantify but it must be considerable. Peter Brierley calculates that there are some 50,000 places of worship in the UK (Brierley 2011). If, for the purposes of illustration, we assume a very conservative average annual rateable value of 2,000 pounds for each of them and apply the current Scottish business rate poundage across the UK as a whole, the global amount of revenue foregone would be some 47.1 million pounds

---

Subsequently, in *Church of Jesus Christ of Latter-Day Saints v United Kingdom* [2014] ECHR 227 the European Court of Human Rights held that there had been no violation of Article 14 ECHR taken in conjunction with Article 9. See http://www.lawandreligionuk.com/2014/03/08/lds-temple-worship-non-domestic-rates-and-article-9-echr/ (accessed 3 November 2014).

23 It should be noted, however, that the exemption applies only to those parts of a church building used for church purposes: see *Glenwright (Valuation Officer) and Durham City Council v St Nicholas PCC* [1988] RA 1 at 10, Lands Trib, in which a former vestry used for retail sales by a charitable company run by the PCC was held to be a separate hereditament for rating purposes. For a recent rating and valuation case in which it was held that two rooms in a church that were used as a coffee- and book-shop run by church volunteers *were* 'used in connection with' a place of public worship and therefore attracted the 'charitable use' exemption see *Ebury (Valuation Officer) v Church Council of the Central Methodist Church* [2009] 138 (LC) LT Case no. RA/33/2007 (17 July 2009).

24 The Valuation Roll is searchable online at: http://www.saa.gov.uk/ (accessed 6 November 2014).

(58.9 million euros). In reality, however, the figure must be considerably higher than that.

Semi-Public and Private Funding

The Churches Conservation Trust (formerly the Redundant Churches Fund) was established by the (Church of England) Pastoral Measure 1983, section 44 of which allows for churches which have been made redundant by the Church of England, for which no alternative use can be found and which are of exceptional historic, architectural or archaeological significance, to be vested in the trust by the Church Commissioners.[25] The trust's core funding is provided by the government through grant-in-aid from the Department for Culture Media and Sport and by the Church Commissioners themselves; in addition, the trust seeks donations from members of the public. In 2012–13, the trust was responsible for 347 redundant buildings and its total expenditure was some 6.4 million pounds (8 million euros) (Churches Conservation Trust 2012: 15).

The Historic Chapels Trust fulfils a similar function to that of the Churches Conservation Trust in respect of other redundant places of worship in England that are listed Grade I or Grade II*: non-Anglican churches and chapels, synagogues and buildings of other faiths. Its running costs are partially supported grants from English Heritage and the Heritage Lottery Fund; the balance is provided by grants and donations and it is currently responsible for 18 buildings.

There are also three 'unofficial' charities that care especially for redundant places of worship. The National Churches Trust is a national, independent, non-profit organization which supports church buildings of historic, architectural and community value across the whole of the United Kingdom. Established in 1953 as the Historic Churches Preservation Trust and re-launched under its new name in 2007, it makes fairly small grants to churches of all denominations. Unlike the other national bodies, it receives no funding from government or from the various denominations, relying solely on individual donations and legacies, grants from other grant-giving charities and investment income. Its total expenditure in 2013 was 1.5 million pounds (1.9 million euros) (National Churches Trust 2014). The Friends of Friendless Churches owns over 40 former places of worship, half in England, half in Wales. The activities of the trust in Wales are funded by Cadw and the Church in Wales; in England, however, to fund its work it relies on non-recurrent grants and donations. The National Trust, which was founded as a not-for-profit company in 1894 but was later reincorporated by the National Trust Act 1907, cares for some 50 ecclesiastical buildings in England, Wales and Northern Ireland, including the remains of several important monasteries (some of

25 A statutory body formed in 1948 by the Church Commissioners Measure 1947 as a union of two earlier asset-holding bodies – Queen Anne's Bounty and the Ecclesiastical Commissioners. Its role is to manage the historic assets of the Church of England.

which were incorporated into later domestic buildings), private chapels, churches and shrines.[26]

Finally, there are several private charitable trusts that make grants to support the cultural heritage, some of which go to support religious buildings. The Freemasons' Grand Charity, for example, gives a small number of grants, typically not exceeding 5,000 pounds (6,250 euros), to religious buildings of national importance.

Property Ownership and Management

There is no simple pattern of ownership of religious listed buildings across the entire spectrum of built heritage. Several extremely important church buildings are in private – usually charitable – ownership. For example, the (Anglican) chapels of King's College, Cambridge and of New College and Magdalen College, Oxford, all of which are Grade I listed, are part of the colleges to which they belong and are vested in the colleges' governing bodies. The Grade A St Magnus Cathedral in Orkney and Glasgow Cathedral, both of which are under the ecclesiastical jurisdiction of the Church of Scotland, are vested in their respective local authorities. The Grade A Rosslyn Chapel, which figured in *The Da Vinci Code*, hosts a congregation of the Scottish Episcopal Church but is owned by a private charitable trust.

As to the major denominations themselves, the system of ownership and control depends to a considerable extent on their ecclesiology and governance, as the following examples illustrate.

Many of the smaller denominations hold their property through a series of charitable trusts, either nationally, regionally or at an individual, congregational level. In the Religious Society of Friends (Quakers), for example, all the property in the South East of England is held by Friends Trusts Limited – a charitable company – as custodian trustee and policy and day-to-day decision-making is delegated by Yearly Meeting (the final authority of the Society) to a body with the curious title of Six Weeks Meeting.

Building ownership and control in the Roman Catholic Church operates in accordance with the guidelines issued by the Pontifical Commission for the Cultural Heritage of the Church which, under Article 99 of its statute, 'has the duty of acting as curator for the artistic and historical patrimony of the whole Church' (Wojtyła 1988: Article 99). Much of the work is done through the Patrimony Committee, which has overall responsibility for the care of Roman Catholic churches, oversees the work of the individual diocesan Historic Churches Committees and acts as the interface between government authorities and the Church in relation to planning and heritage matters (Catholic Bishops' Conference of England and Wales 2011).

26 The National Trust for Scotland, also a charity, is an entirely separate institution.

For the Church of Scotland, under the terms of the Church of Scotland (General Trustees) Order Confirmation Act 1921, both its property and investments are held on behalf of the Church as a whole by the General Trustees, who are appointed for that purpose by the General Assembly of the Church. The Church's rules for the care of its property are set out in Acts of Assembly, the most important of which is Act XII 2007 (anent Care of Ecclesiastical Properties).

Perhaps inevitably, much the most complicated provisions are those surrounding the property of the Church of England. As noted above, almost all work to Church of England (and Church in Wales) churches is subject to the faculty jurisdiction except for very minor items. For England, each diocese has a diocesan advisory committee established under the Care of Churches and Ecclesiastical Jurisdiction Measure 1991 and that committee advises on any proposed works to a church. Final decisions on applications are taken by the diocesan chancellor: a secular lawyer with a seven-year general qualification under section 71 of the Courts and Legal Services Act 1990. 'Ownership' is, however, a difficult concept: instead, it is perhaps preferable to think in terms of 'consecrated land'. Generally speaking, it is not possible at common law to alienate land consecrated to the use of the Church of England by a simple transfer of title. Such land must be deconsecrated before it is sold and sections 58 and 59 of the Mission and Pastoral Measure 2011 (which came into effect in 2012 and updated and consolidated the Pastoral measure 1983 and various other subsequent provisions), provide a statutory procedure for closing a redundant church and make provision for removal of the legal effects of consecration and the disposal of land, subject to an order made by the diocesan bishop.[27]

To conclude on this point: only in very limited circumstances is property ownership a decisive parameter in sources of funding. As noted above, there has been specific, though limited, funding from English Heritage for the Church of England's cathedrals – but that is as much as anything because almost all of them are Grade I buildings and some are of major international importance.[28] What is undoubtedly the case, however, is that whether or not a building is listed is crucial in determining whether or not it will attract grant funding, because – as observed earlier – funding for the religious built heritage is for its heritage value, not for its religious significance.

Religious Heritage and Secular Use

Charles George (2002), writing on secular use largely from an Anglican perspective, observes that the fact of consecration of a piece of land for use by the Church of England changes its legal status in a manner that is very difficult

27 Paragraphs 20.30-20.44 of the associated *Code of Recommended Practice* deal with demolition.

28 Two cathedrals – Canterbury and Durham – are part of World Heritage sites.

to reverse. Canon F15(1) forbids the use of a Church of England church for 'temporal objects inconsistent with the sanctity of the place' and Canon F16(1) allows plays, concerts and films that are 'consonant with sound doctrine and make for the edifying of the people'. For Roman Catholics, Canon 1210 of the *Codex Iuris Canonici 1983* permits only activities that 'serve to exercise or promote worship, piety and religion. Anything which is discordant with the holiness of the place is forbidden'. The Ordinary may, however, permit other uses 'provided they are not contrary to the sacred character of the place'. Similarly in the Church of Scotland: Act II 2000 [Consolidating Act anent Ministry] governs the use of church buildings and '[i]n deciding for what uses the church may be granted the sacred character of the building shall be kept in view'.

But it is not clear what any of this might mean in practice. In reality, Churches welcome tourism, partly because it presents a pastoral opportunity to engage with visitors and partly because it can often be a welcome source of funding. Moreover, there is an emerging consensus that if a church is kept open, it will be less prone to vandalism and theft.[29] The Cathedral and Church Buildings Division of the Church of England (ChurchCare 2012) advises its parishes that:

> … more churches are attacked when they are locked than when they are open, possibly as criminals feel they are less likely to be disturbed in a closed church than one where anyone could appear at any time. Wherever possible churches should be kept open rather than locked.

And, as noted above, it is a specific requirement of the Heritage Lottery Fund's scheme of Grants for Places of Worship that a recipient place of worship must subsequently be kept open for at least 40 days outside normal service times: in this case, the public interest appears to coincide with good practice in relation to the security of the building.

Management in the Future

Declining congregations – particularly in rural areas as a result of changing settlement patterns – and the ever-increasing costs of maintenance have inevitably led the major denominations to think very hard both about the current use that they make of their buildings and possible alternative uses. Part of the attraction of the latter is the possibility of cost-sharing but part, also, is that a building is likely

29 In the past few years a particularly serious problem has been the theft of lead from church roofs, not only because of the cost of replacement but also because of the often devastating effects of the resulting internal water damage. In order to tackle the issue, the Scrap Metal Dealers Act 2013 significantly increased regulation of the market by banning the cash purchase of scrap metal in England and Wales and requiring all dealers to verify the photo identity and address of every person selling scrap metal to them.

to remain in better physical condition if it is not left locked and unheated for the greater part of each week. In addition, in some rural areas (and, for that matter, in some deprived urban communities), a local church building may often be the only available space big enough to host community events.

Several denominations have been exploring additional uses for their buildings. For example, the Cathedral and Church Buildings Division and the National Rural Officers for the Church of England, the Methodist Church and the United Reformed Church have been encouraging churches and chapels to host community shops, particularly in isolated rural communities. Similarly, there are currently at least 35 sub-post-offices operating in churches, chapels and church halls (ChurchCare 2012) as a substitute for commercial sub-post offices that have closed because they had become financially unviable. Perhaps that is the shape of the future, particularly for churches in rural areas.

Conclusion

If any conclusions can be drawn from this brief survey of public institutions and charities concerned with funding and caring for the ecclesiastical built heritage they are these:

First, there is no central body in the United Kingdom, nor even in each of its four constituent parts, charged with maintaining religious buildings (nor, indeed, the built heritage generally). Instead, there is a patchwork of overlapping agencies, charities and grant-giving bodies with little or no formal coordination between them.

Secondly, although we should not forget the funding that religious organizations receive as charities and the relief from non-domestic rates given to places of worship, they nevertheless face a constant struggle to maintain buildings that are often of considerable heritage value with extremely limited resources.

Thirdly, that situation is not going to get any better in the foreseeable future. The result of the Comprehensive Spending Review undertaken by the incoming Coalition government in the wake of the international financial crisis of 2007–2008 was budget cuts (or, at any rate, no real terms increases) for almost all government departments and non-departmental public bodies, followed by a policy of strict controls on public expenditure; and it is clear that, in the current economic climate, no charitable group, however important its work, can rely to any great extent on help from public funds. Or as the outgoing Chief Secretary to HM Treasury, Liam Byrne, put it in his memorable (if extremely ill-judged) note to his successor after the Labour Party had lost the 2010 General Election, 'Dear Chief Secretary, I'm afraid there is no money. Kind regards – and good luck!' (BBC 2010).

Interestingly by way of comparison, in France where there is, theoretically at least, an absolute separation of church and state, a large number of religious buildings were taken over by the *communes* or by the state itself in 1905 and are kept in repair at public expense as part of the French national heritage. In the

United Kingdom on the other hand, with two national Churches established by law (albeit on different statutory foundations) and no concept whatsoever of *laïcité*, funding for religious built heritage remains hand-to-mouth.

References

Books and Articles

Andreae, S. (2009), 'A Catholic perspective', *Conservation Bulletin*, 61, 8–10.

BBC (2010), 'Treasury chief's note to successor' (published online 17 May 2010), available at: http://news.bbc.co.uk/1/hi/uk_politics/8688470.stm (accessed 15 January 2014).

Brierley, P. (2011), *Major UK Religious Trends, 2010 to 2020* (Tonbridge: Peter Brierley Consultants).

Catholic Bishops' Conference of England and Wales (2011), 'Patrimony', available at: http://www.cbcew.org.uk/CBCEW-Home/Departments/Christian-Life-and-Worship/Patrimony/Patrimony-Committee (accessed 15 January 2014).

Chadwick, Sir E. (1842), *Report from the Poor Law Commissioners on an Inquiry into the Sanitary Conditions of the Labouring Population of Great Britain* (London: Wm Clowes for HMSO).

Church of England (2012), *Mission and Pastoral Measure 2011 Code of Recommended Practice*, available at: https://www.churchofengland.org/clergy-office-holders/pastoralandclosedchurches/mpm2011code.aspx (accessed 3 November 2014).

ChurchCare (2012), 'Opening Up Your Church', available at: http://www.churchcare.co.uk/churches/guidance-advice/opening-up-your-church-building (accessed 15 January 2014).

Churches Conservation Trust (2012), *Review 2011–12*.

Cranmer, F. and García Oliva, J. (2010), 'The cultural heritage of faith-communities in the United Kingdom', *Derecho y Religión*, 5, 289–312.

Department of Culture, Media and Sport (2010), 'The Operation of the Ecclesiastical Exemption and related planning matters for places of worship in England: Guidance' (published online July 2010) available at: https://www.gov.uk/government/uploads/system/uploads/attachment_data/file/77372/OPSEEguidance.pdf (accessed 6 November 2014).

Department of Culture, Media and Sport (2012), 'Upcoming changes to the Listed Places of Worship Grant Scheme: Changes to be introduced from 1 October 2012' (published online August 2012), available at: https://www.gov.uk/government/uploads/system/uploads/attachment_data/file/78325/Upcoming_Changes_to_the_LPW_Grant_Scheme.pdf (accessed 15 January 2014).

English Heritage (2013), 'Conservation Area Consent', available at: http://www.english-heritage.org.uk/professional/advice/hpg/consentandplanningpermission/cac/ (accessed 3 November 2014).

George, C. (2002), 'Shared use of church buildings or, is nothing sacred?', *Ecclesiastical Law Journal*, 6, 306–17.

Glanville, A. (2011), 'The view from the Church in Wales', *Historic Churches*, 18, 2–4.

Goodchild, J. (1995), 'The inspection of Church of England churches', *ICOMOS Canada Bulletin*, vol. 4/3.

Historic Scotland (2011), *Scottish Historic Environment Policy* (published online December 2011), available at: http://www.historic-scotland.gov.uk/shep-dec2011.pdf (accessed 15 January 2014).

HM Revenue & Customs (2011), *Reference Notice 708: Buildings and Construction* (published online November 2011), available at: http://customs.hmrc.gov.uk/channelsPortalWebApp/channelsPortalWebApp.portal?_nfpb=true&_pageLabel=pageVAT_ShowContent&id=HMCE_CL_000513&propertyType=document (accessed 15 January 2014).

HM Revenue & Customs (2012), *Gift Aid Small Donations Scheme*, available at: http://www.hmrc.gov.uk/charities/gasds/ (accessed 8 November 2014).

HM Revenue & Customs (2014), *UK Charity Tax Relief Statistics 1990-91*, available at: https://www.gov.uk/government/uploads/system/uploads/attachment_data/file/324070/Commentary.pdf (accessed 8 November 2014).

National Churches Trust (2012), 'Supporting You – Finding Funding', available at: http://nationalchurchestrust.org/supporting-you/overview.php (accessed 15 January 2014).

National Churches Trust (2014), *Annual Review 2013–14.*

Northern Ireland Environment Agency (2009), 'Building Grant FAQs' (published online in December 2009, last updated September 2014), available at: http://www.doeni.gov.uk/niea/built-home/conservation-2/historic_buildings/historic_buildings_grants-2/building_grant_faq.htm (accessed 15 January 2014).

Office of National Statistics (2012), *Religion in England and Wales 2011* (published online 11 December 2012), available at: http://www.ons.gov.uk/ons/dcp171776_290510.pdf (accessed 15 January 2014).

Taylor, J. (2010), 'Listed Places of Worship' (published online May 2010: updated September 2012), available at: http://www.buildingconservation.com/articles/listprot/listprot.htm (accessed 15 January 2014).

Tsivolas, Th. (2014), *Law and Religious Cultural Heritage in Europe* (Springer).

Walker, P. (2006), 'Snapshot survey of listed churches', *Church Building*, 98, March/April.

Wojtyła, K.J. [Pope John Paul II] (1988), *Pastor Bonus* (Rome: Libreria Editrice Vaticana).

Cases

Church of Jesus Christ of Latter-Day Saints v United Kingdom [2014] ECHR 227.

Ebury (Valuation Officer) v Church Council of the Central Methodist Church [2009] 138 (LC) LT Case no RA/33/2007.

Gallagher (Valuation Officer) v Church of Jesus Christ of Latter-day Saints [2008] UKHL 56.
Glenwright (Valuation Officer) and Durham City Council v St Nicholas PCC [1988] RA 1 Lands Trib.
R v Registrar General ex parte Segerdal & Anor [1970] 3 WLR 479 CA.
R (Hodkin & Ors) v Registrar General of Births, Deaths and Marriages [2012] EWHC 3635 (Admin).
R (Hodkin & Anor) v Registrar General of Births, Deaths and Marriages [2013] UKSC 77.

Primary and Secondary Legislation

Act II 2000, Consolidating Act anent Ministry [Church of Scotland].
Act XII 2007, anent Care of Ecclesiastical Properties [Church of Scotland].
Care of Churches and Ecclesiastical Jurisdiction Measure 1991 (no. 1).
Charities Act 2009 (no. 6) [Ireland].
Charities Act 2011 (c. 25).
Charities Act (Northern Ireland) 2008 (c. 12).
Charities and Trustee Investment (Scotland) Act 2005 (asp 10).
Church Commissioners Measure 1947 (no. 2).
Church of Scotland (General Trustees) Order Confirmation Act 1921 (c. xxv).
Council Directive 77/388/EEC of 17 May 1977 on the harmonization of the laws of the member states relating to turnover taxes – Common system of value-added tax: uniform basis of assessment.
Courts and Legal Services Act 1990 (c. 41).
Ecclesiastical Exemption (Listed Buildings and Conservation Areas) Order 2010 (SI/2010/1176).
Electoral Registration and Administration Act 2013 (c. 6).
Enterprise and Regulatory Reform Act 2013 (c. 24).
Housing, Town Planning &c. Act 1919 (c. 35).
9 December 1905 Act on the Separation of Church and State [*Loi du 9 décembre 1905 concernant la séparation des Églises et de l'État,* France].
Mission and Pastoral Measure 2011 (no. 3).
National Planning Policy Framework 2012.
National Trust Act 1907 (c. cxxxvi).
Pastoral Measure 1983 (no. 1).
Places of Worship Registration Act 1855 (c. 81).
Planning Act 2008 (c. 29).
Planning etc. (Scotland) Act 2006 (asp 17).
Planning (Listed Buildings and Conservation Areas) Act 1990 (c. 9).
Planning (Listed Buildings and Conservation Areas) (Scotland) Act 1997 (c. 9).
Planning (Northern Ireland) Order 1991 (SI/1991/1220).
Planning Policy Wales 2012 (Edition 7, July 2014).
Scrap Metal Dealers Act 2013 (c. 10).

Small Charitable Donations Act 2012 (c. 23).
Town and Country Planning Act 1947 (c. 51).
Town and Country Planning (General Permitted Development) Order 19959 (SI/1995/418).
Town and Country Planning (Scotland) Act 1947 (c. 53).
Town and Country Planning (Scotland) Act 1997 (c. 8).
Valuation and Rating (Scotland) Act 1956 (c. 60).

Chapter 6

From Previous Intertwinement to a Future Split in Governance Structures in Cultural and Religious Use of Buildings: On Danish Funding of Religious Heritage

Lisbet Christoffersen[1]

Introduction

The general title of this publication – funding of religious heritage – opens up for analysis three different questions: who funds religious buildings once established and needing to be maintained? When are religious buildings seen as heritage and whose decision is it? And does being labelled as 'religious heritage' change the basic funding scheme?

These questions are rather new in a Danish context, but arise in very timely fashion. While this chapter was being prepared, there was a huge debate on the topic, not least related to a change of reality. Whereas the Danish *Folkekirke*,[2] the Catholic Church of Denmark and Muslim communities have been marked over

---

1 I thank the editors of this volume, the reviewer, Associate Professor Benny Grey Schuster (Theological Pedagogical Centre in Løgumkloster), Mr Jørgen Engmark (Press Officer in the Danish Ministry of Gender Equality and Ecclesiastical Affairs), Associate Professor Dr. teol. *honoris causa* Hans Raun Iversen, University of Copenhagen, and my colleagues, Assistant Professor Inger Marie Conradsen and PhD student Idamarie Svendsen, Department of Globalization and Social Sciences, Roskilde University, for kind comments to the first drafts of this chapter. All judgements as well as all mistakes are of course my responsibility only. I also thank the Theological Pedagogical Centre in Løgumkloster, where I worked on the first draft of this chapter and the review, for the excellent working conditions.

2 The translation of the Danish name for the majority church, of which 78 per cent of the Danes are members, is difficult. The church is identified by the Constitution (Article 4) as Evangelical-Lutheran and named *den danske folkekirke*. It is this concept – *Folkekirke* – which is not easy to translate, at least into English, since there are connotations of 'church of the people'; 'people's church'; 'national-church'; 'nationwide church'; 'popular church'; 'church of the commoners'; 'folk church' and many others. Most Danish scholars now use the Danish term also in international contexts: see, for example, Christoffersen (2010: 145) and Lodberg (2012: 67).

the last 50 years by the development and construction of new churches, mosques and other places of worship, the current period is also characterized by a new tendency to take church buildings out of use, not least in order to fund new ones in other areas.

This has, however, sparked debate on precisely the questions in this volume: which buildings are (religious) heritage and what are the rules for funding religious heritage? Who owns buildings (as well as the assets they contain and cemeteries) seen as religious heritage and what are the legal relations between ownership, use and funding? How are religious buildings seen as heritage used in regard to tourism and religious uses and how is this possible conflict regulated? What are the special requirements for the use of religious buildings seen as (protected) heritage and what changes could be foreseen in regard to these questions on managing religious heritage?

As is the case in many such analyses, it should be noted that there is a general legal, practical and financial distinction between the management of buildings, assets and cemeteries that constitute part of the Danish *Folkekirke,* on the one hand, and all other dimensions of religious heritage in the country on the other. The overall structure of this chapter will be based on this distinction. Hence the first part will present overall legislation on historical and cultural heritage which applies to religious buildings and assets belonging to religious communities outside the *Folkekirke*. The second part then focuses on special legal systems, regulating the maintenance of churches, other religious buildings and assets within the *Folkekirke.* The third part of the chapter consists of a general discussion based on theoretical considerations related to current and future features of Danish religious heritage.

Funding Religious Heritage of Faith Communities outside *Folkekirken*

Legislation on Historical and Cultural Heritage

The listing criteria

In Denmark, 'the idea of protecting buildings was first introduced approximately one hundred years ago' and took form, *inter alia*, in the Preservation of Buildings Act of 1918 (Lunn and Lund 2009: 75).[3] Nowadays, enforceable legislation on historical buildings mainly resides in the Listed Buildings and Preservation of Buildings and Urban Environments Act.[4] Pursuant to this Act, all Danish buildings

---

3 For further details on Danish heritage legislation and history, see Lunn and Lund (2001) and Stubbs and Makaš (2011).

4 Consolidated Act no. 685 of 09 June 2011 on Listed Buildings and Preservation of Buildings and Urban Environments, available at: http://www.kulturstyrelsen.dk/fileadmin/user_upload/kulturarv/english/dokumenter/Bygningsfredningsloven_ENG__camera_ready.pdf (accessed 18 January 2014).

from before 1536 (that is before the Reformation in Denmark) are automatically listed by law as monuments and thus preserved, unless they serve as churches within the Danish *Folkekirke* and are consequently covered by the legislation concerning these churches.[5] The Minister for Cultural Affairs may list a building, provided that it is more than 50 years old and of substantial value, either from a cultural, historical or an architectural perspective. All buildings, including those less than 50 years old, can be listed if they are of outstanding value, represent historical events or have special cultural value. In practice, proposals to list a building are handled by the Danish Agency for Culture. Listing needs the approval of a Historic Buildings Council of 12 members. The ultimate competent institution is the government, as represented by the minister.[6]

There are no special criteria concerning religious buildings, such as synagogues, Catholic churches, churches for other Christian communities or mosques and so on. All these buildings and, for example, cemeteries (related to these churches or owned by the municipalities) are listed according to the criteria concerning representation of substantial or outstanding value in regard to architectural or cultural historical perspectives. This also means that if a church building or a cemetery, previously used for a congregation within *Folkekirken* is no longer in use, then the general criteria for listing buildings are applied.

Legal Consequences of Listing for Preservation

The legal consequences of having a building and/or a landscape listed as preserved may seem 'classical' and very similar to how legal rulings are implemented in other European legislations. The owner is obliged, *inter alia,* to keep the building in good maintenance (2011 Act, § 9) and has to obtain approval from the Minister for Culture before making any major changes to the building. If the owner wants to demolish a listed building, this is also conditional upon obtaining approval from the minister (2011 Act, § 11). Secular, privately owned monuments can be taken over by the state, should the demolition permit be refused; this possibility is, however, not open to – among others – churches (2011 Act, § 13,1).[7] What this concept of 'churches' includes here is not clear. The question is whether 'churches' also includes religious buildings outside *Folkekirken*. The legal consequences of listing churches outside *Folkekirken* are thus not totally clear, although the question has not been of practical relevance so far.

---

5 The Act on Listed Buildings precisely provides that 'Sections 3 and 4 shall not apply to church buildings to the extent that they are subject to legislation relating to the Danish National Evangelical Lutheran Church.' (§5). See below Part II.

6 See http://www.kulturstyrelsen.dk/english/cultural-heritage/listed-buildings/how-does-a-building-become-listed/ (accessed 18 January 2014). Approximately 7,000 buildings are listed.

7 Consolidated Act of 09 June 2011, chapter 3.

The owner of a listed building can take the building out of use, but shall still maintain it – that rule also applies to churches under this legislation, namely churches outside *Folkekirken*.[8]

Listed Buildings Belonging to Religious Communities

Places of worship outside Folkekirken

All buildings from before 1536 are, as mentioned, listed. None of them are of course today identified as Catholic, since 1536 was the year of the Lutheran Reformation in Denmark. All churches from before 1536 were originally built to be what is now called Catholic, but have since the Reformation been under Lutheran use. As a result, none of the buildings owned by the Catholic Church or other religious communities in Denmark are automatically listed. In order to be listed, they have to meet the legal provisions.

The Catholic Church in Denmark owns two churches built before the Constitution of 1849.[9] The first was built in 1767 in Fredericia, as part of the regime of religious freedom applicable in this city, established as an exemption to the general absolutism of 1683.[10] The second was constructed at the Austrian Embassy in Copenhagen in 1842, just before freedom of religion was established by the Constitution of 1849 (Christoffersen 2010). Forty-five Catholic churches and chaplaincies were built after 1849 and are thus meeting the more than 50-year-old listing criterion in theory, while around 20 are less than 50 years old. The Catholic Church also owns school buildings, monasteries and other buildings that may be relevant for listing. However, among Catholic buildings, only the Church of Saint-Ansgar, the Catholic Cathedral in Copenhagen, is listed by decision.[11] The church was erected in 1842 to extend the premises of the Austrian Embassy and was listed in 1973.

Also the synagogue in Copenhagen, which opened in 1764 and was rebuilt in 1830–1833 (after the burning of the city centre), has been listed by decision since 1939. The Reformed Church in Copenhagen (built in 1688) was listed in 1939. The Orthodox Alexander Nevskij Church in Copenhagen, built in 1881 on the initiative of the Danish-born Russian Tsarina Dagmar, was listed by decision in 1981, whereas the Anglican Church of St Alban in Copenhagen, which was built in the late nineteenth century upon the initiative of the sister to the tsarina,

8 The extent to which these rules also apply to churches within *Folkekirken* will be discussed in Part II.

9 Information available on the Catholic Church in Denmark website: www.katolsk.dk (accessed 18 January 2014).

10 The city of Fredericia (literally meaning 'Free City') was founded by Frederick III in 1650 and benefited from special privileges, including freedom of worship and exemption from taxes.

11 The website https://www.kulturarv.dk/fbb/fredningsliste.pdf provides a list of buildings, preserved by decision (accessed 18 January 2014).

the Danish-born Queen Alexandra, has not been listed.[12] Nor is, for example, the Methodist Church of Jerusalem listed. The aforementioned 'free city' of Fredericia experienced a regime of freedom of religion even in absolutist Lutheran Denmark. There, the first Reformed (Calvinist) church building in Denmark, built in 1735, as well as its surrounding walls, is listed.

Finally, many rectories and other remarkable buildings belonging to the *Folkekirke* are listed, since the exemptions for the *Folkekirke* cover, as we shall see, only churches used for religious services.

Cemeteries outside Folkekirken

Landscapes can also be listed following the same criteria. It is, however, possible to list a building without the landscape or vice versa – that is, for example, to list a (Catholic or Baptist) church without the cemetery surrounding it or vice versa. This means that it is possible to list a whole area of special value, such as a cemetery, as a preserved area.

Most cemeteries in Denmark belong to the *Folkekirke*[13] and all Danes have a right to be buried there.[14] Some religious communities, such as the Catholic churches and Jewish congregations, have also established cemeteries. Some of the Jewish cemeteries are very old. Two cemeteries (one in Fredericia and one in Copenhagen) belonging to the Jewish community are listed. This is also in accordance with the Jewish faith, in which a graveyard can never be abolished. Additionally, some cemeteries, belonging to either the Catholic Church in Denmark or a few other religious communities have had cemeteries belonging to them listed.

---

12 It has not been possible to find an explanation for this difference. The historical background for the two Churches should have led to a parallel listing; however the governance of the two Churches is of course in the hands of two very different legal institutions and they might have different interests regarding listing.

13 The legal status of the cemeteries belonging to the *Folkekirke* in regard to listing will be discussed below.

14 Since still above 80 per cent of Danes are members of the *Folkekirke* (78 per cent) and other Christian Churches (around 2 per cent), this system does not entail problems for the majority of the population. A ceremony related to burial is held within the church building if the deceased person was member of a Christian Church; if not, a ceremony can be held in the premises of the cemetery. The very small Jewish population has cemeteries of its own. The system has however given rise to problems for the rapidly growing Muslim population, now nearly 5 per cent of the population. That is why it has become essential to establish premises catering for their needs. Thus the Muslim communities have a right to establish cemeteries of their own; the first one was established in 2006 (in Brøndby). Besides, certain areas within the cemeteries governed by the *folkekirke* or by the municipalities, are marked out for burials of Muslim citizens.

Funding Religious Heritage Belonging to Religious Communities outside Folkekirken

The state can decide to subsidize the maintenance of listed buildings and the preservation of assets in the buildings through grants, loans, technical support and by other means, possibly conditional upon the future use of the building (2011 Act, § 16). For religious communities, the preservation of a listed building thus can imply support and subsidies from the state, not least including technical support on how to preserve the building. Listing may also be synonymous with an indirect acknowledgement of the building and provide a sort of symbolic visibility, which – in a country with a clearly dominant majority religion – can be of interest *per se* for minority churches and religious groups. On the other hand, listing also means clear limits to the use and preservation of the building. And even though the state *might* provide funding and support, this support does not necessarily cover all the costs and it is not automatically granted. This means that listing also can be a (financial) burden for a religious community, since the state requires special preservation without necessarily paying for it via the state budget.

To give an idea, 'the Heritage Agency distributes approximately 40 million DKK a year for the restoration of listed buildings'.[15] This possibility is, however, just an exception from the general rule, which is that the establishment and maintenance of religious buildings is a burden solely on the shoulders of the private owner, and in this regard, the religious community and its members. Religious communities outside the *Folkekirke* are funded solely by their members.[16] Religious communities are exempted from paying taxes. Apart from that, the state does not fund religious communities outside the *Folkekirke*. Not that such a possibility is prohibited by the Constitution – state-funding of religious communities is, however, neither supported nor obliged by the Constitution. Pursuant to Article 4 of the Constitutional Act, instituting the general scheme of state support for the *Folkekirke*, public financial support is granted to the *Folkekirke*, but none of the other religious communities are mentioned as possible targets for support. Even though funding of other religious communities cannot be seen as unconstitutional, such a proposal has never been raised in parliament.[17]

Religious buildings belonging to religious communities outside the *Folkekirke* are thus maintained solely by their members. Seen from this perspective, the

15 Information available at: http://european-heritage.coe.int/sdx/herein/national_heritage/voir.xsp?id=3.3.1_DK_en (accessed 29 May 2013).

16 An individual member of a religious community receives indirect state support by being allowed to deduct the money, given to the church, from the person's income tax. This does not, however, change the situation for the religious community: it is funded solely by its members.

17 For example, the then Minister of Ecclesiastical Affairs proposed in 2001 that the state should guarantee funding to establish a Muslim cemetery. The financial committee of the parliament rejected this proposal.

possibility of being subsidized, whether by obtaining technical advice from experts (for example, from the National Museum or from the Ministry of Cultural Affairs) without having to pay for it or else by direct funding, could be an incentive for a religious community to try to have a religious building listed. Major restoration can by this route become much more feasible for mostly the small religious communities and at least the technical dimensions of such a restoration would run more smoothly if the necessary support was given by the state for free. On the other hand, many are hesitating, since listing also entails many limitations, not only to restoration, but also in regard to changes of building style, such as liturgical adjustments.

The question is currently under discussion with pros and cons for the different religious communities in Denmark.[18]

Funding Religious Heritage within *Folkekirken*

Legislation on Funding Folkekirken *Buildings*

A local church – the building in use by the local congregation – is very visible in the Danish landscape. It usually includes three to four buildings:

1. A rectory, which in the countryside very often has the form of an old freehold farm. The rectory is, legally speaking, an independent body governed by the local congregational council.
2. Many local church communities have recently built community centres (*sognegårde*), used for popular meetings, teaching children, and so on. Sometimes these community centres have been established by rebuilding parts of the local rectory formerly used for farming.
3. Buildings on the local cemetery: here we firstly find, a house, often very small, called 'the chapel' (also in the Danish language), but in the countryside only used to keep the deceased there until the funeral takes place (whereas the religious ceremony in these situations will take place not in the 'chapel', but in the church). In other areas, this building could really be a chapel in use for ceremonies in relation to the funeral. All cemeteries will also contain a small house, in use for the practical needs of the staff maintaining the cemetery. These two sets of buildings in the cemetery are owned by the cemetery as an independent body and managed by the cemetery's governing body, which most frequently is the local congregational council, or by the municipality – as in Copenhagen and

18 Oral information from a series of meetings in the Danish Association for Ecclesiastical Law concerning legal status for religious communities outside the *Folkekirke*, see www.kirkeret.dk (accessed 18 January 2014).

other major cities with cemeteries – run by the municipal council (see below on cemeteries within the *Folkekirke*).

4. The most central building that identifies *the Church* in the Danish landscape is called *kirken*. This church building is the place of worship (directed towards the east, with an altar, a baptismal font, a pulpit, benches and an organ, with a cross on the wall, paintings and so on, that is all the different assets that traditionally identify *kirken*).

Thus, the noun 'the Church' in Danish means a small community of these four sets of buildings. They have certain very clear characteristics which all Danes know and, as mentioned, they form part of the landscape and much local culture in the village or community takes place in the church buildings. By shaping so clearly landscapes and minds, they then form part of the cultural heritage outside the enforcement of legislation on listed buildings.

There is no legal identification of who owns the church buildings. Many of the church buildings within *Folkekirken* were originally privately owned (by the local noblemen, for example) and private owners were responsible for maintaining and keeping them. This was changed by law in 1922, when these church buildings legally became identified as self-governing independent bodies (*selvejende institutioner*).[19] They are maintained (but not owned) by the local congregational council under the supervision of the deanery.

The local members of *Folkekirken* pay church taxes, levied by the congregations and the deanery councils (with technical support from the local municipality) and used in the local deanery to, *inter alia*, maintain church buildings, the rectory and other buildings in use in local church life and also to maintain the churchyards. The church taxes are collected together with taxes for the municipality and the state.[20]

The state also supports the *Folkekirke* with 1/6 of the total budget allocated to the church. This support is, however, not used for maintenance of buildings, but

---

19 The general legislation on protection of church buildings was revised in a major change to the law on churches in 1922 as part of the changed legislation after re-uniting with Schleswig (the southern part of Denmark, German from 1864–1920). Some of the 'German' legislation was introduced into general legislation on churches in Denmark. There were other historical arguments for a major change to the law, related to expropriation of land from, among others, churches; this will however be too much to explain in this chapter. The relevant legislation is now the Act on Maintenance and Use of the Churches within the *Folkekirke* (*Lov om bestyrelse og brug af folkekirkens kirker m.m.*), consolidated Act (*Lovbekendtgørelse,* hereinafter LBK) no. 330 of 29 March 2014, https://www.retsinformation.dk/Forms/R0710.aspx?id=162459 (accessed 16 May 2014), chapter 1 and the Act on Church buildings and cemeteries within the *Folkekirke* (*Lov om folkekirkens kirkebygninger og kirkegårde*), LBK no. 329 of 29 March 2014.

20 Act on the Economy of the *Folkekirke* (*Lov om folkekirkens økonomi*), LBK no. 298 of 14 March 2013, https://www.retsinformation.dk/Forms/R0710.aspx?id=145604 (accessed 18 January 2014). A general explanation of the Danish Church economy is forthcoming in Christoffersen (2015).

is specifically allocated to funding salaries for pastors and bishops, who are civil servants. It follows that the maintenance of each one of the approximately 2,350 Danish churches in use within *Folkekirken* is by and large funded by members of each local congregation. Funding for those areas that have a combination of many (medieval) churches and few inhabitants (and thus providing low income tax rates) is balanced out by financial support from richer deaneries (*udligningsordning*).

The same system of funding applies, be it for the building of new churches or the restoration of old churches.[21] In these cases, too, the funding weighs solely on the shoulders of members of the local church within the deanery – and they do not have the right to deduct the payment from their income and thus pay less tax, as do the members of other religious communities.

The initiative to build a new church is taken locally, by the existing congregational council supported by the deanery and bishop and approved by the Minister of Ecclesiastical Affairs. If a church is to be demolished, this decision also has to be approved by the minister. There is currently no clear ruling on who can take the initiative to take a church out of use if the local congregational council is against it. Some congregational councils argue that it can be decided only on the initiative of the local congregational council, whereas councils at diocesan level do not trust a local congregation when the closing of its own church building is at stake. In September 2013, the (then) Minister of Gender Equality and Ecclesiastical Affairs announced clarification of legislation on competences, when it comes to closing down churches.

As an example of the distribution of the financial burden, consider the restoration of the tower of Our Saviour's Church in Copenhagen in 1991–1995 (costing 50 million DKK). Subsequently the building itself, originally a Baroque church built in 1696, has been restored (at a cost of another 50 million DKK), and lastly it turns out that the roof needs to be repaired … Even though this is one of the major tourist attractions in Copenhagen, all these expenses are paid for solely by members of the *Folkekirke* in Copenhagen, where coincidentally only 50 per cent of the population are members – although also with limited assistance from private funding.

The state does support restoration of church buildings through a special account, which is subject to the discretion of the Minister of Ecclesiastical Affairs, and mostly used for restoration of churches in poorer districts or remarkable churches. This fund is, however, limited to 15 million Danish krone only. The Cathedral in Roskilde has its own account, since it is both world heritage and the current burial place for the royal family.

---

21 Funding the construction of new places of worship *via* church taxes paid by local congregation members has been legally permitted since 1961. Before that, building of new churches within the *Folkekirke* was funded through privately and publicly collected means, with support also from the municipalities, the state and the Crown as well as from individual private groups and charities.

Churches within Folkekirken *as Heritage*

All initiatives concerning maintaining, using and changing church buildings are taken by the local congregational council, which is obliged to inspect the buildings yearly.[22] This council does, however, not decide these matters on its own. The dean supervises – through regular inspections every fourth year – the maintenance and quality of the church building and other Church-owned local buildings. Equally, both the diocesan administration and the bishop have access to and authority to approve some local decisions in this area.

However, certain decisions (such as removing pieces of art, changing the colours of painted furniture) can only be taken after advice from, or subject to conditions stipulated by, the National Museum, the Royal Building Inspector and the Academy of Arts. Some other decisions need approval from the Minister of Ecclesiastical Affairs. Church buildings and cemeteries are regulated under the Act on Church Buildings and Cemeteries within the *Folkekirke*.[23] According to this Act, no major changes can be made to churches and religious monuments without the approval of regional and/or state authorities. The role of the National Museum as well as of state authorities is to preserve the general cultural heritage of the buildings alongside their religious use. That means that the museum very often will argue for a 'cultural heritage' dimension in regard to for example displaying older assets, opposing a congregational council that might wish to opt for more modern functions or art. In its choice of modern art, the museum would argue for using respected and (inter) nationally renowned artists, whereas a local congregational council could argue for the use of a local artist with relations to the church. Among the motives of these provisions is thus the purpose to preserve and protect cultural values alongside upholding the buildings' practical use as places of worship.

As mentioned in Part I above,[24] the Act on Listed Buildings does not apply to church buildings in use regulated by the Act on Church Buildings within *Folkekirken.* The background to this exemption is naturally not that they do not deserve being kept according to cultural values. The reason is that they need to be in use for religious purposes at the same time as being preserved. Thus, the local congregational councils have a dual purpose when they maintain church buildings: they shall both maintain them as monuments of cultural values and make them fit for use for Sunday services and other religious uses.

This legislation thus balances the influence of cultural history with the primary theological purpose of buildings, namely to be used as churches for the

22 Much attention has been paid to the upkeep of old church buildings as part of the obligations of congregational councils and there are many examples of guidance on doing this; see, as the most recent example, a booklet sent out by the Diocese of Roskilde in 2013 with pictures focusing on where church buildings from the Middle Ages need special preservation, see Bahn et al. (2013).

23 LBK no. 329 of 29 March 2014.

24 See footnote 4 and the related text.

local congregation.[25] As an example of this regulatory system, even though the local congregational council is responsible for preservation and maintenance of *mural frescoes* within a church building, such restoration can only be undertaken following a proposal by the National Museum.[26]

It is against this background that buildings used for worship within *Folkekirken* do not fall within the scope of the Act of Preservation.[27] The idea is simply that legislation concerning *Folkekirken* upholds the same purposes but balances them with the current use of the buildings. If the church, however, does not serve as a place of worship any more, then the building is covered by the same legislation on preservation as other buildings in the country. This has an impact on both function and economy in *Folkekirken.*

Churches Built in Different Periods, Owned by Different Partners – and their Future Use

Pursuant to the Act on Listed Buildings, all Danish buildings established before 1536 are, as mentioned, automatically listed as preserved. Moreover, buildings which are more than 50 years old and of substantial value can be listed. Lastly, all buildings – irrespective of their age – can be listed 'by decision', provided that their cultural or architectural value is outstanding. Two-thirds of Danish church buildings within *Folkekirken* were built before 1536. It follows that, if taken out of use as places of worship, these church buildings still must be maintained, but now as listed, preserved buildings.

These buildings have no owners or, in other words, they are independently owned. A few of them were part of estates and were privately owned until 1922, when they were handed over to congregational councils for future maintenance. Others were originally built by kings as part of castles, by city councils or private citizens. They were, however, all left for the congregational councils for future use and maintenance in 1922 as part of a major change to the general funding of the church from tithes and other former taxes to a system of church taxes. The previous church owners gave up their ownership and were rewarded with church property and from that time the buildings were funded through church taxes.[28] As independently owned, this means that the buildings do not have any owners apart from themselves.[29] They are governed by congregational councils and funded by the members of the congregations through church taxes.

---

25 LBK no. 330 of 29 March 2014 and LBK no. 329 of 29 March 2014, § 1, no. 1 and no. 3.

26 LBK no. 329 of 29 March 2014, § 4.

27 Act on Preservation, LBK no. 685 of 9 June 2011, § 5.

28 There is of course much more to say about a general shift from funding churches through tithes and so on to funding through church taxes. This is however not the place to explain that further.

29 Comparable to UK charities.

The problem arises if these church buildings are taken out of religious use. In such cases, there is no owner to take care of the cultural heritage that these buildings represent, many of which are automatically listed as a result of being built before 1536. Here, the current understanding is that a former church building, even if taken out of religious use, would still be left to the congregational councils for them to take care of and maintain and preserve, now however for listed preservation. One such example is the deanery of *Sydthy* in the north-western part of Jutland (Viborg Diocese), where 90 per cent of the citizens are members of *Folkekirken*. They do not, however, amount to more than 14,153 people and they have 16 churches to take care of, most of which were built before 1536 and are extremely valuable.[30] It ensues – and does not seem fair – that the congregation shall maintain cultural heritage on behalf of the entire population if they themselves do not need that many church buildings for their religious purposes any more, since the need of places of worship has severely decreased due to a fall in the general population. As another example, the Diocese of Copenhagen identified 16 church buildings and suggested that they be taken out of religious use and desacralized in the light of demographical changes and a fall in members of *Folkekirken* in the area. The diocese also wanted to take these church buildings out of use in order to be able to build three new churches in areas where new housing had been constructed.

The proposal caused a number of challenges, of which a couple are relevant here. First, the Ministry of Cultural Affairs announced that they – if the church buildings were taken out of religious use – might propose three of the relevant churches as candidates for listing as cultural preservation, with the consequence that the very same congregational councils should still take care of their preservation, now however as listed buildings.[31] This highlights a possible loophole in the legislation on this point which is the disconnection between the administrative decision of listing and funding the buildings' maintenance.

A second challenge regards churches in Copenhagen, where many were built by either the municipality[32] or by a private foundation (*Kirkefondet*).[33] Both categories of churches return to the ownership of the original builder if they are taken out of use as churches. This means that not only the City of Copenhagen, but

30 Dean Jens Munksgaard's contribution to a conference on 23 April 2013 on the National Museum regarding churches within *Folkekirken* taken out of use, see http://miliki.dk/fileadmin/share/dokumenter/nyheder/Jens_Munksgaard.pdf (accessed 18 January 2014).

31 Director Anne Mette Rahbæk's contribution to a conference on 23 April 2013 at the National Museum, regarding churches within *Folkekirken* taken out of use, http://miliki.dk/fileadmin/share/dokumenter/nyheder/Anne_Mette_Rahbaek.pdf (accessed 18 January 2014); see also Toft Jensen (2013).

32 *Magistratskirker* [Churches established by the City Cooperation], that is six churches that were co-funded by the municipality of Copenhagen during the period 1861 to 1890, where the number of citizens in Copenhagen changed very rapidly from around 100,000 to more than 750,000 100 years later. See Ministeriet for Ligestilling og Kirke (2013: 16).

33 It contributed to the building of 48 churches between 1895 and 1978.

also the private foundation, now have to decide what to do with these churches. Being built in the period mentioned, their listing depends on a concrete decision by the Minister for Culture,[34] whereas *Kirkefondet* has opened up the sale of some churches.[35] There is no real discussion about this fallback situation, even though members of the church have paid for the maintenance of these church buildings. However, discussion might arise if the church buildings – also in the public understanding – were representative of cultural heritage and if they were sold for purposes too far removed from the pious use of a church building.

At the end of the day, the Minister of Cultural Affairs (on behalf of the then Minister of Gender Equality and Ecclesiastical Affairs) decided that six of the proposed churches in Copenhagen were to be closed; all were churches in respect of which the congregational council had accepted a proposal. None of the closed churches were relevant for listing as preserved. Six churches are kept for congregational use, contrary to the suggestion by the bishop, and two churches are taken out of congregational use, but are still in use within the *Folkekirke.* Some of the churches closed return to *Kirkefondet* or the city council, which means that the relevant congregational councils, *Kirkefondet* and the city council are now about to decide what the future use of these churches is.[36]

Cemeteries within Folkekirken *as Heritage*

Cemeteries within *Folkekirken* are equally affected by the issue of non-religious reuse. All Danes are, as mentioned, entitled to be buried in the local cemetery, often surrounding or adjacent to the congregational church building, unless they themselves – as, for example, members of a Jewish, Catholic or Muslim religious community – wish otherwise and have access to a burial place of their faith. Most cemeteries are governed and maintained by the local church council and funded through payments for burials (from non-members of the church) and through church taxes (from members). However, 10 of the major cities, including Copenhagen, govern and maintain the churchyards in the city, even though they are consecrated and some of them are placed around churches or at least always have a consecrated *chapel* in the grounds (Roesen 1976: 290–92). Also, as they are consecrated, many cemeteries reserve an area for Muslim burial or burial according to other religious traditions, the idea basically being that not only the church, but also and even more the churchyard, is a *Folkekirke*, having this dimension of being for all the people, unless they do not want to be included themselves.

34 The Ministry has, however, already mentioned some of these churches as relevant for listing: see Toft Jensen (2013).

35 *Brug af kirker, der skal lukkes* [Use in the Future of Churches to be closed], Kirkefondet (2012).

36 http://kum.dk/nyheder-og-presse/pressemeddelelser/2013/september/afgorelse-i-14-kirkelukningssager-i-kobenhavns-stift/ (accessed 18 January 2014).

The culture concerning burials is rapidly changing in Denmark as illustrated by the small *Atheist Association* claiming a right to non-religious cemeteries. Much more influential is the rapid change from burial in a coffin to cremation and hence burial in a cinerary urn, a practice requiring much less space. Former churchyards are thus changed into parks, taken out of use and maybe even re-sold for other purposes.[37] Land originally bought to extend the churchyard, but not yet put into use, can also be resold for farming, building houses and so on.

Also in regard to churchyards, listing for preservation purposes is possible. Listing and other types of preservation are mostly used if the persons buried are well-known cultural or historical figures, such as the place where Hans Christian Andersen or Søren Kierkegaard are buried. *Assistens Kirkegård* in the city of Copenhagen is the main example.[38] The cemetery is run by the municipality and both these cultural figures as well as many others are buried there. Their burial places are preserved and the cemetery is still in active use; it is however also a place with many cultural activities and a popular park. A new metro station is built in a corner of the cemetery. The decision to do so meant that a few burials needed to be moved into a quieter part of the cemetery. Even though individuals reacted against this, the bishop gave his approval and most of the public, however, thought that a necessary balancing of interests had been achieved. This cemetery has been listed by decision in May 2014.

A further topic for discussion is the registration of *memorials on tombs*, which consists of monuments on individual graves. According to legislation from 1986,[39] such monuments can be listed for preservation if they represent the memory of deserving men or women or a certain artistic or cultural heritage (see again the monument on Hans Christian Andersen's grave). The registration is decided upon by the National Museum (or the local museum on behalf of the National Museum) and the consequence of having a monument registered is that it must be preserved in the cemetery, even after closure of the concrete grave. The Minister of Gender Equality and Ecclesiastical Affairs can approve that such a monument be moved to another place than the cemetery. The underlying purpose of this regulation was to establish the legal basis for preserving monuments of significant persons in the local society. This means that the preserved monuments are not only those of Hans Christian Andersen; there are many examples of preserved monuments for a locally well-known teacher or nobleman and so on. What is seen as representing significance and importance, however, changes over a lifetime, and the feeling now is that all too many monuments are preserved in local cemeteries. A working group

37 When a parking lot for a supermarket was established in the town centre of Nykøbing Falster above an old cemetery, it resulted in an outcry because of a feeling of disturbing the peace of the dead, even though of course all formalities were kept.

38 http://www.assistens-kirkegaard.dk/ (accessed 18 January 2014).

39 LBK no. 329 of 29 March 2014 on church buildings and cemeteries within the *Folkekirke*, chapter 4.

has therefore recently suggested that the obligation to register such monuments is reduced in different ways.[40]

Theoretical Considerations on the Current Features of Religious Heritage in Denmark and its Future

Religious heritage generally, if not essentially, proves to be narrowly dependant on the national historical context in which it has been – and is still being – forged. Going beyond the strictly financial approach and bearing in mind the picture of heritage as a reflection of this context contributes to a better understanding of heritage-related legal, administrative or touristic practices and the potential need for change.

Distant and Vicarious Church Buildings

There are around 2,350 church buildings throughout the Danish landscape, which is thus marked by what has been called *the distant church (Den fjerne kirke)* (Jensen 1995). Any romantic picture of the Danish landscape includes, as mentioned, church building, rectory and so on. The idea is that a people made up of individuals who are members of the church not only without believing,[41] but without even believing in belonging (Christoffersen 2011c) is represented culturally by this imagination.

This (romantic) idea is figured out by a white, Danish church building with corbie gables and a certain building style dating back to Romanesque (not Roman, since the Romans never were in Denmark) times. As such, this idea is somehow related to how the vast majority of Danes use the church, namely for rituals in relation to birth, coming of age, marriage and burial and maybe for Christmas Eve services with the family: a distant church building and folk-Church of service, ready when needed and kept and upheld by the commoners for exactly this purpose.

The idea of the distant church is also related to the monarchy and the idea of the 1,000-year-old Danish kingdom, not least embodied by the Church of Jelling, placed besides two huge Viking graves, said to keep King Gorm and his Queen Thyra, parents of King Harald Bluetooth who, on two runic stones beside the church and the Viking graves, gave himself the honour of having christened the Danes. It is this idea of a historical, royal, Christian Danish nation which is also said to be revealed in the first chapter of the Constitution, establishing the people,

40 See Ministeriet for Ligestilling og Kirke (2013). Suggestions are publicized by the ministry in a general hearing after which the minister decides whether or not to propose changed regulation.

41 On this concept, see Davie (1994).

the monarchy, the powers and state support for the church as the four cornerstones on which the Danish nation symbolically rests.[42]

However, a vicarious church does not need to be white and built for small villages. City churches and cathedrals equally have this function of *vicarious religion* for the Danes. The churches are seen as strong centres with open doors, namely buildings filled with spiritual and theological strength not only on behalf of, but also with access for all Danes (Davie 2000). Such a (changed) understanding of the role of the *Folkekirke* is also obvious in the architecture, where, for example, the Cathedral of Copenhagen has installed behind its gates new front doors made of glass, so that it is possible to look into the church from the outside and see the world famous sculpture (by Thorvaldsen) of Christ blessing the congregation – or the world.[43] The gates are, for example, open during late evening when the church is open as *night-church,* a more spiritualized format of services for individualized Danes in the metropolitan way of living, where 'God goes Deep', as the idea is formulated by web-based communication.[44]

The Role of Tourism

Churches within the *Folkekirke* are increasingly also sites to be visited outside of any congregational use and religious services. There is, however, a tendency towards differentiating between cultural and religious use of church buildings that comes not only from the religious side, but also from the cultural side. Of course, Danish churches have a role in tourism, for they add to the historical understanding of the landscape with village churches built in Romanesque times, city churches from before the Reformation (and a few from the Baroque or Rococo periods), cathedrals most of which are also centuries old, albeit maybe rebuilt. This order of churches has shaped the Danish (religious) landscape for centuries. And this landscape is in a very good condition: Danish churches are well-kept and open for a combination of tourism and pilgrimage: a string of more than 400 so-called *vej kirker*, that is churches along the road that are open to the public[45] and invite the tourist in to look at the cultural heritage in the churches. The idea of *vejkirker* is explained in a brochure by the aforementioned *Kirkefondet*; the brochure is helpful for individuals who want to visit their country and its history through visiting the churches. Churches also open for a combined cultural-religious use by providing many cultural events, either related to the ecclesiastical year (concerts for All

42 See Christoffersen, Iversen, Kjærgaard and Warburg (2012) and not least the front page with the picture of the monarch and her husband, the chair of the parliament and the prime minister outside Jelling Church in the official Danish millennium celebration on 3 December 2000.

43 There is a replica of the sculpture on a mountain in Brazil, in the community centre of the Mormon Church in Utah, as well as in several other places around the globe.

44 http://www.natkirken.dk/natcms/index.php (accessed 18 January 2014).

45 http://www.vejkirker.dk/ (accessed 18 January 2014).

Souls, for Advent and Christmas, for Easter and so on) or consisting of public concerts for free during the summer, organized for tourists and Danes in their summer cottages.[46] As a further example of this combined cultural-religious use of the churches, many modern artists have created new ritual clothes for churches, new decorations (painting, carpets) or new mosaics in the windows, paintings in the altarpiece or decided on a new colour for the benches in the church building, a fact that also calls for opening up churches to tourism and which actually invites people to travel around the country to have a look.

The Danish *Folkekirke* is rich, due to very regular funding through church taxes, and the local congregational councils are very willing to use considerable funds to maintain and preserve church buildings and churchyards, as well as for cultural events taking place there. Tourism or fees for cultural events provide for minor replenishment of funds.[47] Some churches therefore require a (small) entrance fee, either for tourist visits or for attending concerts or exhibitions, but this is decided upon at local level and does not contribute much to funding churches' upkeep and most often the idea is that the church is part of the welfare state and should be open for free, at least to members (that is: for most Danes), no matter whether they come to attend a service or to listen to a concert. Very often then, there is no clear cut boundary between cultural and religious uses of the church; they are mixed up into a kind of local life, where it looks natural to all the authorities, that cultural arrangements are part of the contribution by churches to life in the area, not least, for example, in a rural area, where the local church would be the place to be offered a more cultural dimension to life – but still, it is also accepted that major concerts, for example before Christmas, are paid for.

One growing discussion is, however, related to a number of churches, seen as specific cultural *sites*, where tourism, historical heritage and religious use now and then tend to conflict. Examples are the Cathedral of Roskilde (World Heritage), the Cathedral in Ribe, Hover Church (a small village church in West-Jutland) and Our Lady's Church, the Cathedral of Copenhagen (with the Thorvaldsen figures), all part of Danish cultural heritage. Jelling (world cultural heritage) could here serve as an example.[48] The village church is placed between two enormous Viking Era graves and two runic stones containing what has been called 'the baptismal certificate' for Denmark on the front. Here, the newly restored church building is open to the public for free all day long, which means that the congregation pays for cleaning up after groups of interested visitors, be they tourists or guests and locals without distinction. However, the church might be closed also during normal

46 For example this one: http://www.kirkemusikgribskov.dk/ (accessed 18 January 2014). Another example is Søren Kierkegaard's bicentennial in 2013, celebrated in churches throughout the country with lectures, exhibitions and so on.

47 There is no central overview of the income from these cultural arrangements, but the general understanding is that they do not cover much more than what is used in salaries for staff members and so on to organize such arrangements and clean up afterwards.

48 www.jellingkirke.dk (accessed 18 January 2014).

opening hours, due to baptismal services, funerals and so on, thus taking tourists away from the church during services. The tourist interest for Jelling as a historical site is taken care of by an organization managed by the National Museum, called Jelling of the Kings (*Kongernes Jelling*).[49] This organization has been established in a house of its own with, among others, exhibitions, but requires no entrance charge, thus applying the general rule that the National Museum does not charge its visitors. Now a religious community centre (*sognegård*, see above) is to be built in the area and further museum buildings. In the description of the plans for the community centre, the general vision is formulated as follows: 'The goal is to establish and gain clarity in the collaboration between the different dimensions of Jelling, the touristic, the historical and the ecclesiastical.'[50] Even though there is a certain *intertwinement* in the functions, a new wish to be able to distinguish, not only in regard to the age-old question about who provides funds, but certainly more in regard to the equally old question as to who governs and decides and maybe also in regard to the issue of peace around what are termed ecclesiastical functions, has led to this wish for clearer distinctions.

In my view, organizational, financial governance-related distinctions, like in Jelling, are significant in highlighting what is becoming an ever-greater issue.

Church Buildings as Quality Places Versus Community Centres

The question is however to what extent it is possible to try to distinguish between, on the one hand, the locals living around the church (those whom the church is meant for, as it is formulated) and, on the other hand, historically and culturally interested groups of people and tourists. Several developments have changed this idea on distinguishing between *the locals and the globals*. A very common change is that Danes move out from the cities into their summer houses along the coast, not only during July and August, but also over Easter, Christmas and other traditionally religious feasts, and those who go to church at home do so even more in the location of the summer house, which means that local churches with fewer visitors during the dark months might be crowded over summer and Christmas. And these visitors are also 'globals', in that they come from Norway, Sweden, Germany, England and Holland and also want to be part of the local congregation during their holidays. It remains that the churches are (mainly) paid for and (only) governed by the locals.

Another development lies in the briefly mentioned *night-churches*, namely churches in city centres, open until midnight or even longer twice or three times

49 http://natmus.dk/besoeg-museerne/kongernes-jelling/ (accessed 18 January 2014).

50 'At opnå en klarhed I samspillet mellem kirken, monumentområdet og de øvrige omgivelser', see http://www.jellingkirke.dk/fileadmin/group/328/Dokumenter/Juryens_betaenkning_endelig_udgave.pdf (accessed 18 January 2014).

a week, not least related to how the city pulse is.[51] The idea is most often to offer a sanctuary for people who are taking part in late night city life. Most nocturnal services are marked by new spirituality in combination with classical elements such as tide songs. Also the new focus not only on open churches (see above on *vej kirker*), but directly on *pilgrimages* belongs to the same trend. The concept of pilgrimage was originally seen in the Danish context as very Catholic and foreign to Danish ecclesiastical understanding. However, over the last 10–15 years, the *Folkekirke* has appointed special church ministers to organize and facilitate a pilgrimage movement; the newspaper the *Christian Daily* has opened a homepage solely for news and information about pilgrimages[52] and the former Vice-Chancellor of the Pedagogical Centre within the *Folkekirke* (in Løgumkloster), Jens Kristian Krarup, has himself walked more than 2,500 km through Denmark in order to describe what is called *The Danish Monastic Route*,[53] combining the idea of pilgrimage with new knowledge about the landscape and monastic life as it was in Denmark before the Reformation.[54]

These tendencies that have all been obvious throughout the last 20 years are strengthening the *Folkekirke* as a church that keeps pace with traditions and it could be understood as a tendency to interpret church buildings as *quality places*. Such places need to be taken care of in order to keep their quality. They are dedicated to religious use, but certainly a use that is structured under the qualities that the place is keeping. These tendencies could thus be interpreted as ways to restore, even differently, the religious dimension of church buildings, when faced with the secularization of places of worship, whereas the opposite tendency to culturalize places of worship, as has been clear, is also very obvious. The question is whether it is possible to distinguish the two tendencies.

Another, maybe contradictory or at least different, recent approach to church buildings tends to view them as local community centres with combined religious and secular use.

This approach has already started with the many new churches built since the mid-twentieth century, primarily in the suburbs. These churches have been built in new building styles (first *Jugendstil*; later *Modernism*) and have also been seen to reflect a changed theological understanding of the Church's role in society. Also the Catholic Church and other Christian communities in Denmark, such as other Protestant Churches, built many churches in the second half of the twentieth century, in the same two building styles. Finally, one should also notice the building styles reflected in the post-millennium change from buildings to congregations in

51 http://www.folkekirken.dk/folkekirkens-arbejde/natkirker/ (accessed 18 January 2014).

52 www.pilgrimsvandring.dk (accessed 18 January 2014).

53 http://www.klosterruten.dk/ (accessed 18 January 2014).

54 He has opened a website and published seven guidebooks with very detailed maps, helping tourists/pilgrims on foot or bicycle to find their way through the Danish landscape with churches and former monasteries as their guiding principle.

post-secular Protestantism, as well as in the immigrant religious communities (be they Christian or Muslim) taking shelter in former industrial buildings in harbour areas or similar.

Few churches were built in the period from 1700 (when Denmark lost the Scandinavian wars) to the end of the nineteenth century (when people started to move from the rural areas into Copenhagen). Movements among people have, however, generated a need for new church buildings – first in Copenhagen, and after the Second World War in the suburbs of Denmark's major cities.

The churches in *Jugendstil* are characteristic, often with copies of Thorvaldsen figures and very often also with paintings in the altar pieces by artists such as Carl Bloch. It is interesting that copies – and of course original works – by precisely these two late nineteenth century artists are now among the most expensive in the world, because the Mormon Church in the United States sees these works as representing a true religious artistic style.[55] The later period with its *Jugendstil* is also called *Grundtvigian,* representing a lay ideal in regard to church buildings, or there are the so-called *YMCA-churches*, referring to the movements for young men and women from around the industrialized country, where young men and women from the countryside moved to the cities to find work and found shelter in Christian organizations and churches built to make room for religious movements and their work, not only on Sundays, but also during the week.

This was characteristic also for the churches built by *Kirkefondet.* These churches should be small and cheap, not especially fancy, but with plenty of room to be used during the week for children, for women to work, for men to meet after work or for unemployed men. The goal was to build congregations, not to build houses distinguished by high culture. This approach is still clearly visible in these church buildings.

The third generation of people from the countryside, who moved to the capital in the late nineteenth century, moved out of the city again and into the suburbs with their standard package deal houses. They should of course also have access to churches. These huge areas with pre-fabricated houses were often placed just around older villages which already had a village church; they could then conveniently include the new inhabitants too, who knew the look of a village church from their great grandparents. But other areas were simply erected from scratch and here a church building, which better suited the style of the architecture of the newly built houses, was developed. More than 150 churches were built between 1960 and 2010, very often in a rather humble style, but with plenty of space for secondary purposes: lunch and coffee, meals, social gatherings and so on. They were meant to be simple, pragmatic, functional, not difficult for anyone to enter (Schuster 2010: 66 *et seq.*).

---

55 An original painting by Carl Bloch, *Christ at Bethesda*, which hung in the largest missionary hall in Copenhagen, was sold in the late 1990s for more than 10 million DKK to the Mormon Church in Utah, where it is now displayed in their museum and with a copy of it placed in the hall where their social work is organized.

This humble idea of what a church should be has led to the next step in the transition. Indeed, it is true that young people especially, including young families, do not see the need for traditional church buildings (nor the need for collectively organized church life in a European mainstream church, such as the Danish *Folkekirke*). They want to choose their pastor and their leadership on their own, follow their own rituals and sing their own (contemporary) songs, just as they do not want to feel bound to building and using an expensive organ – an electric instrument and a chorus will do much better! Specifically, they do not see why they should spend their money and time on building and keeping artistic, beautiful buildings – a former industrial building on the harbour, with a cross taken out from a cupboard in the wall when the building is in use in order to show the Christian use of the building – such buildings are more than enough for them; they want to build congregations, not to preserve buildings. Due to these anti-traditionalist views, such new congregations are very often established outside the *Folkekirke.* Contrary to the pilgrimage trend this tendency also leads to a certain weakening of mainstream churches such as the *Folkekirke* and thus also to less preparedness to provide for the upkeep of traditional buildings.

Finally, one should mention the influx or the immigration of Christians from churches and congregations never before seen in the Danish context, such as, among others, Syrian Orthodox Christians.[56] Nearly 90 per cent of immigrants into Denmark are now said to come from culturally Christian backgrounds and that immigrants sit on 40 per cent of the benches in churches in Copenhagen each Sunday.[57] A recent change to the Act on Use of Church Buildings within the *Folkekirke* has thus already opened up the possibility of allowing Christian communities outside the *Folkekirke* to use *Folkekirke* church buildings for regular services and for services in relation to weddings and funerals. The communities then pay a rent, based on the actual costs for the use of the church building.

While these religious communities are 'coming of age', they wish to obtain a share of the existing church buildings, since they are very often used to the role of art and beautiful buildings from their countries of origin. It is too early to judge, but it seems as if some of these groups are interested in taking over some of the buildings from the *Folkekirke*; the Church Services for Immigrants thus suggests that two or three immigrant congregations could buy or rent a church building together (Lund 2011) and that they would be able to run their joint communities within that church building for less than 100,000 euros, whereas a common *Folkekirke*-church building with staff costs half a million euros a

56 See the international research program 'Defining and Identifying Middle Eastern Christian in Europe', to which also Professor L.P. Galal, Roskilde University, contributes: https://arts.st-andrews.ac.uk/dimecce/ (accessed 11 November 2014).

57 Oral information provided by Hans Henrik Lund, from Church Services for Immigrants (*Kirkernes Integrationstjeneste*), 5 July 2013.

year.[58] However, this interest from immigrant communities is not widened to church buildings that may be listed by the cultural authorities. As mentioned earlier in this chapter, a church building that is taken out of use within the *Folkekirke* will, from that moment on, fall under the Act on Listed Buildings – and poor immigrant congregations are, just like younger and elder community-oriented Danish congregations, not interested in serving society by keeping up listed buildings.[59]

Management in the Future

To conclude and without sharpening conflicts more than necessary, it might therefore be possible to say that developments within Danish Christianity broadly (within and outside *the Folkekirke*) show two general approaches to church buildings: one oriented towards the maintenance of *classical quality*, the other focused on establishing a current feeling of *community*.

Both these approaches are, however, challenged by broader tendencies in society to require greater efficiency in the use of both century-old and newly built churches, supported by a third tendency becoming much more central than previously, namely a general tendency in society to require documentation of value for money. Within general tendencies to organize public bodies under the concept of *new public management*, the state is now increasingly demanding of congregational councils that they provide information about the cost-effectiveness of tax money used for church buildings.[60] This is of course sometimes rather difficult, due to difficulties in formulating the effects of Christian services (except in numbers of participants) or of cultural heritage (except in numbers of tourists). As a response to this requirement to provide cost-effective governance, some congregational councils have started to argue that it should not be their obligation to maintain buildings as heritage on behalf of a population which has abandoned the position of which these buildings were originally symbols. Others would, on the contrary, argue that the buildings are bearers of classical European cultural symbols, including the cultural and Christian dimensions of the symbols, which in itself could be seen as an argument for keeping and maintaining these buildings. And the third – and maybe most persuasive argument – would then be: but who pays?

As has been shown before, the main answer to this question in the Danish context until now has been that the local congregation pays for all the maintenance and preservation and manages the building at the same time, being this local

58 http://www.kristeligt-dagblad.dk/artikel/516459:Kirke---tro--Indvandrere--Vi-kan-drive-en-kirke-langt-billigere-end-folkekirken (accessed 18 January 2014).

59 http://www.kristeligt-dagblad.dk/artikel/516459:Kirke---tro--Indvandrere--Vi-kan-drive-en-kirke-langt-billigere-end-folkekirken (accessed 18 January 2014).

60 This tendency is investigated in the recently funded cross disciplinary project 'What Money Can't Buy' (2014-2017), see http://teol.ku.dk/cfk/whatmoneycantbuy/ (accessed 11 November 2014).

congregation within the *Folkekirke* or among other religious groups. That is a solution established in a less globalized era with fewer pilgrims, tourists and immigrants and with more classical members of the *Folkekirke* as the local institution for all *rites de passages*. Since it is now no longer always easy to see these different functions as linked and intertwined, it no longer seems fair, on the one hand, that the locals should pay also for the globals and, on the other hand, that only one of the local groups, namely church members, shall decide on behalf of all users.

A bill from the Ministry of Ecclesiastical Affairs and recently passed by Parliament could be interpreted in the light of this context.[61] According to this bill, church buildings belonging to the *Folkekirke* can host also secular uses, as long as these uses are not contrary to the religious purpose of the buildings. Secular purposes could be purely cultural events, such as historical lectures or tourist guided tours – which already take place in local churches. It could however also be to rent the building out to other local groups than religious communities (high schools or the local music school, for example) and in doing so uphold the use as a church building (even occasionally) combined with a local use as cultural meeting place. This could prevent some church buildings from being taken out of use as places of worship – and thus from being regulated under the Act on Listed Buildings, but what seems more central is that it could at the same time broaden the group of locals who pay for the maintenance of the building. The proposal does however not change governance structures; the idea is that the congregational council should still govern the church.

Solutions to questions about funding, governing and maintaining religious heritage in the future could thus also have to do with the changed religious landscape: fewer members (but still many) of the majority Danish Church; immigration by a majority of Christian groups; and a changed understanding of the relevance and need of (preservation of) beautiful buildings, art, certain musical styles … All these dimensions are about to create new and changed scenery for how to organize the funding of religious heritage in the future.

References

Bahn, L., Bollmann, K. and Munck, K. (2013), *Middelalder Kirkens vedligeholdelse* [maintenance of the Church (from the Middle Ages)], with an introduction by bishop Peter Fischer-Møller (Roskilde Stift).

Christoffersen, L., Andersen, S. and Modéer, K.Å. (eds) (2010), *Law and Religion in the 21st Century – Nordic Perspectives* (Copenhagen: DJØF Publishing).

61 Act no. 265 of 25 March 2014 on change of legislation on, among others, church buildings. See https://www.retsinformation.dk/Forms/R0710.aspx?id=162254 (accessed 16 May 2014). This new Act is included in LBK no. 330 of 29 March 2014, § 5 (2).

Christoffersen, L. (2010a), 'State, church and religion in Denmark at the beginning of the 21st century' in Christoffersen, L., Andersen, S. and Modéer, K.Å. (eds), 145–61.

Christoffersen, L. (2010b), 'Et religionsretligt problem og forslag til løsning' [A legal problem and how to solve it – on funding of church buildings within other religious communities than the folkekirke] in Henrichsen, C. et al. (eds), 415–32.

Christoffersen, L. (2010c), 'Not even believing in belonging: States and churches in five north European (post)-Lutheran countries' in Ferrari, S. and Rinaldo, C. (eds), 187–98.

Christoffersen, L., Iversen, H.R., Kærgaard, N. and Warburg, M. (eds) (2012), *Fremtidens danske religionsmodel* [the Danish religion model of the future] (Copenhagen: Anis).

Christoffersen, L. (2015), 'A long historical path towards transparency, accountability and good governance. On financing religions in Denmark', in Messner, F. (ed.).

Davie, G. (1994), *Religion in Britain Since 1945: Believing Without Belonging* (Oxford/UK and Cambridge/USA: Blackwell).

Davie, G. (2000), *Religion in Modern Europe – A Memory Mutates* (Oxford: Oxford University Press).

Eriksson, A.L., Gunner, G. and Blåder, N. (eds) (2012), *Exploring a Heritage. Evangelical Lutheran Churches in the North* (Eugene, OR: Pickwick Publications), Church of Sweden Research Series, vol. 5.

Ferrari, S. and Rinaldo, C. (eds) (2010), *Law & Religion in the 21st Century – Relations between States and Religious Communities* (Farnham: Ashgate).

Henrichsen, C. et al. (eds) (2010), *Ret, Informatik og Samfund. Festskrift til Peter Blume* (Copenhagen: DJØF forlag).

Jensen, Jørgen I. (1995), *Den fjerne kirke. Mellem kultur og religiøsitet* [The distant church/ church building – between culture and religiosity] (Copenhagen: Samleren).

Kirkefondet (2012), 'Brug af kirker, der skal lukkes [Use in the future of churches to be closed down]', available at: http://www.kirkefondet.dk/fileadmin/filer/Billeder/Udgivelser/Kirkefondets_tanker_fremtidig_brug.pdf (accessed 14 January 2013).

Lodberg, P. (2012), 'Burning issues in the Evangelical Lutheran Church in Denmark' in Eriksson, A.L., Gunner, G. and Blåder, N. (eds), 67 *et seq.*

Lund, H.H. (2011), 'Verdens kirker hos os' [World hurches at home in our country], in *Københavns stiftsblad*, October 2011.

Lunn, U. and Lund, C. (2001), 'Denmark', in Pickard, R. (ed.), 73–91.

Messner, F. (ed.) (2015), *Public Funding of Religions in Europe* (Farnham: Ashgate).

Ministeriet for Ligestilling og Kirke (2013), *Rapport fra arbejdsgruppen om folkekirkens kirker, der helt eller delvis tages ud af brug* [Report on the use of totally or partially redundant Folkekirken church buildings], available at: http://miliki.dk/fileadmin/share/publikationer/betaenkninger/Rapport_om_kirker__ud_af_brug.pdf (accessed 14 January 2014).

Ministeriet for Ligestilling og Kirke (2013b), *Hvordan lukker man en kirke? Konference på Nationalmuseet* [how to close a church?], available at: http://

miliki.dk/kirke/nyhedsarkiv-kirke/nyhed-om-kirke/artikel/hvordan-lukker-man-en-kirke/ (accessed 14 January 2014).

Paldam, M. (2012a), 'Church density and the Church membership ratio. The cross-municipal pattern in Denmark. Statistical Background Paper', available at: http://www.martin.paldam.dk/Papers/Rel-trans/Cross-Municipal-Rel.pdf (accessed 14 January 2014).

Paldam, M. (2012b), 'The present churches – age and size distribution', available at: http://www.martin.paldam.dk/Papers/Rel-trans/Present-church-stock.pdf (accessed 14 January 2014).

Paldam, M. (2013), 'An essay on the religious transition. Controversy in the face of facts', 17 p., available at: http://www.martin.paldam.dk/Papers/Rel-trans/Transition-3.pdf (accessed 14 January 2014).

Paldam, M. and Gundelach, E. (2012), 'A model of religious transition', accepted for publication in *Theoretical Economic Letters*, available at: http://www.martin.paldam.dk/Papers/Rel-trans/Rel-Tra-Model.pdf (accessed 14 January 2013).

Pickard, R. (ed.) (2001), *Policy and Law in Heritage Conservation* (London: Spon Press).

Roesen, A. (1976), *Dansk Kirkeret* [Danish Ecclesiastical Law] (Hillerød: Præsteforeningen).

Schuster, B.G. (no date), 'Moderne dansk kirkearkitektur. På sporet af et luthersk kirkerum', available at: http://kirkearkitektur.dk/ (accessed 14 January 2013).

Schuster, B.G. (1993), 'Fra kirkerum til gudstjenesterum. En forfaldshistorie?', *Kritisk Forum for Praktisk Teologi*, 54, 33–54.

Schuster, B.G. (2010), 'Kirkens morfologi. En statistisk-impressionistisk gennemgang af tendenser i moderne dansk kirkearkitektur', *Kritisk Forum for Praktisk Teologi*, 122, 64–85.

Stubbs, J.H. and Makaš, E.G. (2011), *Architectural Conservation in Europe and the Americas* (New Jersey: John Wiley & Sons).

Toft Jensen, H. (2013), *17 Københavnske kirker – en screening*, Kulturstyrelsen, available at: http://kirkenikbh.dk/files/kirkenikbh.dk/attachments/17_koebenhavnske_kirker.pdf (accessed 18 January 2014).

Westergaard, E. (no date), 'Natursyn og mindekultur', available at: http://www.kirkegaardskultur.dk/artikler/natursyn-og-mindekultur/ (accessed 14 January 2013).

Westergaard, E. (2008), 'Lad engle dale og gøre stenen til en stol', available at: http://www.kirkegaardskultur.dk/artikler/lad-engle-dale-og-goere-stenen-til-sin-stol/ (accessed 14 January 2013).

Westergaard, E. (2009), 'Kirkegården som turistmål', available at: http://www.kirkegaardskultur.dk/artikler/kirkegaarden-som-turistmaal/ (accessed 14 January 2013).

PART III
Funding Religious Heritage in Covenantal and Recognized Church Systems

Chapter 7
Funding Religious Heritage in Belgium

Stéphanie Wattier

In Belgium, religion has very much left its mark on history. For this reason, there are many churches and religious buildings in the Belgian landscape, a large number of which are inherited from the medieval period. In addition, most of Belgian religious heritage is Catholic. There are precisely 3,948 Catholic parishes in Belgium: 2,051 in Wallonia, 1,809 in Flanders and 88 in Brussels. Furthermore, there are 150 'non-Catholic parishes' (Coomans 2006: 51).

Legally, the funding of religious heritage raises some important issues in Belgium: the complexity of the repartition of competences between various actors, the incidence of being listed as a monument and the question of the ownership of churches. We must also mention some difficulties pertaining to the conservation of the buildings, a crucial debate about Belgian religious heritage and, lastly, the problem of redundant churches. To understand all those topics, it is important to firstly have a look at the history of religious heritage in Belgium.

Overview of Belgian Religious Heritage

History of Religious Heritage in Belgium

In common with many European countries, Belgium has a rich religious heritage that has existed for more than a thousand years. Most of it belongs to the Catholic Church and has survived many historical events, such as wars and foreign domination.

First of all, during the medieval period, hundreds of Gothic or Roman churches, parish buildings, cathedrals were built. Over the centuries, urban communities grew around these buildings,[1] which were restored, rebuilt, expanded and improved alongside. Many still exist today, which explains the 'high density' (Coomans 2006: 45) of religious heritage in Belgium. Furthermore, the numerous convents and abbeys also belong to religious heritage, however with a different legal status (De Pooter 2005: 169).

In the sixteenth century, many churches were looted and a significant part of the religious heritage was lost. The most fundamental reason was the context

1 On the 'feeling' related to religious buildings in the city nowadays, see Charlier and Moens (2005: 145 *et seq.*).

of the Reform; but iconoclastic Calvinists also played an important role in this context of 'religious wars' (Coomans 2006: 45). The seventeenth century saw the erection of baroque churches and cathedrals. In the following century, despite the influence of the philosophy of the Enlightenment, a very large number of churches, parishes and cathedrals were created and some medieval places of worship were transformed into neoclassical churches (Coomans 2006: 46).

Religious heritage in Belgium has also been influenced by foreign domination. From 1713 until 1795, Belgium was under the control of Austria. Subsequently, Belgium was annexed to the Republic of France from 1795 until 1815 and to the Kingdom of the Netherlands from 1815 until 1830. The French Revolution of 1789 had an important impact on religious heritage insofar as nearly all the religious assets and possessions were nationalized during that period. Then, they were sold and the religious congregations were suppressed. In 1801, Napoleon Bonaparte and Pope Pius VII signed a Concordat that established the separation of church and state. This Concordat also established that worship could be exercised freely and publicly.

Belgium became independent in 1830 and adopted a new Constitution in 1831. During the nineteenth century, economic and demographic development was important and accompanied by the construction of many churches and cathedrals. For this reason, the nineteenth century is called 'the golden age of Catholics' (Coomans 2006: 48). Later, a considerable number of buildings were destroyed during the World Wars of 1914–18 and 1939–45. Finally, the Second Vatican Council (1962–65) initiated an ultimate wave of construction of new churches. The Belgian 'communitarian conflicts' of the 1960s also had an influence on religious heritage: the map of dioceses was adapted to the linguistic border between the French and Flemish communities. Consequently, some dioceses split into two (for example Malines and Liège) or even three parts (for example Malines-Bruxelles), resulting in changes in ownership.

Church Ownership

The term 'church ownership' covers all the buildings and properties that are related to worship. In other words, this definition includes immovable and movable goods like walls, tours, sacristies, baptisteries, organs, bells, altars and so on.

To identify the owner of a church, a distinction must be established between 'churches recognized for the public exercise of worship' (called parishes or public churches) and 'private churches' (Coomans 2006: 54). Most of the time, private churches and chapels belong to religious institutes, schools, hospitals and so on. In general, they have the legal form of non-profit organizations. As far as matters related to 'churches recognized for the public exercise of worship' are concerned, another distinction must be drawn between churches that were built before 1802 – called 'crown churches' – and other churches. In several decisions, the Court of Cassation – the Belgium's highest civil court – judged that 'crown churches' are part of the public domain[2] because they are of public utility (*utilité publique*).[3] Places of worship returned after the Concordat of 1801 belong to municipalities or to the provinces (for the cathedrals). All places of worship built after 1802 belong to the municipalities or to the *fabriques d'églises* (Torfs 2007: 182). The real identity of the builder of the place of worship has no influence on the ownership. The reason is that the building of such churches took place as a result of very complicated financial arrangements (involving the state, municipalities and provinces, but also some private funds from the parish itself) (Coomans 2006: 54).[4]

Contemporary Challenges

The first challenge pertains to the material protection of religious heritage, whose importance makes the task very difficult. Unfortunately, there are a growing number of incidents of burglaries and vandalism in churches. For instance, in 2010, the police registered 977 acts of burglary and vandalism. The problem is that there is no consensus among religious authorities regarding the insurance of churches. For that reason, mechanisms of repression do not work very well and are not satisfactory. To solve this, the idea is to create a *Comité du patrimoine cultuel*, such as existed in France, to improve the situation and find solutions to combat burglaries (Dury 2005: 155).[5]

Besides the problem of burglaries, there are also some illegal disposals of religious heritage, especially involving pieces of art. Journalists do not hesitate to report that 'Belgium is a "turntable" for trafficking works of art'.[6] Furthermore, one of the problems is that there are fewer and fewer people coming to pray. Consequently, this may lead to the closing down of a number of churches.

---

2 Court of cassation, 11 November 1886, *Pasicrisie*, 1886, I, 401; Court of cassation, 6 November 1940, *Pasicrisie*, 1940, I, 279.

3 Court of cassation, 3 May 1879, *Pasicrisie*, 1879, I, 246.

4 During the eighteenth century, some semi-religious buildings that were built in the thirteenth century – such as beguines – were taken over by the administration. Therefore, today, Public Centres for Social Action (*CPAS*) own them.

5 The French *Comité du patrimoine cultuel* – which has stopped working since 2012 – was however not exactly competent on this issue. The *Office central de lutte contre le trafic des biens culturels* (Central Office for the Fight against Traffic in Cultural Goods) 'covers the offences of theft and handling of cultural goods, as well as art forgeries. The Office's mandates include prevention, documentation, prosecution, international cooperation and training. […] the Office is France's "central authority" responsible for implementing the claim and restitution procedures for national treasures that have unlawfully left the territory of one Member state for the territory of another. The Office is in contact with a network of police focal points throughout France.' See: http://ec.europa.eu/home-affairs/doc_centre/crime/docs/Report%20Trafficking%20in%20cultural%20goods%20EN.pdf (accessed 21 January 2014).

6 From the newspaper, *Le Soir*, 10 November 2007.

Fundamentally, problems of burglaries and churches closing down raise a series of other significant issues, such as religious freedom and praying in community. How will people be able to pray in community if there is no religious open space anymore? What about religious freedom, if the government has to adopt legislation to close churches to combat violence and burglaries? Those problems are very much present at the moment in Belgium and are surely one of the current topics that the regional governments have to deal with.

Managing and Funding Religious Heritage in Belgium

The Various Actors Involved in the Management of Religious Heritage

As far as matters related to religious heritage are concerned, various actors have legal authority. At least four types of actors must be mentioned by virtue of Constitutional law. The reason for this is that Belgium became a federal state in 1970.

First of all, the federal state takes charge of salaries and pensions of ministers of religion and of delegates of non-confessional organizations (humanists), pursuant to Article 181 of the Belgian Constitution. To be funded by the state, religious and non-confessional organizations must have been recognized by the state. Concretely, opened up in the nineteenth century to various religious denominations historically located on the territory (Catholic, Anglican, Jewish, Protestant), the funding scheme was expanded in the twentieth century to Islam (1974–2005), to Orthodoxy (1985) and finally to non-confessional philosophical groups (1993–2002).

Secondly, by virtue of Article 6, § 1, VIII, 6° of the Act of 8 August 1980, three regions (Flemish, Walloon and Brussels) are competent for the *fabriques d'églises* and public institutions are responsible for the management of religious buildings.

Thirdly, the three communities (Flemish, French and German) are expressly competent for the cultural heritage by virtue of Article 4, 4° of the Act of 8 August 1980 and Article 127 of the Constitution.

Fourthly, municipalities and provinces are competent for some repairs and restorations of churches. Furthermore, municipalities are competent for cemeteries and provinces are competent for cathedrals. However, it is important to underline that the Belgian doctrine considers that cemeteries are not part of religious heritage.[7] They are rather considered as a public service carried out by the *communes*.

7 According to the doctrine, this interpretation is confirmed by Article 16, § 1, of the Act of 20 July 1971 on funerals and burials, which provides that 'Les inhumations ne peuvent avoir lieu que dans les cimetières communaux ou intercommunaux'. See Christians et al. (2011).

To sum up, the complexity of the legislation and the intertwining of responsible institutions are one of the basic features of religious heritage in Belgium. There is not only one responsible actor and we have to take several elements of Constitutional law into account when analysing the situation. To improve the system, it has been suggested that a coordinating institution needs to be created, at least in Wallonia (Dury 2005: 152). This institution should be – as mentioned before – a kind of religious heritage committee (*Comité du patrimoine cultuel*), such as existed in France. This committee should give advice on protection and conservation of religious heritage.

Being Listed as a Monument

Being listed as a monument is very important in the Belgium legal system applicable to religious heritage. This status can help churches to obtain greater subsidies for repair and restoration. It is also important to mention that, in Wallonia, religious heritage amounts to more than a quarter of listed heritage. There are 2,800 listed buildings in Wallonia, which are divided up as follows: 38 per cent correspond to private property,[8] 30 per cent belongs to religious heritage, 10 per cent are castles, 8 per cent are civil buildings, 7 per cent belongs to minor heritage (kiosks and so on) and 4 per cent belongs to the industrial heritage (Dury 2006: 1).

For the protection of religious monuments, two acts are important to mention: the Royal Decree of 7 January 1835 that created a Royal Commission of Monuments and the Act of 7 August 1931 on the conservation of monuments and sites in Belgium. Until 1970, the conservation of monuments was a federal competence. But then, in 1970, Belgium became a federal state and the process of federalization started. The competence was transferred to the three communities (Flemish, French and German) and the regional competences (environment, *fabriques d'églises* and so on) were given to the three regions (Wallonia, Flanders, Brussels). Finally, in 1994, the German part of Wallonia's competence – which means the territory of the German-speaking region – was transferred to the German community. Consequently, each Community has its own legislation. In Wallonia, provisions pertaining to historic monuments and sites are entrenched in the CWATUP (*Code Wallon de l'urbanisme, de l'aménagement du territoire, du patrimoine et de l'énergie*, Walloon Code of town planning, zoning, heritage and energy), while in Brussels-Capital, they appear in the CoBAT (*Code Bruxellois de l'aménagement du territoire*, Brussel Code of zoning). In the Flemish Region, this topic is regulated by several decrees adopted between 1976 and 1993 (van Ypersele and Louveaux 2006: 48). Pursuant to Article 185 of the Code of Zoning, Planning and Heritage in Wallonia, heritage consists of all 'immovable goods, whose protection is justified due to their historical, archeological, scientific, artistic, social, technical or landscape interest'. No express reference to religious goods appears

8 In the form of private estates, individual houses and so on.

in this text.[9] Nor can this be found in the Brussels-Capital Community where the Brussels Zoning Code applies, in that it provides that immovable heritage means 'all immovable goods which present historical, archeological, artistic, esthetic, scientific, social, technical or folkloric interest' (Article 206).[10]

Once again, all those transfers show the difficulty in comprehending religious heritage in Belgium. Concretely, if the building is a 'public church' – which means that it is dedicated to worship – and if this church is listed as a monument, all the necessary expenses will be publicly funded: 60 per cent will be paid by the region, 20 per cent by the municipality and 20 per cent by the province. If this public church is *not* listed as a monument, it will only receive a subsidy of 30 per cent from the region. The parish itself will have to pay for the other repairs and restoration work. If the church is a 'private church' – which means that it is *not* dedicated to worship – but this church is listed as a monument, it will receive a subsidy of 60 to 80 per cent from the region for its religious heritage. The owner of the church will have to pay for other repairs and restoration work.[11]

Belgian Debate on Funding Religious Heritage

In Belgium, funding religious heritage is controversial: a part of the doctrine considers that the funding of religious heritage *is* indeed part of the global 'public funding of religion', whereas others argue that this is not the case. This question has never been solved by any case law. This controversy can be explained by two different factors. First, the situation is not very clear, due to the number of actors that are competent for religious heritage.[12] Maybe federal, regional and municipal legislators should solve that problem by concluding a 'cooperation agreement' such as already exists for the recognizing and funding religious leaders.[13] The goal of this kind of agreement is to clarify the sharing out of competences between the federal state, the three communities and the three regions. Secondly, the situation is very delicate because of the fact that nearly all Belgian religious heritage belongs to the Catholic Church. Data of 2007 on the allocation of public funds

9 Text available at: http://dgo4.spw.wallonie.be/DGATLP/DGATLP/pages/DGATLP/Dwnld/CWATUPE.pdf (accessed 21 January 2014).

10 Text available at: http://www.unesco.org/culture/natlaws/index.php?&lng=fr (accessed 8 May 2013).

11 Among noteworthy listed religious monuments in Wallonia, we can mention: the *Collégiale Sainte-Gertrude* in Nivelles, the Old Abbeyin Villers-la-Ville, the *Collégiale Saint-Georges et Sainte-Ode* in Liège and the *Cathédrale Saint-Paul* in Liège.

12 See the section *Various Actors* above.

13 See: *Accord de coopération du 2 juillet 2008 modifiant l'accord de coopération du 27 mai 2004 entre l'Autorité fédérale, la Communauté germanophone, la Région flamande, la Région wallonne et la Région de Bruxelles-Capitale en ce qui concerne la reconnaissance des cultes, les traitements et pensions des ministres des cultes, les fabriques d'église et les établissements chargés de la gestion du temporel des cultes reconnus*, in *Moniteur Belge*, 23 July 2008.

dedicated to religious denominations show that most public funds for pensions and property go to Catholic heritage: out of a total of 35.4 million euros allotted to religious heritage, 34.8 million euros are dedicated to Catholic heritage, 0.5 million euros to Protestant heritage, and nothing to that of the other faiths (Husson 2007: 14–16). Hence, should the funding of religious heritage be considered as being part of the overall system of state support for religions, there would be real inequality. Indeed, in case religious buildings were to be deconsecrated and lose their religious nature and, for example, sold, the proceeds from the sale would benefit the Catholic Church.

Redundancy and Deconsecration

The motivation that lies behind the much-debated issue of redundancy and deconsecration of churches is profitability. The concern is about conservation as well, in that the drastic drop in churchgoing no longer allows them to be regularly used. This process has already begun in Belgium and, as a consequence, several churches have been transformed into nightclubs, fruit and vegetable markets, hotels, chip shops and so on. But this is just the beginning of the process.

Deconsecration of churches has given rise to a certain number of rulings. For instance, in Brussels, St Catherine's Church is going to be transformed. This was decided upon in December 2011 in the knowledge that only a few believers come to pray there. The aim is to transform the church into a covered market (of fruits and vegetables) which should be more attractive, according to the City of Brussels. This project should take four or five years and cost five million euros. But some associations have decided to contest that decision. The Council of State will henceforth have to decide whether this decision of transformation is legal or not. As another example, in the case *asbl Pétitions-Patrimoine*, a company had applied for a building permit in order to transform a religious site composed of a church, a convent and other buildings, into a hotel, spa, restaurant, conference centre and parking spaces. The Council of State, the Belgian highest administrative court, held that the material protection of the site could be better achieved through this estate project than through a decision of listing. This was made possible due to the heritage legislation applicable here, which allows a balancing of interests. In addition, it is possible for the government, in charge of listing the buildings, to take into account before doing so, any possible difficulties in reassigning the building if it had not been occupied for a long time (Article 222, §5, 6° of the Brussels Zoning Code).[14]

Over the next 30 years, more than 20 churches in Brussels are going to be reassigned. In Wallonia and Flanders, some religious buildings have already undergone such changes. In Namur, a church was turned into a dance hall. In

14 Council of State, 12 July 2012, no. 220.314, *asbl Pétitions-Patrimoine*.

Tongeren, a church has been reassigned as a chip shop. In Mons, an old convent has been converted into a four-star hotel.

Fundamentally, the issue of redundant church buildings further raises some crucial questions: can a deconsecrated church still be considered a church, that is, as a place of worship? What can be done to preserve the availability of places of worship? And so on and so forth ... This list of issues is certainly not exhaustive.

Conclusion

The Belgian landscape is undeniably marked by religious heritage. We have seen that it raises several difficulties due to federalism, property of churches and on the severe decrease in religious practices. However, the current problem of Belgian religious heritage is surely related to deconsecration and decommissioning.

Nowadays, authorities have to find solutions to avoid closing down churches. This solution would raise one other fundamental question about the *status* of deconsecrated churches. Indeed, as a historical perspective or as a pure heritage question, a deconsecrated church is still a church. Nevertheless, legally and theologically, it is not the case anymore. From that perspective, the question becomes: if Belgium decides to begin a general process of deconsecration and decommissioning of churches, does that mean that the system of religious heritage is moving to a system of *cultural heritage?*

References

Charlier, J.E. and Moens, F. (2005), 'Les églises, biens cultuels, Patrimoine culturel et décision politique. Enseignements d'une enquête sur les lieux de culte catholiques d'une ville belge', in Husson, J.F. (ed.), 137–48.

Christians, L.L., De Pooter, P. and Tilkin, G. (2011), 'Islam et parcelles confessionnelles dans les cimetières en Belgique', *Revue de droit communal*, 2, 2–12.

Coomans, Th., Morisset, L.K. and Noppen, L. (eds) (2006), *Quel avenir pour quelles églises?* (Québec: Presses universitaires du Québec).

Coomans, Th. (2006), 'La propriété et les enjeux: les églises en Belgique', in Coomans, Th., Morisset, L.K. and Noppen, L. (eds), 41–72.

De Pooter, P. (2005), 'Quel avenir pour les lieux de culte en Belgique?', in Husson, J.F. (ed.), 169–78.

Dury, J. (2005), 'La gestion du patrimoine religieux. Aperçu de la situation en Région wallonne', in Husson, J.F. (ed.), 149–56.

Dury, J. (2006), 'La gestion du patrimoine religieux. Aperçu de la situation en Région wallonne', *La lettre du patrimoine*, 2, 1–20, available at: http://www.institutdupatrimoine.be/ (accessed 21 January 2014).

Flores-Lonjou, M. and Messner, F. (eds) (2007), *Les lieux de culte en France et en Europe* (Leuven: Peeters).
Husson, J.F. (ed.) (2005), *Le financement des cultes et de la laïcité: comparaison internationale et perspectives* (Namur: Les éditions namuroises).
Husson, J.F. (2007), 'Le financement public des cultes et de la laïcité', *Politique, revue de débats*, 52, 14–16.
Laffineur-Crépin, M. (2005), 'Conservation, mise en valeur et sécurité du patrimoine mobilier religieux. Vingt ans d'efforts ... pour quels résultats?', *Patrimoine et vie collective*, 191–200.
Torfs, R. (2007), 'Les édifices culturels en Belgique', in Flores-Lonjou, M. and Messner, F. (eds), 181–6.
Van Ypersele, J. and Louveaux, B. (2006), *Le droit de l'urbanisme en Belgique et ses trois régions* (Bruxelles: Larcier).

Chapter 8

Funding Religious Heritage in Estonia: From Sacred Buildings to Sacred Groves

Ringo Ringvee

Introduction[1]

The following chapter is about funding religious heritage in a secular society. Questions like 'Is funding religious heritage at the same time also funding religion?' or 'Is only heritage of traditional religions funded by public money?' are important and often heatedly debated. In the current European context, religious diversity is increasing and the role and presence of any kind of religion in the public sphere and funding of religion either directly or indirectly have become highly contested issues. Europe is a mosaic of varying cultures, tradition and practices with their different histories and experiences. These differences are also reflected in domestic conservation policies. The following chapter focuses on conservation of religious heritage and the related funding in Estonia.

Estonia became part of the Western Christendom after the invasion of the Teutonic Order during the Nordic Crusades in the early thirteenth century. During the Catholic era that lasted until the sixteenth century, Estonia became covered by an infrastructure of churches and monasteries. After the Lutheran Reformation in Estonia during the sixteenth century, the former Catholic church buildings became places of worship for the new Lutheran Church. In the early eighteenth century, the missionary movement of the Moravian brethren from Herrnhut arrived in Estonia. The Brethren were successful among the native Estonian peasants who began to build prayer houses for their religious meetings. After the Great Nordic War in 1721, Estonia became part of the Russian Empire. In the same year, the first Orthodox church was built in Tallinn. The Kazan Church is the oldest wooden church in Tallinn. The Russian Orthodox Church began its missionary activities in the mid-nineteenth century and, from then on, Russian Orthodox church buildings were built across the country. The most important new Orthodox church building was erected in 1900 as a political symbol at Toompea Hill, in uptown Tallinn, that had been the power centre of the Baltic German nobility who had ruled the land since the thirteenth century.

1 This research was supported by the Estonian Ministry of Education and Research, targeted financing project SF0180026s11 and the European Union through the European Regional Development Fund (Centre of Excellence CECT).

In 1918, Estonia was declared independent and it became a democratic republic. Although the Lutheran Church was the majority Church, it did not have any privileges compared to other religious associations. The process toward closer cooperation between the Government of the Republic and the Lutheran and Orthodox Churches ended without much result in 1940, when independence ended and Estonia became part of the expanding Soviet Union. The battles of the Second World War between the Soviet and German troops traversed Estonia in 1941 and 1944. The battles of 1944 completely destroyed the unique seventeenth century Baroque town of Narva, half of the city centre in Tartu and part of the medieval Old Town of the capital city Tallinn. Church buildings were badly damaged all over the country.

The Soviet period that lasted from 1944 until 1991 was accompanied by anti-religious policies aimed at marginalizing religion in society. The most influential anti-religious campaign started in 1957 with the introduction of new Soviet rites of passage and use of the media to ridicule religion and religiosity. Religious associations relied on donations from membership while being taxed at specially high rates by the Soviet authorities. From the 1960s onward, the membership numbers of religious associations started to decline, especially in the countryside. It could be considered a result of different factors, including fast urbanization and industrialization. In 1940, the church buildings were nationalized by the Soviet regime. In later years, some church buildings became considered as architectural or cultural monuments and were thus protected on the same basis as other monuments.

Relations between the State, Religion and Society in Estonia

Article 40 of the 1992 Estonian Constitution stipulates the principles of freedom of religion and states that there is no state church in Estonia. The Minister of the Interior defined the basis for relations between the state and religious associations in 1993 as one of cooperation in areas of common interests (Ringvee 2011: 91–2). The main partners for the state have been the Estonian Evangelical Lutheran Church and the Estonian Council of Churches. Currently, the Estonian Council of Churches include the Evangelical Lutheran Church, Apostolic Orthodox Church, Orthodox Church of Moscow Patriarchate, the Roman Catholic Church, the Union of Evangelical Christian and Baptist Churches, the Methodist Church, the Association of Seventh Day Adventists, the Christian Pentecostal Church, a congregation of the Armenian Apostolic Church and the Charismatic Episcopalian Church in Estonia.

Areas of common interest became defined in 2002, when the Estonian Government and Estonian Council of Churches signed a protocol in which the interests include chaplaincy and spiritual care, rehabilitation, integration and also heritage conservation.[2]

In Estonia, the Churches and Congregations Act (CCA) sets the legal framework for religious associations. The first CCA was adopted in 1993[3] and it was replaced by a new act in 2002.[4] In Estonian legislation, the religious associations registered according to the CCA are legal entities under private law. These associations all have the same privileges and there is no distinction between different religions or religious associations based either on historical, cultural or other reasons.[5] In 1993, the responsibilities for the relations between the state and religious associations were shifted from the Ministry of Culture to the Ministry of the Interior. According to annual religious freedom surveys, Estonia is one of the countries where religious freedom is acknowledged both in legislation and in practice.[6]

At the same time the state has had the closest relations with the Estonian Evangelical Lutheran Church (EELC) that has been the majority Church in Estonia since the sixteenth century. In 1995, the Estonian Government established a joint committee with the EELC and it has had several sub-commissions. In the context of heritage protection, the sub-commission of architectural heritage has been important.

According to several surveys, Estonia is one of the most 'un-churched' societies in Europe. The secularization of Estonian society is reflected in low religious adherence, as well as low participation in religious services on a weekly basis. According to the year 2011 population census, less than one third of the population considered themselves adherents of a religious tradition.[7] According to a survey on religiosity in Estonia from 2010, 16.4 per cent of respondents considered themselves members of a religious association. In 2010, 3.2 per cent of respondents said that they attend religious services at least once a week. Over 57.3 per cent of respondents said that they do not attend religious services at all. To the question 'Why do you attend religious services?' the respondents answered

---

2 *Eesti Vabariigi Valitsuse ja Eesti Kirikute Nõukogu Ühisshuvide Protokoll*, 17 October 2002. [Protocol of Common Interests between the Government of the Estonian Republic and the Estonian Council of Churches. 17 October 2002], available in Estonian at: http://www.siseministeerium.ee/public/EESTI_VABARIIGI_VALITSUSE_JA_EESTI_KIRIKUTE_N_UKOGU_20061219111211.doc (accessed 18 January 2014).

3 *Kirikute ja koguduste seadus* (Churches and Congregations Act), *Riigi Teataja*, I 1993, 30, 510.

4 *Kirikute ja koguduste seadus* (Churches and Congregations Act), *Riigi Teataja*, I RT I 2002, 24, 135.

5 On the legislative framework for religion, see Kiviorg (2011) and Ringvee (2008).

6 See, for example, the International Religious Freedom Report for 2011. Estonia. (US Department of State, Bureau of Democracy, Human Rights and Labor), available at: http://www.state.gov/j/drl/rls/irf/religiousfreedom/index.htm?dlid=192805 (accessed 18 January 2014).

7 Statistics Estonia Website. 2011 population census database, available at: http://pub.stat.ee/px-web.2001/I_Databas/Population_Census/databasetree.asp (accessed 18 January 2014).

that they like old traditions (49 per cent), it is a family tradition (43.3 per cent) or they get spiritual peace from there (33.9 per cent). The fourth most popular reason for attending religious services was that the respondents enjoy the architecture of the building (31.9 per cent).[8]

Religious associations are self-financing organizations in Estonia and their budgets depend on donations. The ageing and declining membership of congregations has been problematic for the EELC, which has the largest number of church buildings, the majority of which need either conservation or different renovation works. Declining member donations sets limits on financial capabilities to do the necessary works. Often the problem is also passive congregation (Niit 2011: 234). Congregations tend to become passive for different reasons: one of them is the general demographic changes that are reflected in the growing age of the congregation members and the churches' inability to attract younger generations.[9] However, the involvement of congregations proves to be not always fortunate. In 2005 when an active congregation with good intentions painted a seventeenth century altar and pulpit with bright, synthetic colours that pleased the pastor but seriously damaged the monument.[10] Due to this incident, the National Heritage Board and the Ministry of the Interior initiated in 2006 an educational programme for the clergy and congregations' representatives on good maintenance of buildings and sacral artifacts. The programme has become regular, has received positive feedback and has resulted in a handbook on the correct maintenance of church buildings.[11]

Heritage Protection in Estonia

The Estonian Republic was declared independent in 1918. Self-organized protection of cultural heritage had already begun in 1919, when the Estonian Central Committee of Cultural Societies highlighted in a memorandum the necessity of protecting cultural monuments (Raal 2011: 149). On 15 April 1919, two art protection committees were formed, one for the North and one for the South of Estonia (Raal 2011: 152). In 1925, the Estonian Parliament adopted the

8 See 'Elust, usust ja usuelust 2010 tulemused' (2012: 298, 301–2).

9 So, for example, according to the 2011 population census 48.3 per cent of the Lutherans are over the age of 65 and only 8.8 per cent of the Lutherans are younger that 30 years of age.

10 National Registry of Cultural Monuments. Monument 15373, Vigala Church. See: http://register.muinas.ee/?menuID=monument&action=view&id=15373 (accessed 18 January 2014).

11 Available at: http://www.muinas.ee/files/Kirikute%20hooldusraamat_.pdf (accessed 11 November 2014).

Antiquities Protection Act.[12] A new version of the Act was implemented in 1936[13] and the first governmental inspector was appointed in the same year. A distinction between secular or religious monuments was not made in the legislation. Research and protection of cultural heritage was volunteer-based, and conducted mostly by professors and students from the University of Tartu. The main interests and focus of research and protection at that time was early Estonian history and the Middle Ages, although already in the 1930s the first Baltic German manors had become listed as cultural monuments (Alatalu 2012: 41).

The first Soviet regulation of conservation and maintenance of monuments was implemented in 1947. In 1961, the Estonian Soviet Socialist Republic adopted the Act on Conservation of Cultural Monuments in the Estonian SSR that was the first regulation of its kind in the Soviet Union.[14] The Act was drafted by experts in the field and followed the principles already functioning in Estonia during the 1920s and 1930s (Alatalu 2012: 42). The first regulation by the central government of the USSR was implemented in 1977. The professional restoration and conservation of church buildings that had started during the Soviet times in the 1950s continued and increased in the 1980s (Alatalu 2012: 118). The 1977 Act had publicized on the one hand the responsibility to conserve monuments and on the other hand had endorsed civic involvement in protection of cultural heritage. As a result, local heritage clubs were established for young people as well as other target groups.

In the 1980s, the heritage protection movement became more important and, during the late 1980s, the heritage movement began to operate as a basis for civic political involvement. During the period of *Perestroika,* the heritage protection movement became organized from below and, in 1987, the Estonian Heritage Society was established as an umbrella organization for 80 different local heritage protection societies.[15] At that time, the heritage movement became an important civic movement for the re-establishment of Estonian independence (Kasekamp 2010: 161).

Drafting new legislation for heritage conservation started in 1990. The first Heritage Conservation Act was adopted in 1994[16] and the second version in 2002.[17] The Act applies to all monuments and there is no distinction between regional and

12 *Muinasvarade kaitse seadus* [Antiquity Conservation Act], *Riigi Teataja* [State Herald] 1925, 111/112.

13 *Muinasvarade kaitse seadus* [Antiquity Conservation Act], *Riigi Teataja* [State Herald] 1936, 67.

14 *Eesti NSV seadus Eesti NSV kultuurimälestiste kaitse kohta* [Estonian SSR Act on Conservation of Cultural Monuments of the Estonian SSR], *Eesti NSV Ülemnõukogu Teataja* [Herald of the Supreme Court of the Estonian SSR] 23, 15 June 1961.

15 Estonian Heritage Society website. History of the Society.

16 *Muinsuskaitse seadus* [Heritage Conservation Act], *Riigi Teataja* [State Herald], RT I 1994, 24, 391.

17 *Muinsuskaitse seadus* [Heritage Conservation Act], *Riigi Teataja* [State Herald], RT I 2002, 47, 297.

national monuments and there is no special category for religious monuments. According to the Act, monuments may be classified as archaeological, architectural, artistic, technical, industrial or historical monuments. In Article 2, the Heritage Conservation Act defines cultural monuments as:

> a movable or immovable, a part thereof, a body of things or an integral group of structures under state protection which is of historical, archaeological, ethnographic, urban developmental, architectural, artistic or scientific value or of value in terms of religious history or of other cultural value and due to which it is designated as a monument.

Immovable monuments include places of worship, burial grounds, cup-marked stones, sacred buildings with artistic value or value in terms of cultural history. Immovable monuments also have protection zones. Movable monuments include among others ethnographic objects and works of visual and applied art having value in terms of religious or cultural history. Proposals to classify objects as a monument are made by the experts of the Heritage Conservation Advisory Panel to the National Heritage Board. According to Article 12, monuments are unlisted by a directive of the Ministry of Culture. Before the decision is made, the proposal must also have been presented to the owners.

In the early 1990s, the heritage protection policy was in transition, as was the rest of society. By the late 1990s, the priorities in heritage protection started to become more focused and target-oriented. In 2001, the state programme 'Schools in Old Manors – Preservation of the Cultural-Historical Complex and Turning it into a Modern Learning Environment' was adopted. The aim of this programme was to turn schools located in former manor houses into modern regional education and cultural centres, thus ensuring that the historical manor houses and cultural heritage contained within them are preserved. In 2003, a state programme for the conservation of places of worship was adopted. This was followed by a programme of 'Rural Architecture and Landscapes' in 2007 and a development programme for the protection of sacred places in nature was introduced in 2008. In 2012, there were 26,076 listed monuments in Estonia (Alatalu 2012: 183).

The State Programme 'Conservation and Development of Places of Worship'

The state programme 'Conservation and development of places of worship' was adopted in 2003 and has been extended up to 2018.[18] In 1995, the Government of the Republic had established a joint-commission with the Estonian Evangelical

18 *Riiklik programm 'Pühakodade säilitamine ja areng'* [State programme 'Conservation and development of places of worship'], available on National Heritage Board website: http://www.muinas.ee/puhakoda (accessed 11 November 2014). The

Church. One of the sub-committees was focused on architectural values. The members of the committee were from different ministries, representatives of the EELC and conservation experts. The responsibility of implementing and supervising the programme was assigned to the National Heritage Board at the Ministry of Culture. The aim of the 'Conservation and development of places of worship' programme is to conserve and renovate culturally and historically important churches and other sacral buildings, churchyards and also movable sacral objects (altars, icons and so on). The programme budget is used for the restoration of places of worship, the preparation of projects, as well as for installations of security alarms and lightning arresters.[19]

The church buildings in Estonia are mostly owned by the religious associations, although there are some exceptions where the buildings are owned by the municipality or by the state. The reasons for this have been either historical from the pre-Soviet period or based on the decision of the religious association during the property reform in the early 1990s when some congregations for different reasons did not claim the church buildings to be returned to their ownership. There are 157 church buildings either owned or used by the EELC that are classified as monuments. The Estonian Apostolic Orthodox Church has 47 such church buildings, the Estonian Orthodox Church of Moscow Patriarchate 13 and the Old Believers have two church buildings listed as monuments. These figures are also reflected in the distribution of programme allocations – between 2004 and 2010, the EELC received 71.3 per cent (4,654,000 euros) of the total programme allocation (Uustalu 2010). This trend has, however, begun to change recently. In 2012 and 2013, the programme budget allocations for the EELC have been around 40 per cent of the total budget. The reason for this decline, if compared to the previous years, is that many of the emergency conservations on the Lutheran churches were finished. Approximately 80 per cent of the programme's budget has been used for the conservation of places of worship that are listed as monuments.

The funding model of the programme has not been based around denominations, although a considerable number of allocations have been used for the conservation of Lutheran churches. By 2012, seven different religious denominations have received funding through the programme. The active use of sacral buildings does not play a role in the board's decisions on funding. Tourism and cultural activities in the churches may provide some financial help for the congregation's finances although such an income does not have a substantial role in the congregations' budgets. However, there has always been a gap between needs and financial means – between 2003 and 2010, the programme budget covered only 17.7 per cent of the actual needs of the programme. Private donors

---

website of the programme includes the programme's annual budgets, as well as other related information.

19 There were occasional tensions between the National Heritage Board and the Rescue Board concerning the placement of fire alarms and other installments related to fire safety required by the law in the protected buildings in the 1990s and early 2000s.

or trusts have had only a minor role in funding certain church restorations, and the main reason for this is most probably that there has not been a tradition of private donors for restoration work in Estonia. Most of the works undertaken in churches within the framework of this programme have been emergency conservation. The programme has been a fruitful framework for collaboration between the National Heritage Board and research institutions like Tallinn Technical University and the Estonian Academy of Arts. One of the results of the cooperation has been the digital archive on church conservation (Uustalu 2010).[20]

Besides governmental initiatives, there have also been regional and municipal programmes that have targeted religious heritage. One large-scale initiative was Tallinn's Church Renaissance Programme from 2002 to 2011 that targeted 22 churches in Tallinn. It has been common practice in Estonia that local governments provide financial support for the conservation of church buildings. In 2008, the Minister of Regional Affairs approved a programme for maintaining the traditions of the Old Believers on the western coast of Lake Peipus. This programme has financed the conservation and restoration of Old Believers churches, icons and manuscripts. Some monuments have received direct allocations from the state and/or local budget for conservation. These have been for example the medieval St John's Church in Tartu, and the Lutheran St John's Church in St Petersburg, Russia, and there are other examples as well. Although the primary aim of the use of public money for the conservation of sacral buildings has nothing to do with supporting religious activities or associations, it has been noted that it also often has political undertones (Alatalu 2012: 118–19).

The Development Plan 'Historical Natural Holy Places in Estonia'

One year after the adoption of the 'Conservation and development of places of worship' programme, the first initiatives for a similar programme for the protection of historical sacred places in nature were undertaken by the House of Taara and Native Religions (HTNR). The HTNR was founded in 1995, formed of two indigenous religious traditions – Taara-faith that dates back to the 1920s and Earth-faith (*maausk*) that emerged during the national reawakening in the late 1980s.[21] *Maausk* is defined by the HTNR as the indigenous, ethnic Estonian religion. The Estonian indigenous pre-Christian religious tradition could be described as animistic and the sacred places of the indigenous traditions are situated in nature. Some of these traditions relating to nature have been preserved up to today, like the cross-trees that are marked during funerals in certain south-eastern parts of

20 Available at: http://kirikud.muinas.ee (accessed 18 January 2014).

21 For the background and history of the House of Taara and Native Religions, see Vakker (2012) and Västrik (1995).

Estonia, and there are also other holy or sacred places in nature (trees, groves, springs, stones) that are still in use.[22]

In 2008, the Estonian government approved the state development plan for the protection of historical sacred places in nature.[23] This programme was the outcome of the activities of the HTNR that resonated with the general Estonian nature-related identity and obtained political support. In 2008, there was a one and a half million kroon (approximately 100,000 euros) allocation from the state budget for the *Hiite Maja* Foundation for the implementation of the plan, resulting from the politics of the Estonian Green Party that was represented in the Parliament from 2007 to 2011.[24]

The development plan 'Historical Natural Holy Places in Estonia' for 2008–12 considered sacred places historical if they had a history of more than 100 years, and their historicity verified by archival or other materials.[25] This plan on natural sacred places was largely modeled on the 2003 state programme for the conservation of places of worship. The interest of the state has been in preserving the buildings as cultural, architectural or other monuments. The responsible institution for the development plan is the National Heritage Board. The Board of the programme includes representatives from the National Heritage Board, Ministry of Culture, Ministry of Agriculture, Ministry of Environment, Ministry of the Interior, University of Tartu and of the House of Taara and Native Religions. The focus of the programme is on the historical sacred sites (that is groves, springs, trees and so on) in nature that are considered an important part of heritage, as well as of Estonian identity. In Estonia, there are approximately 2,800 historical sacred places in nature. Similar to the 2003 programme, there is also a shortage of financial means. Between 2008 and 2012, the programme obtained only 19 per cent of its planned funds (Kaasik 2013: 7).

The process of implementing the development plan for the conservation of sacred sites in nature has raised new questions for lawmakers and the state. Unlike sacral buildings that are either owned or rented by religious associations and are used primarily for religious services, none of the sacred sites are owned by religious associations. As conservation of church buildings sets rules and limitations for the owner, the protection of sacred sites sets limits on economic activities. And here

22 On this issue, see Jonuks (2009 and 2012), Kõivupuu (2009) and Valk (2009).

23 Ministri käskkiri, 1 April 2008, no. 146. *Valdkonna arengukava 'Eesti ajaloolised looduslikud pühapaigad. Uurimine ja hoidmine' aastateks 2008-2012 kinnitamine.* [Ministry of Culture, Decree no. 146, 1 April 2008. Approval of the development plan 'Historical Natural Holy Places in Estonia' for 2008–12], available at: http://www.muinas.ee/files/pühapaikade%20arengukava%20kk.pdf (accessed 12 April 2014).

24 Minutes of the Finance Committee of the Riigikogu no. 152, 7 December 2008. Searchable from http://web.riigikogu.ee.

25 Valdkonna arengukava 2008–2012 'Eesti ajaloolised looduslikud pühapaigad. Uurimine ja hoidmine' [The development plan 'Historical Natural Holy Places in Estonia. Study and Maintenance' for 2008–12], available in Estonian at: http://www.muinas.ee/files/Pühapaikade%20arengukava.doc (accessed 12 April 2014).

differing interests easily collide, as the court cases show. The HTNR established a *Hiite Maja* (House of the Groves) foundation for the implementation of the development plan, which has highlighted the need for a new legal Act to protect historical sacred places in nature.[26]

Some of these sacred places became protected as early as the 1920s, after Estonia had established its independence. This process continued during the Soviet period. However, these places are currently under protection according to two different legal Acts: the Heritage Conservation Act and Nature Conservation Act.[27] Some of these sacred places and objects are protected for their cultural value, some of them as archaeologically important places; some are protected to preserve natural environments of cultural or aesthetic value or some elements of them. Thus, there are several categories under which the wide ranges of holy places and sites are protected. In 2012, 14 per cent of all holy sites in nature were protected as cultural monuments, 1.96 per cent were protected according to the Nature Conservation Act, 1.96 per cent of the sites were protected both according to the Heritage Conservation Act and the Nature Conservation Act, while 82 per cent of the known sacred sites were without any protection (Kaasik 2013: 5). At the same time, several places that are protected do not have fixed borders or, even if they do, the borders are debated. Often these debates are very emotionally charged. There have been four court cases (2012, 2008, 2007, 2006) in which the HTNR or the House of the Groves have protested against economic activities in the sacred space in nature that violate the traditional principles of conduct for the sacred space/holy place.[28] However, here the reliability of evidence or proof that the places have been ancient holy places is often questioned.

In this process, the question of protection of sacred sites not only as physical objects, but also as a spiritual space, has been raised. Here, the already difficult questions on fixed borders of the sacred space in nature to be marked on the map/cadaster for protection becomes even more complicated with the issue of protecting also the spiritual space. Although it is a deep philosophical question, it seems to be extremely difficult, or even impossible, to regulate in law the protection of sacred space in nature. Where does sacredness start and where does it end? The subjectivity of the experience of the sacred becomes unpleasantly mixed with legal regulations.

---

26 See Hiite Maja Foundation website: www.hiis.ee (accessed 12 April 2014).

27 *Looduskaitse seadus* [Nature Conservation Act], *Riigi Teataja* [*State Herald*] RT I 2004, 38, 258.

28 House of Native Religions website. Press releases, available at: www.maavald.ee/press.html?op=rubriik&rubriik=24 (accessed 12 April 2014).

Conclusion

The conservation and funding of religious heritage on the same basis as other heritage and the non-differentiation between religious and non-religious monuments has been part of conservation policy in Estonia since the 1920s. Current policy and practice in conservation of religious heritage is the outcome of interaction between the state and municipal officials from different fields on the one hand and different religious communities on the other.

In conservation, the religious aspect of a monument is an irrelevant criterion. The state programme 'Conservation and development of places of worship' is sometimes criticized as funding not only religious heritage and its conservation, but also as a form of financing Christian associations and especially the Lutheran Church. This criticism has come mostly from the HTNR. It is true that, until 2011, the EELC received most of the programme's allocations and it is centred on the Christian churches. It is a pragmatic approach, as most of the listed monuments that are churches belong to the EELC. At the same time, Orthodox icons, buildings, as well as Russian Old Believers manuscripts, have been funded by this programme, also through different governmental and local initiatives. As religious associations are self-financing associations, one serious problem has been the shrinking numbers of donors among EELC members, but also ongoing urbanization that affects smaller local congregations.

In the European context, we must understand and agree that most religious heritage is Christian heritage, most of the buildings under protection are Christian churches and so on, for historical reasons. In Estonian context the reproaches that churches would get funding because of their religious importance could be considered groundless. The church does not become more valuable as cultural/architectural heritage than a mansion or a castle because of its religious connection and vice versa. Although the majority of conservation and protection include Christian related objects this does not mean that the heritage of other traditions than Christian could be neglected if it has similar historical, architectural, cultural or other values. Until the funding of religious heritage is not based on religious concerns, but on general principles of conservation and policies of funding cultural heritage, the discussions on the legitimacy of using public money for it are not relevant.

References

Alatalu, R. (2012), *Muinsuskaitse siirdeühiskonnas 1986-2002: rahvuslikust südametunnistusest Eesti NSV-s omaniku ahistajaks Eesti Vabariigis*. [*Heritage in Transitional Society 1986-2002: From Nation's Conscience in the Estonian SSR into the Harasser of Private Owner in the Republic of Estonia*] (Tallinn: Eesti Kunstiakadeemia).

Bergmann, S., Scott, P.M., Jansdotter Samuelsson, M. and Bedford-Strohm, H. (eds) (2009), *Nature, Space and the Sacred. Transdisciplinary Perspectives* (Farnham: Ashgate).

Elust, usust ja usuelust 2010 tulemused [Survey 'On life, faith, and religious life 2010' results] (2012), in Jõks, E. (ed.), 283–317.

Estonian Heritage Society Website. History of the Society, available at: http://www.muinsuskaitse.ee/index.php?page=1&id=25 (accessed 18 January 2014).

Hansson, J. and Heikki Ranta, H. (eds) (2011), *Archeology and History of Church in Baltic Region. Symposium June 8-12, Visby, Sweden* (Visby: Gotland University).

Jõks, E. (ed.) (2012), *Astu alla rahva hulka. Artikleid ja arutlusi Eesti elanikkonna vaimulaadist* [*Step Down to the People. Articles and Essays on the Spirituality of Estonian Population*] (Tallinn: Estonian Council of Churches).

Jonuks, T. (2009), 'His Sites in the Research History of Estonian Sacred Places', *Folklore. Electronic Journal of Folklore*, vol. 49, available at: http://www.folklore.ee/folklore/vol42/jonuks.pdf (accessed 18 January 2014).

Jonuks, T. (2012), 'From Holy Hiis to Sacred Stone: Diverse and Dynamic Meanings of Estonian Holy Sites', in Rountre, K., Morris, C. and Peatfield, A. (eds), 163–83.

Kaasik, A. (2013), *Eesti ajaloolised looduslikud pühapaigad. Uurimine ja hoidmine. Valdkonna arengukava 2008-2012. Koondaruanne.* [Estonia's Historical Sacred Natural Sites. Research and Maintenance. Development Plan 2008–2012. Summary Report] (Tartu: University of Tartu).

Kasekamp, A. (2010), *A History of the Baltic States* (Basingstoke, New York: Palgrave Macmillan).

Kiviorg, M. (2011), *Religion and Law in Estonia* (Alphen aan den Rijn: Kluwer Law International).

Kõivupuu, M. (2009), 'Natural sacred places in landscape: an Estonian mode', in Bergmann, S., Scott, P.M., Jansdotter Samuelsson, M. and Bedford-Strohm, H. (eds), 223–34.

National Heritage Board Website (2012), available at: http://www.muinas.ee/sinule/omanikule/puhakodade-programm (accessed 18 January 2014).

Niit, R. (2011), 'The State of Church Buildings in Estonia, Good Economic Management of a Church' in Hansson, J. and Heikki Ranta, H. (eds), 233–6.

Raal, M. (2011), 'Kunstiväärtuste kaitsmine Eestis 1919-1921' [*Protection of Artistic Valuables in Estonia 1919-1921*], in Randla, A. (ed.), 140–74.

Randla, A. (ed.) (2011), *Mälu.* Eesti Kunstiakadeemia Toimetised 20 (Tallinn: Estonian Academy of Arts).

Ringvee, R. (2008), 'State, Religion and the Legal Framework in Estonia', *Religion, State and Society*, 36, 181–96.

Ringvee, R. (2011), *Riik ja religioon nõukogudejärgses Eestis 1991-2008.* [*State and Religion in Post-Soviet Estonia 1991-2008* (With English Summary)] (Tartu: Tartu University Press).

Rountre, K., Morris, C. and Peatfield, A. (eds) (2012), *Archaeology of Spiritualities* (New York: Springer).

Statistics Estonia Website. 2011 population census database, available at: http://pub.stat.ee/px-web.2001/I_Databas/Population_Census/databasetree.asp (accessed 18 January 2014).

Uustalu, K. (2010), 'Funding places of worship by the state and local governments in Estonia', Paper presented at *Conference on Christian Values*, Tallinn, 19 November 2010.

Vakker, T. (2012), 'Rahvusliku religiooni konstrueerimise katsed 1920–1930. aastate Eestis – taara usk' [Efforts to construct a national religion in Estonia in the 1920s-30s – Taara belief. With summary in English], *Mäetagused*, 50, available at: http://www.folklore.ee/tagused/nr50/vakker.pdf (accessed 18 January 2014).

Valk, H. (2009), 'Sacred Natural Places of Estonia: Regional Aspects', *Folklore. Electronic Journal of Folklore,* vol. 42, available at: www.folklore.ee/folklore/vol42/valk.pdf (accessed 18 January 2014).

Västrik, E.V. (1995), 'The heathens in Tartu in 1987-1994: Heritage Protection Club Tõlet. Some comments on Zhivile' Ramoshkaite-Sverdioliene's speech 'The Archaic Patterns of Modern Life' at the Conference of Contemporary Folklore in Tartu, 3 November 1995', available at: http://haldjas.folklore.ee/rl/pubte/ee/cf/cf/8.html (accessed 18 January 2014).

Chapter 9
Funding Religious Heritage: The Italian Case

Alessandro Ferrari

Introduction

The vast majority of cultural heritage in Italy, about 70 per cent, is of a religious nature or of religious interest and belongs, in many cases, to the Catholic Church. Statistics refer to 110,000 churches and chapels, 85,000 of which are technically considered part of the national cultural heritage (1,535 monasteries, 5,500 libraries, 26,000 archives, 700 collections and ecclesiastical museums and thousands of paintings and sculptures).[1] Furthermore, cataloguing the whole religious heritage, as promoted by the Italian Catholic Episcopal Conference, is extremely difficult and has not yet entirely been completed.[2] This gives an idea of the special and unique role played by Catholicism in the Italian scene.[3] Consequently, public funding does not depend on the nature of the owner, but on two different conditions: the cultural value of the artwork and its public 'openness' or public availability.

In this context, the religious nature and/or the ecclesiastical ownership of cultural artworks is not an obstacle to public funding, but, on the contrary, forms the basis for their shared protection by the state and religious authorities. The 'concordatarian style' of the relationships between the Italian state and religious communities, in fact, extends its influence in this matter, focusing the debate not

1 See Conferenza Episcopale Italiana, Servizio per la promozione del sostegno economico alla Chiesa (April 2012: 9), summary for the press, in http://www.8xmille.it/rendiconti/rendiconto2014.pdf (accessed 11 November 2014) and Grasso (2004). In 2008, the Italian Episcopal Conference doubled the funding allocated to places of worship, from 40 to 80 euros, for each building catalogued by the dioceses in their inventory of cultural artworks, with a view to fostering the inventory process.

2 Since 1996, the National Office of Ecclesiastical Cultural Heritage of the Italian Episcopal Conference promotes, coordinates and supports the activities of inventory of movable historical and artistic artworks (paintings, sculptures, furnishings, vestments and so on …) of the Italian dioceses. The inventory, as required by the Code of Canon Law (can. 1283, 2nd), is aimed at the protection and enhancement of ecclesiastical heritage and must be drawn up in a uniform way throughout the country following the method indicated by the above National Office and agreed with the Central Institute for Cataloguing and Documentation of the Ministry of Cultural Heritage.

3 See Ferrari (2010).

on whether to allocate public resources for the protection of cultural heritage belonging to religious groups, but, rather, on the contents and conditions of the agreements between public and religious authorities in order to protect and enhance this specific heritage. Consequently, a precise analysis of the specific framework in which religious heritage is managed should precede a focus on the financial aspects of the Italian system.

The Legal Framework of – Religious – Cultural Heritage

According to Article 9 of the Italian Constitution, 'the Republic promotes the development of culture and of scientific and technical research. It safeguards the natural landscape and the historical and artistic heritage of the Nation'. This article places the burden of safeguarding the 'heritage of the Nation' not on the state but on the 'Republic', consequently emphasizing not only central and local state responsibilities, but also the duty of civil society as a whole, including private actors, in this mission. Likewise, this same burden is referred to as the cultural heritage of the 'Nation' – and not just of the state – regardless of property titles.[4] In turn, Article 117 of the Constitution specifies the division of responsibilities among the different public institutions, assigning the state exclusive legislative powers for the 'protection' of cultural heritage and attributing to the regions the 'concurring legislation' for its 'enhancement'. In the latter case, legislative powers are vested in the regions, except for the 'fundamental principles', which are laid down by the central state.[5] Nevertheless, not being easy to exactly separate what can be referred to as protection and what concerns, instead, enhancement, central government and local authorities must cooperate in this matter in accordance with the 'principle of loyal cooperation' established by Article 120 of the Constitution. As will be seen in greater detail below, regions play an important role in 'religious heritage'.

In addition, religious heritage is subject to a specific legal regime within legislation applicable to cultural heritage, which mainly resides in the Code of Cultural Heritage (Legislative Decree no. 42 of 22 January 2004).[6] According to Article 2-2 of this text, 'cultural property consists of immovable and movable things which, pursuant to Articles 10 and 11, present artistic, historical, archaeological, ethno-anthropological, archival and bibliographical interest, and of any other thing identified by law or in accordance with the law as testifying to the values of civilization'. It falls within the competence of the Ministry of

4 See Crisafulli (1952: 36 *et seq.*) and Merusi (1995: 21–8).

5 See especially Articles 4 to 8 of the Code of Cultural Heritage promulgated by Legislative Decree no. 42 of 22 January 2004. See, in particular, Pastori (2004 and 2007), Aicardi (2005: 1072 *et seq.*), Cocozza (2006: 63 *et seq.*), Severini (2012: 65 *et seq.*), Ainis, Fiorillo (2008: 241 *et seq.*) and Bolgiani (2012a).

6 Text available at: http://www.unesco.org/culture/natlaws/media/pdf/italy/it_cult_landscapeheritge2004_engtof.pdf (accessed 11 November 2014).

Culture to establish the guidelines on the verification of cultural interest. However, the legislative decree expressly designs a specific regime for 'cultural property of religious interest' in that it provides that 'the Ministry and, where applicable, the Regions shall attend to the exigencies of cultural property of religious interest belonging to bodies and institutions of the Catholic Church and of other religious denominations, according to the needs of worship, and in agreement with the respective authorities' (Article 9).

In fact, although the same Article 117 of the Constitution confers on the central state the exclusive competence for relationships between the 'Republic and religious denominations', nevertheless religious cultural heritage is the subject of several local agreements between regions and religious institutions.[7] This is possible because the prevailing interpretation of Article 117 allows cooperation between regions and religious communities in relation to matters falling within regional competence and, consequently, also in relation to the 'enhancement' of cultural heritage existing in the regions.[8] As a result, for the protection and enhancement of religious cultural heritage, the Italian Constitution sets up a trilateral relationship between state, regions and religious denominations, which has its roots in history.

Something Special: Religious Cultural Heritage in Recent History

The Constitution unitarily considers the cultural heritage of the Nation, without mentioning its possible religious nature and, consequently, without envisaging a specific category for religious cultural heritage. Nevertheless, Italian law had taken into consideration the religious interest of artworks, their links with worship and with the life of religious communities very early on.[9] This consideration has given rise to a special system of protection for religious artworks where public authorities have never ignored either that most of them belong to the Catholic Church or their liturgical and pastoral use, which has made it impossible to consider them as mere 'museum pieces'. This explains the 'denominational character' of the Italian

7 Consideration should also be given to the special autonomy enjoyed by some local bodies resulting from their statutes (see Article 116 of the Constitution and Article 8 of the Code of Cultural Heritage of 2004). Among the latter, the Region of Sicily and the provinces of Trento and Bolzano of the Region Trentino Alto Adige have exclusive general competence in matters of cultural heritage: see Roccella (2001: 923–4); Di Prima (2010).

8 Pastori (2003: 3 *et seq.*) and Milani (2005: 202 *et seq.*).

9 See Roccella (2005: 2041) and Cardia (2007: 32), who observes how religious cultural heritage was considered 'public' also because of the 'public' position recognized by the *Ancien Régime* in respect of the Catholic Church.

model of protection of 'religious cultural heritage', basically characterized by stable and formal cooperation between state and religious authorities.[10]

The 'Liberal' Age

The politics of the liberal state towards religious cultural heritage was greatly influenced by the fact that the state had become the owner of a large part of it. In fact, while suppressing religious orders with the Acts of 1855 and 1866, the state confiscated many ecclesiastical properties. Consequently, more than 700 churches, including those of San Domenico in Bologna, Santa Croce and Santa Maria Novella in Florence and Santa Maria in *Ara Coeli* in Rome, became the property of a special state body called first, from 1855 to 1866, the Ecclesiastical Coffers (*Cassa ecclesiastica*) and then, from 1866 to 1987, the Fund for Worship (*Fondo per il Culto*) and Fund for Places of Worship (*Fondo Edifici di Culto*) from 1987 to date.[11] This situation forced the public authorities to reconcile their liberal, abstract separatist ideology with the need to preserve their new artworks for their religious purposes. As a result, the state agreed to provide for the maintenance of the religious buildings that it owned, which were open to the public and considered indispensable for the pastoral care of the faithful.[12] These places kept their original religious purpose and were often entrusted to those managing provinces and municipalities. In this way, behind the exclusive relationship between the central state and local authorities, a third partner emerged: the religious institutions directly involved in worship, which had to agree the concrete terms of use of these churches with city authorities.[13]

The same accommodationist approach and the same combination of culture and worship that characterized religious cultural heritage also emerged in the attitude of the state towards the places of worship and cultural artworks owned by the church. In fact, their openness to public worship assimilated them to state properties, allowing tax exemptions and public contributions.[14] In particular, Article 237 of the Communal and Provincial Act no. 2248 of 20 March 1865 considered it 'compulsory' for municipalities to maintain 'buildings serving for public worship', Catholic or not, provided that no other private funding was available. Similarly, various acts provided exemptions from property tax (Acts no. 1831 of 15 July 1864, no. 2136 of 26 January 1865 and no. 3718 of 18 July 1867), income tax (Royal Decree no. 2078 of 13 September 1874) and tax on movable

10 See Margiotta Broglio (2000), Renna (2003), Roccella (2004) and Chizzoniti (2008; 2010).

11 See Bellini (1967: 179–87) and Dalla Torre (1997: 15 *et seq.*).

12 See Cardia (2008: 13).

13 See Petroncelli Hübler (1988: 14 *et seq.*).

14 Gioli (1997).

goods (Act no. 4021 of 28 August 1877) 'churches and any other buildings devoted to worship', without denominational distinctions.[15]

In addition, the first decade of the twentieth century was marked by the promulgation of the first Organic Act on Cultural Heritage, Act no. 364 of 20 June 1909, modified in 1912 and implemented by Royal Decree no. 363 of 30 January 1913.[16] The Act of 1909, entirely centred around affirming the role of the state as the absolute guarantor of national heritage, established: the inalienability, without the permission of the Ministry of Education, of artworks belonging to the state, municipalities and provinces, but also to vestries and ecclesiastical legal persons (Article 2); the obligation for parish priests and church rectors to provide a 'descriptive list' of the artworks under their administration (Article 3); the possibility for the Ministry of Education to remove these artworks from their location and/or to order their restoration at the expense of the owner, except if the latter was not able to provide for it (Articles 4 and 7) and the prohibition on removing, changing or restoring these artworks without the permission of the same ministry (Article 12). The Executive Decree of 1913, reiterating state primacy, limited devotional practices such as lighting and candles dangerous for artworks (Article 51) and foresaw the obligation for churches and other 'sacred buildings' to make artworks 'freely visible to everyone'. Nevertheless the same decree also specified that this last duty could be fulfilled by opening 'in determined hours' and with the possibility of 'limitations' due to the 'specific character (of these buildings)' (Article 28).[17]

Thus, even in a context opposed to any form of 'concordatarian approach' between state and religious institutions and formally inspired by a form of merely negative and abstentionist religious freedom, the nineteenth century liberal state funded restoration of religious cultural heritage regardless of its ownership, recognizing the need to balance the protection and accessibility of this heritage with the requirements of worship.

The Lateran Pacts

It was with the Lateran Pacts between the state and the Catholic Church of 11 February 1929 that religious cultural heritage received formal recognition.[18] In

---

15 Royal Decree no. 2169 of 24 November 1919 also exempted the same buildings with all their assets and libraries and non-trading galleries from the special progressive income tax on property. See Mauro (1995: 20).

16 The Act of 1909 develops and systematizes what was established by the first law of the twentieth century specifically devoted to cultural heritage, Act no. 185 of 12 June 1902.

17 See Mattaliano (1975).

18 The Treaty, still in force, recognizing the 'noble artistic tradition of the Catholic Church' (Art. 16, § 2) gives the Holy See total freedom in relation to important religious heritage in its exclusive ownership and including not only the Vatican, but also other important artistic buildings, such as the basilicas of San Giovanni in Laterano, San Paolo

fact, the bilateral approach of the Pacts also influenced the manner of protection of religious cultural heritage, becoming the golden rule in this field. This bilateral approach was made evident in Act no. 1089 of 1 June 1939 on the Protection of Historic and Artistic Heritage. The Act, confirming the more important measures of the liberal age, including the possibility of public funding for cultural goods belonging to religious communities, obliged for the first time the Minister of National Education to obtain the agreement of the 'ecclesiastical (Catholic) authority' in relation to the 'needs of worship' and this 'when an artwork belonging to a Catholic religious entity was at stake' (Article 8).[19] Similar attention to the needs of worship of the Catholic Church was also formalized in the Civil Code of 1942, which is still in force, where the use of the building for public Catholic worship is a legitimate limitation of the right of ownership, both for public or private owners (Article 831, § 2).[20]

'Religious Cultural Interest' in Present Times: 'Extended' Bilateralism

The contemporary pluralistic societal framework recognized by various European legal state systems after the Second World War has brought important changes to the protection of religious heritage. In particular, the new pluralistic framework has deeply influenced relationships between the state and civil society and also between the former and religious communities, increasingly present in the public arena. This statement applies to religious heritage as it is managed in Italy.

The Concordat of Villa Madama: Shared Protection of Religious Cultural Heritage?

As regards Italian Catholic heritage, these changes were evident in the new Concordat of 1984, which, for the first time, explicitly includes cultural heritage among the matters of bilateral cooperation between state and the Catholic Church. Article 12 of the Concordat of Villa Madama, in fact, establishes two important principles. First, the recognition of the principle of cooperation between the Italian

---

and Santa Maria Maggiore with all their contents (Arts. 13–15). The Treaty also guarantees visitors and researchers accessibility to artistic and scientific 'treasures' in the Vatican City and in the Lateran Palace on the basis of rules freely determined by the Holy See itself (Art. 18). The Concordat handed the Holy See the basilicas of Santa Casa in Loreto, of San Francesco in Assisi and San Antonio in Padua (Art. 27) and guaranteed the Holy See, in exchange for its financial commitment, full accessibility to the Christian, but also the Jewish Catacombs (Art. 33).

19 See Finocchiaro (1967: 649–50). A different position has been expressed in some case law (Council of State, sect. VI, 7 March 1950, no. 73) for which the agreement between state and ecclesiastical authorities is not a condition for the lawfulness of administrative measures: see, in the same vein, La Croce (1998: 503–6).

20 See Berlingò (1992: 191 *et seq.*).

Republic and the Holy See, in their respective spheres of competence, for the protection of historic and cultural heritage as a whole. This broad state–church cooperation, which ignores the ownership of the single artworks and the specific religious character of the cultural heritage, is considered an implementation both of Article 9 of the Constitution and of Article 1 of the Concordat itself. The latter, in fact, envisages that the state and the Catholic Church work together 'for the good of man and of the country'.[21] Secondly, Article 12 requires that Italian law is harmonized with 'religious needs' through agreements to establish 'appropriate provisions' for the preservation, enhancement and enjoyment of artworks of religious interest belonging to ecclesiastical bodies and institutions. In this way, Article 12 has inaugurated a system of coordination between state and ecclesiastical authorities in order to apply Italian law to cultural heritage with 'religious interest' belonging to the church. Moreover, by substituting the more specific 'worship interest' of the Act of 1939 with the generic 'religious interest', the new Concordat seems to expand the borders for cooperation between the state and the Catholic Church. This cooperation, in fact, should cover not only the strictly liturgical aspects of the church cultural heritage but all 'pastoral' possible uses of this latter.[22] Furthermore, when an artwork belonging to the church has some 'religious interest' the state will have to obtain the cooperation of the church not only regarding its protection and safeguarding – already considered, in relation to the 'worship interest', by the Act of 1939 – but also, more extensively, regarding its 'enhancement and use' (Bordonali 1995: 98). Finally, Article 12 provides 'that the conservation and consultation of archives of historical interest and the libraries of the same organizations and institutions will be encouraged and facilitated on the basis of agreements between the competent authorities of the two Parties'.[23]

Article 12 of the 1984 Concordat has had a fundamental impact on the Italian system of protection of religious cultural heritage. The bilateral approach has, in fact, encouraged the perception of the specificity of this heritage, influencing the new Code on Cultural Heritage (Legislative Decree no. 42 of 22 January 2004) and fostering a widespread implementation of the cooperation drafted by the Concordat, not only at central, but also at local level.[24] To the agreements between the Italian Episcopal Conference and the Italian Ministry of Cultural Heritage have, in fact, been added those signed by the Regional Episcopal Conferences and the regions.[25]

---

21 Pastori (1995: 30–31) and Cardia (1995: 62).

22 See Chizzoniti (2012: 144 *et seq.*; 2010: 176–8).

23 See Crosetti (2010); Boni (2005); Roccella (2003).

24 See Dalla Torre (1993), Bordonali (1995: 83), Finocchiaro (1995), Cardia (1995), Roccella (2004 and 2008), Pastori (2005).

25 See Roccella (2006a) and Bolgiani (2012a: 87 *et seq.*) On the agreement signed in 2010 between the Region of Sicily and the Sicilian Ecclesiastical Region, see Di Prima (2012), who points out the atypical elements of this covenant, which reveals the special prerogatives enjoyed by the regional government and the presence of particular rules that

The agreement signed on 8 March 2005 between the Department of Cultural Heritage and Landscape of the Ministry of Cultural Heritage and the National Office for the Ecclesiastical Cultural Heritage of the Italian Episcopal Conference has been an important example of this implementation. This covenant, apparently of minor importance, establishes, in fact, a specific procedure for the identification of the cultural interest of buildings belonging to ecclesiastical institutions, also envisaging regional agreements between local state and ecclesiastical authorities 'on the amount, priority and periodicity of the requests for the verification of the cultural interest of buildings belonging to ecclesiastical institutions in the territory under their jurisdiction' (Article 1). This institutional and hierarchical system guarantees ecclesiastical heritage a specific procedure for its listing as cultural asset, different from that envisaged for other private artworks and on which state and religious authorities agree in respect of the classification of artworks belonging to the Catholic Church as a cultural asset. In particular, this specific procedure is more certain in its timing and, above all, has better chances of achieving a positive result.[26]

This bilateral and institutional approach, particularly coherent with the Italian system of religious freedom, has also been extended in its general features to non-Catholic religious groups.

Bilateralism for Non-Catholic Religious Heritage

The Code on Cultural Heritage of 2004 has extended the special recognition initially only offered to the cultural heritage of the Catholic Church to cultural artwork with religious interest belonging to 'legal bodies and institutions' of 'other religious communities'. Article 9 of this code, extending to these groups the provisions of the former Act no. 1089 of 1939, requires the state and the regions to proceed 'through agreements with the religious authorities' when 'needs of worship' are involved. Although the provision of the code, only considering

do not totally reflect the model of national agreement (*Intesa*) of 2005, also revealing autonomous regional guidelines compared to the Concordat of *Villa Madama*.

26 A note of October 2011 by the General Direction for the Landscape, Arts, Architecture and Contemporary Art of the Ministry of the Cultural Heritage explains that 11,207 procedures of verification of the cultural interest of ecclesiastical buildings were undertaken between March 2005 and August 2011. Forty per cent of them ended with positive result, 'with a higher rate than that observed for artworks belonging to other public bodies and private legal bodies', in http://www.chiesacattolica.it/cci_new_v3/s2magazine/AllegatiArt/2475/tutela_patrimarchitettonico.pdf. The agreement of 8 March 2005 is available at http://www.benitutelati.it/moduli/Accordo_8_marzo_2005_DipartimentoBC_CEI.pdf. See on this topic Rivella (April 2005) in http://www.olir.it/areetematiche/1/documents/Rivella_Interesse_culturale.pdf and Consulta Nazionale per i Beni Culturali Ecclesiastici (of the Italian Bishop Conference), *Verifica dell'interesse culturale dei beni immobili*, at http://www.chiesacattolica.it/cci_new/UfficiCEI/AllegatiArt/11/Verifica.pdf (all documents accessed 11 November 2014); see also, more generally, Ferretti (2007).

'needs of worship' and not broader 'religious' interests, is more limited than the concordatarian rule, it nevertheless inserts non-Catholic cultural heritage, at least when it belongs to organized groups, within the bilateral framework traditionally envisaged for the Catholic Church.[27]

The soft bilateral approach envisaged by the code represents one of the cases where unilateral state legislation appears to be more convenient than the specific general agreements (*intese*) signed by the state with single religious groups. The latter, in fact, have not asserted any specific obligation for the state to make its legislation respectful of the 'religious interest' of the cultural heritage of the signatory religious communities. Apart from the agreement signed in 1987 with the Union of the Italian Jewish Communities, which envisages broad cooperation, giving a precise deadline for the establishment of a specific bilateral commission,[28] the other agreements have been much more generic and only concerned with a simple duty 'to cooperate in the protection and enhancement of the assets related to the historical and cultural heritage' belonging to these groups.[29] Not until 8 August 2013 was a specific agreement signed between the Ministry of Cultural Heritage and the Waldensians Table in order to cooperate on the cataloguing and enhancement of the Waldensians' and Methodist cultural heritage. This covenant finally establishes the mixed commission already envisaged in the general agreement (*intesa*) of 1984 and, following the traditional Waldensian approach to state–church relationships, which tend to emphasize more cultural than directly religious aspects,[30] it does not widen consideration of the religious interest already envisaged by the Code of 2004, but it aims at ensuring specific technical state support for the management and protection of the particular heritage of these religious traditions.

In any case, the particular attention to Jewish heritage has already been unilaterally displayed by Act no. 175 of 17 August 2005, on the safeguarding of cultural Jewish heritage in Italy. This Act initially provided five million euros of funding for the years 2005–07 and subsequently prorogated it for the years 2008–09 in Article 50, no. 1 of the Legislative Decree no. 248 of 31 December 2007 (implemented by Act no. 31 of 28 February 2008); it has established a

27 See Pastori (2005: 195).

28 See Article 17 of Act no. 101 of 8 March 1989 and Tedeschi (1995).

29 See the agreements with the Adventists (Art. 34, Act no. 516 of 22 November 1988), Assemblies of God (Art. 26, Act no. 517 of the same day), Baptists (Art. 18, Act no. 116 of 12 April 1995), Orthodox (Art. 12, Act no. 126 of 30 July 2012), Mormons (Art. 16, Act no. 127 of the same day), Apostolic Church in Italy (Art. 29, Act no. 128 of the same day), Buddhist (Art. 17, Act no. 245 of 31 December 2012) and Hindu (Art. 18, Act no. 246 of the same day).

Only the agreements with Waldensians and Lutherans envisage the establishment of a special commission (but without specifying any deadline) also for the inventory of their cultural goods (Arts. 17 and 16 of Act no. 449 of 11 August 1984 and no. 520 of 29 November 1995).

30 See Long (1995).

system of protection of Jewish cultural heritage centred around the role played by religious Jewish authorities as representatives of the whole of Judaism. The Act allows public subsidies for works annually decided by decree of the Minister of Cultural Heritage, after consultation with the Union of Italian Jewish Communities, which could also be the direct recipient of this funding.[31] The same bilateral – and denominational – approach was also followed, at regional level, by the agreement signed on 8 June 2005 by the Union of the Jewish Italian Community and the Sicilian Region, which envisages extensive cooperation for the safeguarding and enhancement of Jewish heritage in this region.[32]

Various Degrees of 'Religious Interest'

In conclusion, in the same unitary category of cultural heritage, it is possible to identify four different degrees of consideration of 'religious interest'. The first degree concerns cultural heritage with a subjective and an objective religious interest: it is the case of buildings dedicated to religious purposes and belonging to the Catholic Church. In this case, use for worship limits the rights of private and public owners and becomes the basis for the 'bilateral protection' of buildings by the state and religious authorities. The second degree concerns cultural heritage that has a subjective religious interest, because it belongs to the Catholic Church. The protection and enhancement of these goods have to be balanced with the extensively considered pastoral needs. The third degree regards the religious cultural heritage belonging to non-Catholic denominations. In this case, the need for a bilateral agreement, unilaterally envisaged by the Code on Cultural Heritage of 2004, will only concern artworks specifically devoted to 'worship needs'. Finally, the fourth degree of 'religious interest' is very general and generic and surfaces in the general concordatarian commitment undertaken by the Italian Republic and the Holy See to cooperate, within their own legal system, to protect the entirety of national cultural heritage.

31 Art. 5, no. 2 of Act no. 112 of 7 October 2013 has also allocated four million euros for the years 2013–14 for the continuation of construction works on the National Museum of Italian Judaism and the Holocaust already envisaged by the Act of 17 April 2003, no. 91.

There is nothing similar at regional level for other 'religious heritages', generally protected, apart from the provisions of the 2004 Code and of single agreements with the state, in a more cultural way: see, for example, the project 'Pinerolo and Valleys: Freedom's Walk between Art and Culture', in a region characterized by the historical presence of Waldensians; the Waldensian Cultural Centre is part of the project management together with other institutions, including the Catholic diocesan office for cultural heritage: see http://www.fondazionevaldese.org/documenti/progetti/Cammini%20di%20liberta_descrizione%20del%20progetto.pdf (accessed 11 November 2014).

32 See Sveva Mancuso (2006).

Funding Religious Cultural Heritage: Unilateral and Bilateral State Support

Confirming the approach already established at the time of the liberal era in the nineteenth century, Article 1 of the Code of Cultural Heritage of 2004 does not consider the religious use of an artwork or its ecclesiastical ownership as reasons for preventing public funding. On such grounds, Italian legislation envisages two different streams, bilateral and unilateral, for publicly funding religious cultural heritage. The bilateral legislation is contracted by the state and religious groups with the first aim of guaranteeing and promoting religious freedom. In this framework, funding religious cultural heritage is a dimension of this latter right and, consequently, it will be read in light of it and subordinated to it. Unilateral state legislation, on the contrary, is principally focused on safeguarding cultural heritage: in this case, the first interest is cultural, although religious interests can also be considered.

Unsurprisingly, Catholic artworks are the biggest beneficiaries of these two channels of public funding. This is both due to their huge number and the particular role played by the Catholic Church in the country, a role that is not only religious, but also cultural, as a key player in national history and identity. The '*Orientamenti*', dictated in 1992 by the Catholic Episcopal Conference on the subject of religious heritage, very clearly illustrate this reality. In fact, if they suggest that dioceses ask funding first of all from local Christian communities, they also suggest asking the state and other public bodies in the name of the full participation of church heritage in the republican heritage, a participation that has been confirmed by the concordatarian duty of cooperation between church and state for the promotion of the good of the country.[33]

The Bilateral Sources of Funding

The first bilateral source of funding for cultural religious heritage is the Concordat itself. The latter in fact completely redrafted public funding for the church, also influencing the matter of cultural heritage. The Concordat established the 'eight per thousand' system, which allows taxpayers to give part of their tax on individuals to the Catholic Church. The agreements (*intese*) between the state and non-Catholic religious groups, apart from that with the Mormons, have all adopted this very beneficial model.

With the 'eight per thousand' system, the Catholic Church received about one billion euros in 2013 and the National Episcopal Conference has specifically allocated to the protection of its cultural heritage 60.5 million euros. To this sum should also be added part of the 122.5 million euros allocated by the same Conference specifically for religious buildings as places of worship and part of the 43.35 million envisaged for the 'needs of national relevance', which

33 See Volpe (1998).

includes enhancement, census and safeguarding of the sacred art.[34] The 'eight per thousand' funding for cultural heritage is attributed to the dioceses, which must submit specific projects to the National Episcopal Conference and which are also responsible, through the bishops, for heritage belonging to religious orders. The rule for the allocation of these funds is that the necessary use reflects a specific and clear religious interest of the artwork for which funding is requested. The list of admissible fees drawn up by the National Episcopal Conference highlights, in fact, more than generic and merely artistic sensitivities, rather a major and specific interest for needs of worship and, consequently, for cultural heritage clearly connected with religious community life.[35] The restoration of places of worship is at the centre of the church's concerns. Safeguarding archives, libraries and ecclesiastical museums is the other main concern.

Apart from the money directly received through the 'eight per thousand' system, religious cultural heritage, especially Catholic, could also be funded by the 'eight per thousand' collected by the state. This latter, in fact, is the only 'secular' actor that competes with the religious communities having agreements within this system of funding. The amounts collected by the state through the 'eight per thousand' can only be used for specific purposes, such as natural disasters, world disease and the protection of cultural heritage. If the state never complied with these limits,[36] at least until 2012, a good part of these funds was devoted to

---

34 http://www.8xmille.it/rendiconti/ripartizione2014.pdf (accessed 11 November 2014).

35 In 2011 requests for funding made by dioceses to the Italian Episcopal Conference numbered 1,634. Four hundred and eighty-two projects concerned the restoration and consolidation of buildings of worship and the adjustment of their appliances, 457 related to anti-theft security-systems, 246 conservation and consultation of libraries, 191 archives, 156 enhancement of diocesan museums, 82 the restoration of pipe organs and 20 for the care, protection and enhancement of places of worship by volunteers. See http://www.avvenire.it/Chiesa/Pagine/otto-per-mille-e-progetti-tutela-beni-ecclesiastici.aspx (accessed 11 November 2014). Also for the financial years 2012–13, contributions by the Italian Episcopal Conference to religious cultural heritage have been exclusively allocated for the following activities: a) computerized census of the churches of the Italian dioceses and computerized inventory of their artistic and historical artworks; b) installation of anti-theft security systems; c) conservation and consultation of diocesan archives and libraries and enhancement of diocesan museums; d) purchase of buildings of worship for the purpose of their safeguarding; e) restoration and consolidation of buildings of worship and adjustment of their appliances; f) restoration of pipe organs of historic and artistic interest and g) initiatives for the care, protection and enhancement of places of worship promoted by the diocese using volunteers, at http://www.chiesacattolica.it/beniculturali/richieste_di_contributo__norme_e_modulistica/00006244_Richieste_di_contributo__norme_e_modulistica.html (accessed 11 November 2014).

36 In 2011, about half of the 145 million euros perceived by the state through the 'eight per thousand' system, were allocated to civil protection for the needs of the fire-fighting fleet (64 million euros) and to the construction of prisons and to improve living conditions in the latter (57 million euros), at http://www.governo.it/Presidenza/Comunicati/dettaglio.asp?d=66024 (accessed 11 November 2014).

Catholic cultural heritage and, in particular, to the restoration of places of worship, considered part of national cultural heritage.[37]

The Unilateral Sources of Funding

Among the unilateral forms of funding there are different channels, both at national and local level, which can be devoted to religious cultural heritage. Nevertheless, in times of economic crisis, the huge number of possible sources is not enough for the immense and increasingly fragile Italian religious heritage.

In any case, a decision to list artwork of cultural interest is necessary to benefit from this funding. For artworks belonging to the Catholic Church, this declaration is regulated by a specific bilateral administrative procedure, agreed in 2005 by the state and the church, that envisages the intervention by the competent authorities of these same institutions. Usually, the procedure of funding also envisages a specific agreement between the state and competent religious authorities in order to establish the specific religious dimension of the intervention.

The Catholic Church is, not surprisingly, the principal beneficiary of this funding. Once again, in fact, Catholic heritage can count not only on its specific religious dimension, but on all its mixed cultural, religious, folkloric and touristic value. In this regard, the legislation passed at the time of the Jubilee of 2000 has been paradigmatic.[38] The latter was in fact the occasion for hundreds of generous interventions during the course of which the state and regions have supported several projects led by ecclesiastical authorities, occasionally linked more to the hotel reception for tourists than to the protection and enhancement of religious heritage. Anyway, regions and municipalities play a crucial role in relation to this funding: these authorities are, in fact, closest to, and directly responsible for, the fulfillment of the local interest condition, which also includes religious and cultural interests and allows financial support.

Articles 35 and 36 of the Code of Cultural Heritage contemplate two forms of public funding: direct funding, which consists in repaying private owners, including religious owners, who have undertaken restoration work; and indirect funding, which consists in ensuring low interest rates for private owners who provide for the protection of cultural heritage. Other direct funding has been envisaged by the law on the national lottery and, more specifically, by two laws that funded an extraordinary intervention in order to ensure efficient security systems for cultural assets and for private and ecclesiastical archives.[39]

Other pieces of legislation provide a detailed system of tax incentives for private benefactors, individuals and companies. In this way, those who fund the restoration and enhancement of cultural heritage can deduct from their taxes 19

37 See Pistolesi (2006: 182) and Fiorita (2012).

38 See Act no. 651 of 23 December 1996 and Act no. 494 of 16 December 1999 (Art. 8). On this topic, see Acciai (1998).

39 See Gallucci (2000).

per cent of the cost of their investment.[40] The same philosophy inspires another older law that reduces to 10 per cent the value-added tax due for the restoration of buildings (but without a detailed consideration of the cultural nature of the property)[41] and Act no. 53 of 28 February 1983, which exempts from the state tax of 22 per cent the insurance premium for the protection of historical or artistic buildings. Finally the Municipal Tax on Real Estate (IMU) of 2011–13 reduced by 50 per cent taxable income in the case of buildings qualified as historic or artistic under Article 10 of the Code of Cultural Heritage.

As has already been pointed out, not only the central state, but also regions provide important funds for religious heritage. Economic reasons explain why the central state is not particularly protective of its exclusive competence in this financial field. In fact, if it is already difficult to distinguish between funding destined for the protection (which is part of the exclusive state competence) and funding earmarked for enhancement (which is, on the contrary, part of concurring legislation in the regions). It is also true that, when a region intervenes to support cultural heritage, the central state is generally not so sharp-eyed in evaluating whether or not the regional intervention respects the strict borders of regional competence.

In any case, funding for places of worship is included within regional competences. This is another case where worship and culture are strictly connected, especially in relation to Catholic buildings that often represent an ancient and historical heritage. Not only the central state,[42] but also Regions are promoters of *ad hoc* provisions regarding religious cultural heritage linked with regional history. Typical occasions for this funding are the centenaries of saints: for the sixteenth centenary of Saint Ambrose, the Region of Lombardy has completely restored the homonymous basilica, other local places and individual artworks linked with the saint.

Other regional interventions are the consequence of natural calamities. In 1997 the Region of Piedmont restored the Turin dome and the chapel of the Holy Shroud, seriously damaged by a fire. Region Emilia-Romagna is engaged in supporting the difficult restoration of the religious heritage destroyed by the 2012 earthquake. Also in this case the first recipients of public funding are the places of worship directly connected with the needs of the population and which are traditionally qualified as 'political' and 'public'. The restoration of less 'popular' cultural religious heritage will follow or will become part of previous interventions.

---

40 See also with reference to contributions of private companies, Art. 13 bis, g and h and Art. 65, c-ter, c-quarter and c-nonies of the Decree of the President of the Republic no. 917 of 22 December 1986.

41 See no. 127-terdecies and quaterdecies of the Third Part of the Table attached to the Decree of the President of the Republic no. 633 of 26 October 1972.

42 See, for example, Art. 7 of Act no. 237 of 12 July 1999 which envisaged funding for the Basilica di Noto, a jewel of the Sicilian Baroque damaged by a crash. On this *ad hoc* funding, see Roccella (2005: 378–9).

Regional contributions often follow agreements signed between regional authorities and Catholic episcopal regional conferences. In fact, almost all Italian Regions have signed these agreements, which are drafted on the model of Article 12 of the Concordat and of national agreements signed between the Italian Episcopal Conference and the Ministry of Cultural Heritage.[43] These regional agreements have in general two different parts: one 'procedural', where regional competent authorities both for the state and for the church are indicated and one more 'substantial', where the specific engagements are detailed. One agreement signed in 1997 by the Sicilian Region and the local regional episcopal conference was particularly broad, recognizing the 'religious interest' of Catholic cultural heritage that gave rise to the obligation of a specific agreement between ecclesiastical and civil authorities. This 'religious interest' was in fact considered to include all 'theological, philosophical and canonical aspects'.[44]

A specific chapter on funding of religious cultural heritage is connected to the state maintaining about 2,000 churches of the Fund for Places of Worship (*Fondo Edifici di Culto*), established after the expropriations of the nineteenth century and which has replaced the *Fondo per il Culto* (see *The Liberal Age* section above). As has already been said, part of the religious buildings expropriated at that time, especially convents, passed to the municipalities and they were used in different ways, including as a space for local museums. The churches, on the contrary, were in general maintained in line with their use and are in most cases still used for worship. Their legal status is sometimes very complicated. On the one hand, the entity, public or private, which has ownership, is not always clearly identified; on the other, these places of worship are part of trilateral relationships between the state, as the owner, the municipality, as the concrete leaser and the dioceses, responsible for worship. Quite often a special convention between these different parties also details the financial responsibilities generally borne by secular institutions.

---

43 Bolgiani (2012b).

44 See Article 9 of the Agreement of 11 June 1997, at http://www.regione.sicilia.it/bbccaa/soprintp/SBCA_Trapani/normativa/03%20INTESA%20regione_chiesa.pdf (accessed 11 November 2014). This agreement was abrogated and substituted by another covenant of 2010. The preamble of the latter states that the regional cultural religious heritage belonging to the church constitutes a 'decisive heritage and particularly' not only – as in 1997 – for the 'historical memory' of the region, but also, more in general, for its 'identity'. This new agreement does not expressly mention theology, but Article 9 broadly states that 'restorations or adjustments are negotiated at the local level (…) with reference to the religious interest and the needs of worship'; on this agreement, see footnote no. 25.

Funding and Control

The public funding of religious cultural heritage is very often linked to specific agreements between the public sponsor and the beneficiary religious group. The Code of Cultural Heritage and an agreement signed on 26 January 2005 between the National Episcopal Conference and the Ministry of Cultural Heritage establish the general framework of these covenants.[45] A general rule has, in any case, to be followed: the restored or enhanced religious artworks have to be kept accessible to the public. This need has to be balanced with the specific 'religious interest' granted to each single religious artwork. The Code of Cultural Heritage relies on the specific agreements between the owner and the public administration to find the balance between this interest and the public opening of the artwork restored or enhanced with public funding. This balance is not difficult for Catholic places of worship due to the traditional openness of Catholic churches.[46] Nevertheless, it has been a more delicate task regarding libraries and, above all, archives, because of both the greater difficulties to fulfill all the conditions to secure their enjoyment and traditional ecclesiastical discretion.

The bilateral agreement signed in 2005 between the National Episcopal Conference and the Ministry of Cultural Heritage considers three main specific needs: 1) the need for a form of cataloguing of cultural heritage belonging to the Catholic Church compatible with the cataloguing in use for state cultural heritage; 2) the need for cultural religious artworks to be maintained in their original locations (and, in this regard, there is the growing question of the dismissed churches); 3) the need for a permanent consultation between the two parts in order to programme interventions of maintenance and enhancement.

The same agreement has also established other important points. First of all, the conferment of the decision upon a higher hierarchical level when the local bishop and local public administration do not reach an understanding in respect of an intervention, for example, regarding conservation works to be undertaken. Secondly, the requirement that places of worship subject to these latter local covenants be opened to the public, be it for worshippers or tourists. Moreover, the 2005 agreement seems to suggest that this opening, finalized in respect 'of the religious needs', should involve the exclusion of entrance tickets. In this regard, the state has always been particularly demanding, although the agreement of 2005 does not contain any specific norm likely to impede a practice that is particularly annoying in the Italian context in which the Catholic Church receives a huge amount of money through the 'eight per thousand' system. Therefore, the National Episcopal Conference also formally agrees with this opposition to

45 See Madonna (2007), Chizzoniti (2005) and Roccella (2006a).

46 See, in any case, Feliciani (1997: 14): clarification would have perhaps been appropriate in this regard, given that 'it appears unrealistic to think that the right of access and visitation could effectively be insured for all the artworks that are the subject of the agreement'.

entrance tickets, even if about 80 places of worship especially in popular locations envisage this form of payment, only providing for strict 'free areas' – in general far away from artworks – for 'religious people' who will have to find their own spiritual inspiration without the help of the religious heritage.[47] Finally, the 2005 agreement imposes that the works for liturgical adequacy respect Italian law on cultural heritage. If the latter often allows the prevalence of the religious interest, it is anyhow possible that 'conservative people' try to use Italian law against canonical liturgical reforms.[48]

Some Conclusions

Five concluding observations can be made. First, it is impossible to separate Italian cultural heritage from Catholic cultural heritage. The relevance of this latter is at the same time religious, cultural, folkloric, touristic and linked with a religious community that fiercely refuses interpretations that are too cultural and neutralizing. Secondly, not only is a ban on funding cultural artworks belonging to the church unthinkable, but equally unthinkable are public interventions that have as a consequence a new secularization of protected heritage. The religious interest is, in fact, explicitly taken into account, both in concordatarian and unilateral laws. Thirdly, due to the growing role of regions, one future challenge will be the coordination of the different levels, national and local, of the bilateral relationships between church and public administrations. The present double procedure for the two distinct levels of cooperation, between church national authorities and state national authorities on the one hand and between church regional authorities and regional authorities on the other will probably require integration through trilateral coordination where all three actors could sit at the same table. This trilateral approach could also help to overcome the worries of the Catholic Church about being excluded by state and regions from the rooms where decisions are taken. Consequently, some regional agreements signed with the regional episcopal conferences establish rooms open to the presence of all these three actors. In this framework, where the Catholic Church is almost considered a

47 See Feliciani (2010). The note *Access in the churches*, approved by the Permanent Council of the Italian Episcopal Conference on 31 January 2012 specifies how the principle of gratuitousness 'should be maintained even in the presence of significant flows of tourists, allowing free access in the churches (…) except, in exceptional cases, in the judgment of the diocesan bishop'. The adoption of an entrance fee, then, should be 'allowable only for guided tours of parts of the complex (crypt, baptistery, bell tower, cloister, single chapel and so on), clearly distinct from the building of the church, which must remain available for prayer'.

48 See the note by the Italian Episcopal Conference, *The adaptation of churches according to the liturgical reform*, of 31 May 1996, at http://www.diocesiverona.it/s2ewdiocesiverona/allegati/196/ADEGUAMENTO%20Chiese.pdf (accessed 11 November 2014).

public body, the discussion whether public funding for religious cultural heritage is possible or not becomes really abstract.[49] Fourthly, the protection of Catholic cultural and religious heritage is the model followed by the state for considering the religious and cultural heritage of other religious denominations. Consequently, these would have to orient their competent institutions (also) in this field along the same central and local axis encountered in the relationships between the state and the Catholic Church. Fifthly and finally, the present economic crisis does not leave many resources for cultural heritage and, in addition, religious heritage is starting to experience this general, and often dramatic, situation.[50] One might then ask whether *quod non fecit res publica* against religious cultural interest *faciet mercatus*.

References

Acciai, R. (1998) 'Grande Giubileo del 2000. L'intervento finanziario pubblico fra evento religioso e business turistico, *Quaderni di diritto e politica ecclesiastica*, 1, 181–204.

Aicardi, N. (2005), 'Commento agli artt. 4 e 5', in Trotta, G., Caia, G., Aicardi, N., Commentario del Codice dei beni culturali e del paesaggio, *Le Nuove Leggi Civili Commentate*, 5–6, 1072–83.

Ainis, M., and Fiorillo, M. (2008), *L'ordinamento della cultura. Manuale di legislazione dei beni culturali* (Milano: Giuffrè).

D'Avack, P.A. (ed.) (1967), *La legislazione ecclesiastica. Atti del Congresso celebrativo del centenario delle leggi amministrative di unificazione* (Vicenza: Neri Pozza).

Bellini, P. (1967), 'Le leggi ecclesiastiche separatiste e giurisdizionaliste (1848–1867)', in D'Avack, P.A. (ed.), 179–87.

Berlingò, S. (1992), *Enti e beni religiosi in Italia* (Bologna: Il Mulino).

Bolgiani, I. (2012a), *Regioni e fattore religioso. Analisi e prospettive normative* (Milano: Vita & Pensiero).

49 See Colaianni (2012) and, previously, Guerzoni (1993).

50 In this context, it is possible that religious cultural heritage will benefit, more, from other forms of intervention such as, for example, the free loan of public buildings than from financial public support. Such was the case with the decision of 2 August 2013 by the municipality of Milan to assign to the diocesan museum premises in the prestigious royal palace of the city for 25 years, http://www.olir.it/ricerca/getdocumentopdf.php?lang=ita&Form_object_id=6164 (accessed 13 September 2013). This situation, which has also led the national legislature in very recent times to more precisely regulate private contributions that can financially support public ones as 'sponsorship', helping the activity of the latter in matters of protection of cultural heritage: see the new Articles 26 and 199 bis and the technical implementation established by the Decree of the Ministry of Cultural Heritage of 19 December 2012: see Chieppa (2013) and Casciu (2013).

Bolgiani, I. (2012b), 'I beni culturali di interesse religioso tra Intesa nazionale e accordi regionali ('vecchi' e 'nuovi')', *Stato, Chiese e pluralismo confessionale*, 5 November (accessed 13 February 2013).

Boni, G. (2005), 'La collaborazione fra Stato e Chiesa cattolica in materia di archivi ecclesiastici di interesse storico', in Dalla Torre G. (ed.), 213–25.

Bordonali, S. (1995), 'L'art. 12 del nuovo Concordato', *Quaderni di diritto e politica ecclesiastica*, 1, 75–100.

Cammelli, M. (2007) (ed.), *Il Codice dei beni culturali e del paesaggio* (Bologna: Il Mulino).

Cardia, C. (1995), 'Tutela e valorizzazione dei beni culturali di interesse religioso tra Stato e Chiesa Cattolica', in Feliciani (ed.), 55–75.

Cardia, C. (2007), 'Lo spirito dell'accordo', in Madonna, M. (ed.), 29–48.

Cardia, C. (2008), 'La condizione giuridica', in Daniele Persano (ed.) (2008), *Gli edifici di culto tra Stato e confessioni religiose* (Milano: Vita e Pensiero), 13.

Casciu, S. (2013), 'Il tema delle sponsorizzazioni/erogazioni liberali visto dalla parte delle Soprintendenze: difficoltà, equivoci, burocrazia, mentalità', *Aedon – Rivista di arti e diritto on-line*, 2.

Chieppa, R. (2013), 'Il nuovo regime delle erogazioni liberali e delle sponsorizzazioni: il settore dei beni culturali e l'intervento delle fondazioni', *Aedon – Rivista di arti e diritto on-line*, 2.

Chizzoniti, A.G. (ed.) (2003), *Le carte della Chiesa* (Bologna: Il Mulino).

Chizzoniti, A.G. (2005), 'L'intesa del 26 gennaio 2005 tra Ministero per i beni e le attività culturali e la Conferenza Episcopale Italiana: la tutela dei beni culturali di interesse religioso appartenenti a enti e istituzioni ecclesiastiche tra continuità e innovazione', *Quaderni di diritto e politica ecclesiastica*, 2, 387–98.

Chizzoniti, A.G. (2008), 'I beni culturali di interesse religioso: la collaborazione tra istituti pubblici ed ecclesiastici nell'attività di valorizzazione', in Degrassi, L. (ed.), 63–93.

Chizzoniti, A.G. (2010), 'La tutela dei beni culturali di interesse religioso nell'ordinamento giuridico italiano', *Derecho y Religión*, V, 171–98.

Chizzoniti, A.G. (2012), 'Bienes culturales eclesiásticos en Italia', in Vega Gutiérrez, A.M., del Mar Martín García, M., Rodrígez Blanco, M., José Maria Vázquez Garcia-Peñuela, J.M. (eds), 139–54.

Cocozza, V. (2006), 'Sub art. 4 – 5', in Leone, G., Tarasco, A. (eds), 56–65.

Colaianni, N. (2012), 'La tutela dei beni culturali di interesse religioso tra Costituzione e convenzioni con le confessioni religiose', *Stato, Chiese e pluralismo confessionale*, 11 June (accessed 12 February 2013).

Conferenza Episcopale Italiana, Servizio per la promozione del sostegno economico alla Chiesa, *Otto per mille. Destinazione ed impieghi 1990–2011*, updated April 2012 summary for the press, in http://www.8xmille.it/rendiconti/rendiconto.pdf (accessed 11 February 2013).

Crisafulli, V. (1952), *La Costituzione e le sue disposizioni di principio* (Milano: Giuffrè).

Crosetti, A. (2010), '*I beni archivistici e librari d'interesse religioso', Aedon – Rivista di arti e diritto on-line*, 3.
Dalla Torre, G. (1993), 'I beni culturali ecclesiastici. Appunti per una riflessione', *Quaderni di diritto e politica ecclesiastica*, 1, 109–21.
Dalla Torre, G. (1997), 'Il Fondo per il culto: ascesa e declino di un Istituto giurisdizionalistico', in Ministero dell'Interno, Direzione generale degli affari dei culti (ed.), 9–19.
Dalla Torre G. (ed.) (2005), *Annali 2002–2004* (Torino: Giappichelli).
Degrassi, L. (ed.) (2008), *Cultura e istituzioni. La valorizzazione dei beni culturali negli ordinamenti giuridici* (Milano: Giuffrè).
del Carmen Caparrós, M., del Mar Martín, M., Salido, M. (eds) (2010), *XXX Años de los acuerdos entre Esp*aña y la Santa Sede. Actas del IV Simposio Internacional de derechoconcordarario (Almería, 18–20 de novembre de 2009) (Granada: Comares).
Di Prima, F. (2010), 'La tutela del patrimonio storico e artistico d'interesse religioso nelle autonomie speciali. Due esempi a confronto: Sicilia e Catalogna', in del Carmen Caparrós, M., del Mar Martín, M., Salido, M. (eds), 362–70.
Di Prima, F. (2012), 'La nuova Intesa con la Regione Ecclesiastica Sicilia sui beni culturali ecclesiastici alla luce del sistema concordatario italiano: l'atipicità diventa tipica?', *Revista General de Derecho Canónico y Derecho Eclesiástico del Estado*, 30, 3, 1–33.
Domianello, S. (2012), *Diritto e religione in Italia. Rapporto nazionale sulla salvaguardia della libertà religiosa in regime di pluralismo confessionale e culturale* (Bologna: Il Mulino).
Feliciani, G. (ed.) (1995), *Beni culturali di interesse religioso* (Bologna: Il Mulino).
Feliciani, G. (2007), *Introduzione*, in Madonna (ed.), 5–14.
Feliciani, G. (2010), 'La questione del ticket d'accesso alle chiese', *Aedon – Rivista di arti e diritto on-line*, 3.
Ferrari, A. (2010), 'Civil religion in Italy: 'A mission impossible', *The George Washington International Law Review*, 41, 4, 839–59.
Ferretti, A. (2007), 'Verifica dell'interesse culturale: spunti di riflessione su aspetti problematici delle limitazioni soggettive', *Aedon – Rivista di arti e diritto on-line*, 1.
Finocchiaro, F. (1967), 'Il regime del patrimonio storico e artistico degli Enti Ecclesiastici nel diritto dello Stato', in *Per la salvezza dei beni culturali in Italia. Atti e documenti della Commissione di indagine per la tutela e la valorizzazione del patrimonio storico, archeologico, artistico e del paesaggio*, 638–52.
Finocchiaro, F. (1995), 'Le norme pattizie sui beni culturali di interesse religioso e il sistema delle fonti', in Feliciani, G. (ed.), 41–53.
Fiorita, N. (2012), 'Il pluralismo in materia religiosa nel settore del finanziamento pubblico delle confessioni', in Domianello, S. (ed.), 75–86.
Gallucci, L. (2000), 'L'intervento finanziario dello Stato', *Aedon – Rivista di arti e diritto on-line*, 1.

Gioli, A. (1997), *Monumenti e oggetti d'arte nel Regno d'Italia. Il patrimonio artistico degli enti religiosi soppressi tra uso e riuso, tutela e dispersione. Inventario dei "Beni delle Corporazioni religiose" 1860–1890* (Roma: Ministero per i beni culturali e ambientali – Ufficio centrale per i beni archivistici).
Grasso, G. (2004), Chiesa cattolica in Italia e beni culturali degli enti ecclesiastici: alcuni problemi, *Aedon – Rivista di arti e diritto on-line*, 3.
Guerzoni, L. (1993), 'Nuovo Concordato e beni culturali: profili politico-istituzionali della «bozza» d'intesa', *Quaderni di diritto e politica ecclesiastica*, 1, 123–43.
La Croce, 'L. (1998), I beni culturali d'interesse religioso e l'intesa sull'art. 12 dell'Accordo del 1984', *Il Diritto ecclesiastico*, 3, 503–6.
Leone, G., Tarasco, A. (eds) (2006), *Commentario al Codice dei beni culturali e del paesaggio* (Padova: Cedam).
Limiti, G. (ed.) (1975), *Ricerca sui beni culturali*, I, *Quaderni di studi e legislazioni della Camera dei Deputati – 17* (Roma: Grafica Romana).
Long, G. (1995), 'Tutela e valorizzazione del patrimonio culturale nelle intese con le confessioni diverse dalla cattolica', in Feliciani, G. (ed.), 89–97.
Madonna, M. (ed.) (2007), *Patrimonio culturale di interesse religioso in Italia. La tutela dopo l'Intesa del 26 gennaio 2005* (Venezia: Marcianum Press).
Margiotta Broglio, F. (2000), 'I beni culturali di interesse religioso (art. 19 d. lg. 490/1999)', *Aedon – Rivista di arti e diritto on-line*, 1.
Mattaliano, E. (1975), 'Il movimento legislativo per la tutela delle cose di interesse artistico e storico dal 1861 al 1939', in Limiti, G. (ed.), 3–89.
Mauro, T. (1995), *L'evoluzione della normativa sull'edilizia di culto,* in Chiara Minnelli (ed.), *L'edilizia di culto*, Vita e Pensiero, Milano, 19–32.
Merusi, F. (1995), *Beni culturali, esigenze religiose e art. 9 della Costituzione*, in Feliciani, G. (ed.), 21–8.
Milani, D. (2005), 'La tutela degli interessi religiosi delle comunità locali tra riforma della Costituzione e nuovi statuti regionali', *Quaderni di diritto e politica ecclesiastica*, 1, 201–44.
Minelli, C. (ed.) (1995), *L'edilizia di culto* (Milano: Vita e Pensiero).
Ministero dell'Interno, Direzione generale degli affari dei culti (1997), *Il Fondo edifici di culto: chiese monumentali, storia, immagini, prospettive* (Roma: De Rosa).
Pastori, G. (1995), '*L'art. 12* dell'Accordo 18 febbraio 1984 nel quadro dell'ordinamento giuridico italiano', in Feliciani, G. (ed.), 29–40.
Pastori, G. (2003), 'Regioni e Confessioni religiose nel nuovo ordinamento costituzionale', *Quaderni di diritto e politica ecclesiastica*, 1, 3–12.
Pastori, G. (2004), 'Le funzioni dello Stato in materia di tutela del patrimonio culturale (art. 4)', *Aedon – Rivista di arti e diritto on-line*, 1.
Pastori, G. (2005), 'I beni culturali di interesse religioso: le disposizione pattizie e la normazione più ricente', *Quaderni di diritto e politica ecclesiastica*, 191–200.
Pastori, G. (2007), 'Commento all'art. 4', in Cammelli, M. (ed.), 65–8.

Per la salvezza dei beni culturali in Italia. Atti e documenti della Commissione di indagine per la tutela e la valorizzazione del patrimonio storico, archeologico, artistico e del paesaggio (1967) (Roma: Casa Editrice Colombo).
Petroncelli Hübler, F. (1988), *I beni culturali religiosi. Quali prospettive di tutela* (Napoli: Jovene).
Pistolesi, I. (2006), 'La quota dell'otto per mille di competenza statale: un'ulteriore forma di finanziamento (diretto) per la Chiesa cattolica?', *Quaderni di diritto e politica ecclesiastica*, 1, 163–82.
Renna, M. (2003), 'I beni culturali di interesse religioso nel nuovo ordinamento autonomista', *Aedon – Rivista di arti e diritto on-line*, 2.
Roccella, A. (2001), 'Regioni e beni culturali ecclesiastici', *Il diritto ecclesiastico*, 3, 919–31.
Roccella, A. (2003), 'Conservazione e consultazione degli archivi di interesse storico e delle biblioteche degli enti e istituzioni ecclesiastiche tra ordinamento canonico e ordinamento statuale', in Chizzoniti, A.G. (ed.), 29–110.
Roccella, A. (2004), 'I beni culturali ecclesiastici', *Quaderni di diritto e politica ecclesiastica*, 1, 199–232.
Roccella, A. (2005), 'Beni culturali di interesse religioso e interventi finanziari pubblici', in *Studi in onore di Giorgio Berti*, vol. III, 2041–86.
Roccella, A. (2006a), 'La nuova intesa con la Conferenza episcopale italiana sui beni culturali di interesse religioso', *Aedon – Rivista di arti e diritto on-line*, 1.
Roccella, A. (2006b), 'Le intese delle Regioni con le autorità ecclesiastiche sui beni culturali d'interesse religioso', *Le Regioni*, 6, 1105–25.
Roccella, A. (2008), 'La conservazione: gli artt. 18–52', *Aedon – Rivista di arti e diritto on-line*, 3.
Sandulli, M.A. (ed.) (2012), *Codice dei beni culturali e del paesaggio* (Milano: Giuffrè).
Severini, G. (2012), 'Artt. 6–7', in Sandulli, M.A. (ed.), 50–77.
Studi in onore di Giorgio Berti (2005), vol. III (Napoli: Jovene).
Sveva Mancuso, A. (2006), 'L'intesa della Regione siciliana con l'Unione delle Comunità ebraiche italiane', *Nuove Autonomie*, 2–3, 383–98.
Tedeschi, D. (1995), 'Tutela e valorizzazione del patrimonio culturale dell'ebraismo italiano', in Feliciani, G. (ed.), 77–88.
Vega Gutiérrez, A.M., del Mar Martín García, M., Rodrígez Blanco, M., José Maria Vázquez Garcia-Peñuela, J.M. (eds) (2012), *Protección del patrimonio cultural de interés religioso* (Granada: Editorial Comares).
Volpe, G. (1998), 'Finanziamento dei beni culturali di interesse religioso', *Quaderni di diritto e politica ecclesiastica*, 1, 99–109.

Chapter 10
The Spanish System of Funding Religious Heritage[1]

Carmen Garcimartín

Spanish heritage is one of the great treasures of the country. The history of Spain and the blend of cultures that has occurred in its territory, among other factors, have contributed to the development of a rich heritage across the length and breadth of the country. Catholic cultural heritage constitutes, by far, the biggest part: it comprises almost 75 per cent of all Spanish cultural and historical heritage sites and embodies an important contribution to the configuration of the Spanish identity.

Religious buildings and other works of art continue to play an important role in Catholic worship, but they also form an invaluable part of the fabric of Spanish culture. These items, then, have a dual value. On the one hand they are not understandable in disregard of their religious significance and deprived of their function of worship; on the other hand, civil communities have played a major role in the safeguarding and protection of these buildings and objects. Therefore, although they belong to the Catholic Church, they are also part of the common heritage and, as such, they must be available for general benefit. These two aspects should be harmonized in the regulation of the religious cultural heritage.

Due to historical and cultural reasons, there is little religious heritage associated with other religious denominations. Indeed we could affirm it is virtually non-existent. Jews and Muslims were expelled from Spain at the end of the fifteenth century and were not allowed to return until the second half of the twentieth century. Until 1978, there was no full religious freedom and before 1967 (when the first, yet limited, Religious Freedom Act was enacted), religious denominations other than the Catholic Church could not have legal existence, nor, consequently, own goods in the country.

For a better understanding of the legal framework of the Spanish religious heritage, we should also recall that the Catholic Church enjoys a particular status as an international juridical entity, which entails, among other things, that agreements with the state are regarded as international treaties, while agreements

1 This work has been funded by the Spanish Government – Ministry of Economy, within the framework of the Project DER 2012–34765, 'La religión en el espacio público: conflictos y soluciones jurídicas', led by the author.

with other denominations, despite previous negotiation, are approved by state law. Their respective implementation, therefore, requires different instruments.

General Legislation on Cultural Religious Heritage

The Spanish Constitution contains two sections which constitute the legal framework governing religious heritage: section 16 and section 46. The first one has to do with the principles governing the relation between church and state; it states the separation of civil and religious powers, but at the same time it provides that 'public authorities shall take into account the religious beliefs of Spanish society and shall consequently maintain appropriate cooperative relations with the Catholic Church and other confessions'.[2] Two main features can be highlighted in this section. The principle of neutrality goes side by side with the principle of cooperation; it means that the state cannot ignore the religious element of society, but it may cooperate with religious denominations in those issues of shared interest. Religious heritage is undoubtedly among them, as we will see. The other feature is that the article expressly names the Catholic Church. That is not a kind of disguised endorsement or covert establishment of the Catholic Church, but a recognition of the social and historical factors that have shaped Spanish society.

The other section of the Constitution, section 46, is devoted to Spanish heritage specifically. It provides that:

> The public authorities shall guarantee the preservation and promote the enrichment of the historical, cultural and artistic heritage of the peoples of Spain and of the property of which it consists, regardless of their legal status and their ownership. The criminal law shall punish any offences against this heritage.

This section pertains to the chapter that deals with the principles governing economic and social policy; although it is within Part 1, related to the fundamental rights and duties, it encompasses slightly weaker protection than the fundamental rights and freedoms. Some issues arise from the content of this norm.

First, the wording of the section has been widely criticized, because it is generally accepted that 'cultural heritage' is a broader concept that includes historical and artistic pieces as well as other manifestations – documentary, ethnographical and so on. Secondly, the statement in section 46 is not an empty declaration. It entails compulsory action by public authorities in the protection and development of heritage, therefore giving the highest rank to the norm that

---

2 Section 16-3 of the Spanish Constitution, 27 December 1978: 'No religion shall have a state character. The public authorities shall take into account the religious beliefs of Spanish society and shall consequently maintain appropriate cooperation relations with the Catholic Church and other confessions.'

imposes this positive mandate (Álvarez Cortina 2012a: 80).[3] Besides, the state and regional and local authorities will have jurisdiction over this issue, each one within its powers. Nonetheless, the Constitution stresses the unity of the heritage, referring only to *Spanish heritage* and not to multiple heritages. Finally, it endorses an objective concept of the heritage; a certain item will belong to it according to its value, regardless of who the owner is. Both public and private items may be part of Spanish heritage.[4] In the case of the latter, the social function of the piece or property and the right of access to it may result in the imposition of certain duties or restrictions on the ownership and, as such, will affect the right to private property.

Section 46 of the Constitution was developed through the Spanish Historical Heritage Act (SHA) and the Royal Decree approving the regulations relating to the Act.[5] This Act follows the Constitution in adopting an objective definition of the heritage; still, its scope is broader than the constitutional one and more than the title might suggest, because it comprises not only items of historical significance, but also those with artistic, paleontological, archeological, ethnographical, scientific or technical value. The Act applies to museums, archives and libraries of general interest as well.

Law and Organization at State Level

State Legislation on Heritage

The regulation of heritage at state level is covered mostly by the SHA and the aforementioned Royal Decree provides additional guidance for regulation of this area. This legal framework applies to all assets regardless of what the ownership,

3 The author points out that Section 46 must be construed in the framework of section 44, that recognizes the right of access to culture (1. 'The public authorities shall promote and watch over access to culture, to which all are entitled. 2. The public authorities shall promote science and scientific and technical research for the benefit of the general interest'), and Section 9-2, that, as a general rule, requires public powers 'to promote conditions ensuring that freedom and equality of individuals and of the groups to which they belong are real and effective, to remove the obstacles preventing or hindering their full enjoyment, and to facilitate the participation of all citizens in political, economic, cultural and social life'.

4 Section 33 of the Constitution: '1. The right to private property and inheritance is recognized. 2. The social function of these rights shall determine the limits of their content in accordance with the law. 3. No-one may be deprived of his or her property and rights, except on justified grounds of public utility or social interest and with a proper compensation in accordance with the law.'

5 Act 16/1985 of 25 June 1985 on Spanish Historical Heritage and Royal Decree 111/1986 of 10 January 1986, partially implementing the 16/1985 Act. Translation in English available at: http://www.unesco.org/culture/natlaws/media/pdf/spain/spa_law_16_1985_engtof.pdf (accessed 12 November 2014).

nature or function of the property or item may be. These norms do not provide specific guidelines for the management and regulation of items of religious heritage, despite the remarkable importance and the specific problems of such asset.[6] The legal framework stated in the general legislation is the same for all heritage, irrespective of the provenance of the item in question. Only two articles apply directly to items of religious heritage or to Catholic properties in particular. However, the interpretation of the law should take into account the function and usage of religious items, so as to reconcile the legitimate interests of all entities.[7]

We can distinguish three different groups of actions with direct or indirect impact on the funding of the heritage. The first one refers to the preservation and protection of the goods and premises; the second includes access for supervision, research and enjoyment; and the third conveys all kind of actions designed to promote and enrich the heritage.

Preservation and protection

Public authorities will provide, through accurate technical means, for the preservation and improvement of items of cultural interest or included in the general inventory (Article 39 SHA). When those items belong to religious entities, any measure should be carried out in accordance with their authorities.

One of the measures regulated in the Act is a precautionary control in the case of additions, repairs and the like. Monuments with a cultural value cannot be modified, either totally or partially, without the express consent of the public authorities (Article 19-1 SHA). This general rule encounters a limitation when applied to religious monuments. It should be understood in the sense that if the proposed reform is demanded for liturgical reasons, public powers will have no discretion in granting permission. Otherwise, the aim of worship would be omitted, when in fact, it was the main role of the building.

More specific is the ban on displaying placards, banners or any kind of signs on the façade of the buildings (Article 19-1 SHA). This ban cannot, however, affect the symbols of faith placed in the buildings, as well as those announcements of the religious services or any other advertisement related to the activities that will be held in the building. In any case, it must be done in such a way as to minimally affect the aesthetic of the building.

The main restrictions on religious heritage relate to transferring ownership or property rights to prevent such items becoming private property. According to the Act, the movable items declared to be of cultural interest and those included in the general inventory possessed by religious entities can only be sold or donated or the

---

6 Some authors have criticized this option because they understand that the religious function should deserve special consideration that should be reflected in the Law, as happens in other European countries. See Álvarez Cortina (2012b: 84–5) and literature cited.

7 The Supreme Court issued a ruling on the issue on 10 February 2009 (RJ 2009/975). It states that both aims – cultural and of worship – should be protected; but if it comes to the crunch and one of them must prevail, it would be that of worship.

property transferred to public entities or other religious entities. Private owners or companies cannot acquire them. This restriction applies today to all movable items of Spanish heritage that belong to ecclesiastical entities.[8] It is a much stricter regime than the norms in force for private owners, who are not bound by such limits. It is not clear why the Catholic Church must undergo such rigorous restrictions, especially if we consider that sales of religious items have special warranties in Canon Law.[9] The article refers to items possessed by religious entities, not only those they own. This detail is important in Spain because during the period of seizure of Catholic properties by the government in the nineteenth century, a number of these properties were formally transferred to private ownership to avoid confiscation. As a result, private people are the formal owners, however, the goods are possessed in different ways and means by the Catholic Church.

Besides, the SHA provides that all documents older than 40 years possessed by religious entities belong to Spanish Heritage (Article 49 SHA).[10] Nonetheless, this norm should be interpreted together with section 1 of the Agreement with the Holy See on Juridical Affairs,[11] which considers them inviolable.

Access to items belonging to the heritage

The Catholic Church, and religious entities in general, must facilitate access to works pertaining to cultural heritage in the terms stated in the Act for all items of cultural heritage. Generally, the owners, or those who are in charge of the items with a juridical entitlement, must grant access to the authorities to supervise them and to researchers who request it and justify the need for access with a fair reason. The Act conveys two different dispositions, depending on the kind of protection they deserve.

On the one hand, as regards movable items and premises that had been declared of cultural interest through the special procedure regulated in the Act, free entrance shall be allowed under the conditions and according to a schedule stated in the regulations, for a minimum of four days every month. Public authorities, however, must release owners from this obligation totally or partially, if a justified reason exists (Article 13-2 SHA). This general rule has to be adjusted when it refers to an item pertaining to the Catholic Church, because the religious function cannot be

---

8 Article 28 and Additional Disposition 5 SHA; Act 42/1994 of 30 December 1994 on Tax, Administrative and Social Actions, DT 1, extended this period for another ten years.

9 See canon 1290 *et seq.* especially, canon 1291: 'The permission of the authority competent according to the norm of law is required for the valid alienation of goods which constitute by legitimate designation the stable patrimony of a public juridic [sic] person and whose value exceeds the sum defined by law'; canon 1292: '§2. The permission of the Holy See is also required for the valid alienation of goods whose value exceeds the maximum amount, goods given to the Church by vow, or goods precious for artistic or historical reasons.' On this issue see Motilla (2012: 56).

10 See Cano (2012: 188).

11 Agreement between the Holy See and the Kingdom of Spain of 3 January 1979.

superseded by the cultural function. The right of public access has to be reconciled with the religious goal, and, for example, visits might be restricted or forbidden during liturgical functions; visitors could be required to comply with certain rules inside the buildings – silence, wearing appropriate clothes and so on. Nonetheless, public access may be forbidden due to religious reasons, for example, visits to the interior of cloisters may be not allowed.

On the other hand, owners of movable items included in the general inventory shall lend them for public exhibition with the corresponding warrants, for periods of time not exceeding a year (Article 26-6 SHA). Again, this norm should be construed in accordance with the specific features of the religious heritage. This way, religious authorities will not be obliged to lend items that carry a high religious significance where they are placed, enhancing a religious function in that specific place, and when their transfer or relocation is not justified solely for cultural reasons. A typical example is the burial of St Jacques (St James), which draws a large number of pilgrims.

Improvement and promotion

The Constitution states that the public authorities must promote and enrich heritage, but it does not say how. Therefore, the state can establish both direct and indirect measures in order to fulfill this aim (Pedreira Menéndez 2004: 26). I will summarize the ways and means to promote religious heritage, setting aside the detailed study of the legal framework of every item mentioned.

1. *Public allowances.* These include two main features. The first is the provision that grants preferential access to public loans for payment of conservation work and maintenance in respect of items of cultural interest (Article 67 SHA). The owners can also have access to down-payments for such investments, but only if the public authorities had previously required them to proceed with the work (Article 36-3 SHA). The other is the so-called 'cultural one per cent'. It means that 1 per cent of the budget for public investment in infrastructure, whenever the total amount is 600,000 euros or more, will be destined for conservation or improvement of Spanish heritage ('preferentially on the actual site of the work or in the immediate surroundings' pursuant to Article 68 SHA). Works related to public services or defence are excluded from this requirement.
2. *Tax benefits.* Religious entities can obtain tax benefits specially reserved for them in the Agreements with Religious Denominations; other benefits are due to their status as non-profit entities, according to the Act of Patronage;[12] and others can be obtained as long as they have ownership rights over items of cultural interest, as a compensation for the duties and burdens imposed on the owners (Article 69 SHA). The following are the main ones:

12 Act 49/2008 of 23 December 2002 on the tax regime of non-profit organizations and tax incentive for trusts.

- Deduction of a percentage of the amount invested in the acquisition, maintenance, reparation or exhibition of cultural goods from income tax.
- VAT exemption for the import of certain items of cultural interest, as well as for those operations stated in the law.[13]
- Exemption from wealth tax.[14] This tax, however, only applies to individuals, not to entities; therefore, as a general rule, it will have no bearing on the items of religious heritage.
- Exemption from local taxes. Premises belonging to the heritage or included in the General Inventory will be exempt from Real Estate Tax.[15] Besides, works of restoration, conservation and improvement of these monuments will have a 95 per cent discount in respect of Maintenance Tax.

3. *Acceptance in lieu.* The option of using cultural and historical items of Spanish heritage as payment in lieu of tax is permitted under the SHA (Article 73). Although its primary objective was precisely to prevent the sale of such goods to pay tax debts, the scheme has been highly criticized for a number of reasons (Beneyto 2012: 315). First, there is the fact that public authorities are often unable to place the items in an appropriate environment and must also assume the cost of maintenance and conservation of said items, thereby placing a financial burden on the state (Martín Retortillo 2001: 44). Secondly, there is some evidence to suggest that some major corporations are taking advantage of this loophole to reduce their tax burden and, as such, make a profit on the purchase of these goods through the guise of phony patronage. Therefore, some scholars defend the stance that only in very special cases of bankruptcy or similar should this special payment be allowed (Martín Retortillo 2001: 44). Religious entities, however, do not usually avail of this mechanism insofar as they have significant fiscal benefits, but they would have the right to do so.
4. *Donations.* More important is the option religious entities have to accept donations of items of cultural interest, with tax benefits for those making them.[16] Donors can transfer the title of the item, but they can establish a usufruct or another real right without reward as well. The latter is an interesting way of patronage, insofar as the owner retains ownership of the item, while simultaneously enjoying the fiscal benefits (Beneyto 2012: 321).
5. *Other means of patronage.* Since the enactment of the Act of Patronage in 2002 the General State Budget can establish preferential activities of patronage that will enjoy greater tax benefits. From that year on, the Acts

13 Article 54 Act 37/1992 of 28 December 1992 on Value Added Tax.

14 Article 4 Act 19/1991 of 6 June 1991 on Wealth Tax.

15 Article 62-2-b Royal Legislative Decree 2/2004 of 5 March 2004 approving the revised text of the Act Regulating Local Tax.

16 Article 17 and Additional Disposition 9 of the Act 49/2002 of 23 December 2002 on tax regime of non-profit organizations and tax incentive for trusts.

> that approved the General State Budget have included among those activities the conservation, restoration and rehabilitation of the items belonging to specially mentioned Spanish heritage. This has been advantageous for religious denominations, mainly for the Catholic Church due to the number of premises and monuments it owns (Rodriguez Blanco 2005: 105),[17] but it has also benefited other religious communities that have signed agreements with the state.

Despite the economic crisis, the Government has maintained this disposition. Among the properties that have benefited are, for example, the Mosque of Córdoba, the Cathedrals of Seville, Zaragoza and Burgos and a number of other monuments.[18] The same applies to the General State Budget for 2013.[19]

Finally, the Act of Patronage regulates the pacts for cooperation between a religious entity that has an agreement with the state and a company. They stipulate that the company will provide funding for a certain activity or initiative and that the religious entity will advertise that support. Religious entities have signed these kinds of agreements mainly to foster conservation, restoration and rehabilitation of heritage and to maintain places of worship, mostly cathedrals.[20] Such is the case of the Agreement between the Spanish Conference for Bishops and BBVA in 1995, for the conservation of churches and cathedrals, and Endesa in 1998, renewed for the fourth time in July 2012, that funds 50 per cent of the lighting of the cathedrals. At local level, there are also a number of agreements between the trustees of certain premises – again, usually cathedrals – and private companies.[21] In this regard, one unique case is the restoration of the Cathedral of Vitoria. To this end, the dioceses and the local and regional governments created a non-profit institution, which launched a project to obtain private funds from companies and also from individual donors.[22]

---

17 Not all scholars agree on the power given to the state to decide through the General State Budget the entities that will be able to enjoy those benefits. See Beneyto (2012: 337).

18 Act 39/2010 of 22 December 2010, General State Budget for 2011, and Act 2/2012 of 29 June, General State Budget for 2012.

19 See General State Budget for 2013, Act 17/2012 of December 2012.

20 Article 25 of the Act 49/2002 of 23 December 2002, on tax regime of non-profit organizations and tax incentive for trusts. See on this topic Rodríguez Blanco (2005: 111–12).

21 *Idem.*

22 See Messeguer (2012: 485). More information on the project can be found at: http://www.catedralvitoria.com/index.php (accessed 12 November 2014).

Agreements with Religious Denominations

Agreement with the Catholic Church

The SHA, in the second Additional Disposition, establishes that according to the law the international treaties signed by the state also bind public authorities. This is quite a strange declaration, insofar as there is no need of it, and in the Spanish juridical system, international treaties are not subordinated to legislative norms.

Spain signed an Agreement with the Holy See on Education and Cultural Affairs in 1979. Section XV is devoted to cultural heritage. It affirms in its preamble that the historical, artistic and documentary heritage of the church constitutes a major part of the cultural heritage of the country. It further states that the combined effort of church and state to preserve, foster and ease the enjoyment of that heritage will be determined by circumstance. Following that declaration, Section XV reiterates the church's willingness to display its historical, cultural and documentary heritage in the interest of society. As such, it provides a bilateral legal framework for the preservation, cataloguing and exhibition of the cultural heritage in the possession of the church. This framework thus facilitates the conservation of the works in question, thereby preventing their deterioration while also providing access to them for academic research and study. This section refers to the items in the possession of the church again, and therefore to all those that rely on church authorities for any entitlement. It is interesting to note, however, that these norms do not expressly mention objects with a function of worship, as they form a remarkable part of religious heritage.

The Agreement approved the creation of a joint commission to fulfill these aims,[23] which was established a year later, and which approved the Rules that would govern this matter.[24] Basically, the Catholic Church agreed to open up its heritage to the Spanish population and the state, in exchange, agreed to cooperate technically and financially in the preservation of this heritage according to the following principles:

1. Respect for the liturgical usage of the religious items;
2. Coordination of the purpose of worship with the scientific and artistic goals, and with all actions needed in order to preserve them;
3. Regulation of public access and exhibition of the heritage, balancing cultural and the necessities of worship;
4. All elements belonging to the heritage should be displayed in their original placement. Where this is not possible, they should be gathered together

---

23 In fact, this is the only compulsory statement in the agreement. See Motilla (2012: 57).

24 'Criterios Básicos', jointly approved by the Spanish Conference of Catholic Bishops and the Secretary for Justice, 30 November 1980. See on this matter, among others, Alvarez Cortina (1985: 293).

in collections, museums and other premises that guarantee the safety of the items.

However, the need to acknowledge the right of the regional governments of the autonomous regions to conduct their own affairs has somewhat limited the commission in its remit. Consequently, many of the powers related to heritage were assumed by the regional authorities (Motilla 1995).

Agreements with Other Religious Denominations

There are three agreements in force with Jewish communities, Muslim communities and Evangelicals, all of them approved on 10 November 1992.[25] Agreements with the Jewish and Muslim communities – not with Evangelicals, as there is no protestant heritage – devote Article 13 to the cultural heritage pertaining to those faiths. They only provide that these communities will cooperate with the state in the preservation and the promotion of their cultural heritage. That cooperation will include the creation of an inventory and the creation of trusts or other entities with a cultural aim. There is no other provision regarding the establishment of a joint commission.

Law and Organization at Regional Level

The political structure of Spain, with 17 autonomous regions and two autonomous cities, has an impact on the governing of religious heritage.[26] As a general rule, the Constitution grants powers to the regional governments over museums, libraries and monuments of regional interest.[27] However, there are some elements of uncertainty that may affect the implementation of these powers. For example, there is no indication whether *monument* refers only to a special kind of premises. Neither is it clear on which grounds a monument shall be considered of regional or national interest. In some cases the standard used for this delimitation is the location, while for others the strength of the link to local culture or other factors is taken into consideration.

Additionally, a ruling from the Constitutional Court of 1991 has opened the door to wider regional regulation.[28] Therefore, most regions have enacted legislation on

25 Acts 24, 25 and 26/1992 of 10 November 1992.

26 For the sake of simplicity, I will use the term *region* to refer to the *Comunidad Autónoma*, a Spanish territorial unit with no parallel in other countries – sometimes called *Self-governing Communities*. The *Comunidades Autónomas* have legislative and administrative powers, but no judiciary, in their respective territories.

27 Section 148-1-15 of the Spanish Constitution.

28 Case of the Spanish Constitutional Court, STC 17/1991, 31 January 1991.

cultural heritage in general, or on a particular issue.[29] The final picture, then, is not crystal clear. For the sake of clarity, I will sum up some general features of the regional laws, without going deeper into the situation of each particular region.

Regional Legislation on Heritage

The regional laws usually establish their own means of conservation and fostering the cultural heritage that are essentially similar to those stated in the SHA.[30] At times, these laws use rather imprecise terms with the aim of broadening regional powers, and hence they talk about social, anthropological or industrial heritage. All this is particularly disturbing, because it causes a fragmentation of the protection of the heritage that may result in a weaker efficacy of the means adopted to protect it.

With regards to religious heritage, the general rule is that it is subject to common regulation. However, there are some specific provisions that shape its legal framework. Many regional laws contain a compulsory mandate to cooperate in this field with the Catholic Church, but not so often with other religious denominations. To this end, they provide for the participation of members of religious orders in advisory boards with competence in matters of heritage.[31]

Some regional laws pursue a policy of harmonization in terms of giving equal status to both the religious and the cultural function of items of religious heritage, while acknowledging the primary function of the item as an instrument of worship. This acknowledgement makes up for the lack of clarity in this regard in the SHA. Nonetheless, the cultural function is given preferred status in a number of regional regulations.

The measures adopted in order to promote heritage and particularly funding are again quite similar to the state ones. The only feature that might be highlighted is that certain norms allow public authorities from several regions to give direct aid, in the form of subsidies, when a certain action is needed for the conservation of the items and the owners – whether religious institutions or not – demonstrate that they do not have the means to do so (Tejón 2008: 454).

Regional Agreements with Religious Denominations

The mandate of cooperation between regional authorities and religious denominations, as previously mentioned, is stated in most regional laws. According to this mandate, and due to the high sensitivity around issues of cultural heritage,

29 Regional legislation is gathered in different publications. See, among others, Anguita (2007).

30 In this section, therefore, I will refer only to the special features of the regional laws, setting aside those others which are a replication of state regulations. See on this issue, among others, Aldanondo (2010) and literature cited.

31 A more detailed account of this law and its content is to be found in Álvarez Cortina (2012b: 86–7) and Tejón (2008: 409 *et seq.*).

all the regions have signed agreements with the ecclesiastical authorities of the Catholic Church.[32] The agreements have different nature and form, but there are only slight variations in their structure and content (Rogriguez Blanco 2003). Several elements are worthy of note.

First, the agreements recognize the function of the items as objects of worship belonging to religious heritage, although they do it with different levels of intensity or commitment. Some of them refer to the 'prevalent religious function', while others state that their cultural interest must be considered 'without prejudice' to their function of worship (Álvarez Cortina 2012b: 96).

Secondly, all agreements impose the creation of a joint committee like the one stated in the agreement between the Holy See and the state. These committees have powers to act, to protect and promote heritage in the region, as well as the budget to do so. Certainly, these regional committees have been much more active, insofar as acting at a level closer to the location of the heritage eases the operations and makes them more efficient (Álvarez Cortina 2012b).[33]

Thirdly, another development at the regional level that has had an impact on funding is the signing of sectorial agreements in several regions. They have a narrower scope but the funds can be allocated to specific initiatives that otherwise might remain neglected. These are some examples of this kind of agreements:[34]

- Agreement between the regional authorities and the Dioceses of Oviedo, 15 October 1997, on archives and libraries. The region will partially fund the disinfection, repair and recording of books and documents and the church will pay the other part of the total budget and will grant access to them for study and research purposes.[35]
- Agreement in order to prepare the inventory of the religious heritage of the Basque Country (1991), Murcia (1991), Aragon (2006) and Castile-La Mancha (2008). The church will prepare the inventory of their goods of cultural interest and will send it to the regional authorities, who will pay for the costs of the task.
- Agreements regarding the Diocesan Museums, signed in several Dioceses of Catalonia and Asturias. The museums will be integrated into the local network of museums under the same conditions as the civil ones and the civil authorities will contribute to the conservation of the museum and the training of personnel.
- Agreement between the regional government and the Dioceses of Andalucía (1991) on musical heritage. The regional authorities will fund the restoration of musical instruments and the church will allow the recording

32 See Motilla (2012: 60 *et seq.*) who had assembled all the agreements signed at regional level.

33 See also Motilla (2012: 62).

34 Motilla gives notice of these agreements in Motilla (2012: 63 *et seq.*).

35 A similar agreement was signed in Castilla-La Mancha on 2 July 1998.

of the musical archives of the cathedrals, as well as performances of them in religious premises not open for worship.

Finally, agreements with other religious denominations, although much less numerous, can be found in several regions, mainly in Catalonia and Madrid, and with a more restricted scope than in other regions. They do not aim particularly to protect and foster heritage, but some of them contain a general recognition of Protestant, Jewish or Islamic heritage as part of the regional heritage. Moreover, the agreements between the Jewish community and the regional governments of Madrid and Catalonia state a commitment to cooperate in the protection and development of historic, artistic and literary heritage and archeological heritage, in case some archeological item appear. The same provision appears in the Agreement between the Islamic communities and the Government of Madrid (Tejón 2008: 405).

Law and Organization at Local Level

A reference to the local level is worth mentioning, although the prospective actions that might be developed are less important for heritage, due to the lower levels of both financial means and political power of the councils and other local entities.

The legal tools, in this case, are the agreements, usually established between several local entities of differing level (*ayuntamientos*, *diputaciones* and, on the islands, *cabildos* or *consejos*) and Catholic entities, generally dioceses, but also cathedrals or other entities.

The contents, necessarily related to the powers of the local entities, have to do, to a large extent, with the promotion of tourism. Local entities may fund the salaries of the guides, ushers or security and the church will open the monument up to the public for tours. Sometimes, the guides are employees of the local entity. Another typical initiative is the joint funding of the restoration of a valuable item, for example an altarpiece that must be opened for exhibition once the work has ended. Finally, there are also agreements for the temporal loan of premises or goods for cultural activities – concerts of sacred music, exhibitions of religious works of art and the like, often with the participation of private contributors (Motilla 2012: 168). It is in the context of a similar agreement that a significant series of exhibitions called *Las edades del hombre* took place in various locations around Castile-Leon, widely regarded as one of the richest sites in Europe in terms of religious heritage.[36]

36 See http://www.lasedades.es (accessed 12 November 2014).

Special Initiatives

National Plan for Cathedrals

Cathedrals enjoy special protection in Spain. They are a significant part of the historical and cultural heritage. However, the large amount of funds needed for maintenance, conservation and restoration makes it imperative that there is financial cooperation among all parties involved. It is understandable then that they benefit from particular attention from the public authorities.

In 1997 (25 February), the Secretary for Justice, the regional governments and the National Congress of Bishops of the Catholic Church signed a joint agreement called the National Plan for Cathedrals (Rodríguez Blanco 2003). As of today, 90 cathedrals all over Spain have benefited from this plan. The plan studies the situation in all Spanish Cathedrals and includes a specific project for each cathedral, elaborated with the intervention of the state, region and dioceses. The plan describes the actual state of the cathedral, the actions needed for their protection and repair and the total budget, over a period of eight to ten years.[37] The Spanish Government will fund its share of the programme, and the General State Budget Act includes it as a priority for patronage, granting tax benefits on private contributions to this cause. Other sources of funding are regional budgets, local entities and private patronage. The Church also assumes responsibility for applying for grants from the European Union in addition to appealing for assistance from their own members. The specific plans will state the percentage that corresponds to each share of the financial contribution.

The plan is currently under revision, with the idea of achieving broad cooperation, not only regarding conservation and restoration, but also for the daily management of these monuments (Messeguer 2012: 481).

National Plan for Monasteries, Abbeys and Cloisters

In the wake of the National Plan for Cathedrals, on 25 March 2004, the Secretary for Culture and the National Conference of Catholic Bishops signed the National Plan for Monasteries, Abbeys and Cloisters. It will affect whichever such premises have been declared of cultural interest. The plan will include strategies to deal with the issue of harmonizing the cultural and religious status of these buildings, whilst acknowledging the special nature of monastic life that may preclude provision of public access to these sites. The protection will apply not only to the buildings, but to the entire cultural and material heritage linked to monastic life, such as the music, liturgy and the like.

---

37 Once the individual projects were set up, it became clear that the plan could not reach all Spanish Cathedrals. Therefore, on 21 November 2006, a new partial agreement between the Spanish Government and the Catholic Church established a priority of the cathedrals, stating which ones were in more urgent need of help. See Tejón (2008: 246).

Conclusion

Despite the tough economic situation, Spanish authorities have maintained most of the measures aimed at the protecting and fostering religious heritage, although with an unavoidable cut in funds. However, better management of the existing resources will be needed. Perhaps the main flaw is the overlapping powers of state and regional governments on the cultural heritage issue.

As most scholars and authorities have often pointed out, recognizing the particularities of religious heritage would be highly desirable in order to obtain more accurate protection of cultural heritage that respects the identity and, at the same time, the aims of the religious premises and other issues.

References

Aldanondo, I. (2010), 'El Patrimonio Cultural de las Confesiones Religiosas en España', *Derecho y Religión*, 5, 147–69.

Alvarez Cortina, A.C. (1985), 'Bases para una cooperación eficaz Iglesia-Estado en defensa del patrimonio histórico, artístico y cultural', *Ius Canonicum*, 25, 293–331.

Álvarez Cortina, A.C. and Rodríguez Blanco, M. (eds) (2012a), *La religión en la ciudad. Dimensiones jurídicas del establecimiento de los lugares de culto* (Granada: Comares).

Álvarez Cortina, A.C. (2012b), 'Destino al culto y valor cultural (concurrencia y conflicto)', in Álvarez Cortina, A.C. and Rodríguez Blanco, M. (eds), 75–107.

Anguita, L. (2007), *Código del patrimonio cultural* (Navarra: Thomson-Aranzadi).

Beneyto, R. (2012), 'Régimen tributario de los bienes culturales de titularidad eclesiástica', in Vega, A., Martín, M., Rodríguez Blanco, M. and Vázquez García-Peñuela, J.M. (eds), 245–379.

Cano, I. (2012), 'Patrimonio documental y estatuto jurídico de los archivos eclesiásticos', in Vega, A., Martín, M., Rodríguez Blanco, M. and Vázquez García-Peñuela, J.M. (eds), 177–94.

Martín Retortillo, L. (2001), 'Nuevas perspectivas en la conservación del patrimonio histórico: una recapitulación global', *Revista Aragonesa de Administración Pública*, 19, 31–60.

Messeguer, S. (2012), 'La gestión del patrimonio cultural de titularidad eclesiástica', in Vega, A., Martín, M., Rodríguez Blanco, M. and Vázquez García-Peñuela, J.M. (eds), 475–86.

Motilla, A. (1995), *Régimen jurídico de los bienes histórico-artísticos de la Iglesia Católica* (Madrid: Eurolex).

Motilla, A. (2012), 'Bienes culturales de la Iglesia Católica: Legislación estatal y normativa pacticia', in Vega, A., Martín, M., Rodríguez Blanco, M. and Vázquez García-Peñuela, J.M. (eds), 45–70.

Pedreira Menéndez, J. (2004), *Beneficios e incentivos del patrimonio cultural* (Pamplona: Thomson-Aranzadi).
Rodríguez Blanco, M. (2003), 'El Plan Nacional de Catedrales: contenido y desarrollo', *Ius Canonicum*, 60, 711–33.
Rodríguez Blanco, M. (2005), *Las confesiones religiosas en el marco del régimen jurídico del mecenazgo* (Madrid: EDISOFER).
Tejón, R. (2008), *Confesiones religiosas y patrimonio cultural* (Madrid: Ministerio de Justicia).
Vega, A., Martín, M., Rodríguez Blanco, M. and Vázquez García-Peñuela, J.M. (eds) (2012), *Protección del Patrimonio Cultural de Interés Religioso* (Granada: Comares).

PART IV
Laïcités, Separation between Church and State and Funding Religious Heritage

Chapter 11

A *Dutch Treat*: State Funding for the Maintenance and Restoration of Built Religious Heritage in the Netherlands

Adriaan Overbeeke

In a famous essay published in the journal *De Gids* in 1873, lawyer Victor de Stuers observed that '[o]ur old gothic church buildings, most of them in the possession of the Reformed Protestants, did not get any special attention until now. [...] I have to point at the inadequacy of the governments funding system for the restoration of ancient buildings'.[1] Since then, the situation has dramatically changed in the Dutch religious landscape, but the question of the responsibility of the state remains on the agenda and is becoming more urgent since the number of redundant churches is increasing. There are many stakeholders: church communities and their religious leadership, heritage protection organizations, as well as local and central public authorities. They all have a role to play in the efforts to manage the (still) rich cultural religious heritage that moulded the traditional Dutch landscape. Its skyline is depicted in 'Memory of Holland' (*Herinnering aan Holland)*, a poem by Hendrik Marsman:

> ... .tree clumps, villages,
> truncated towers,
> churches and elm trees
> all wondrously planned.[2]

1 de Stuers (1873: 360 and 382), [authors' translation].
2 Hendrik Marsman (1899–1940).

Churches, chapels and monasteries are, apart from windmills, the most visible part of Dutch-built heritage.[3] A related issue is that of discussions about the heritage value of religious objects, part of the buildings' interior.[4]

The current interest for the fate of religious buildings in the context of policies and budgets regarding built heritage, is the result of the financial burden that maintenance obligations impose on owners, especially in an age of secularization. A high proportion of church buildings are 'oversized' for the local religious community. A growing number of buildings are not needed for their original function anymore, raising the issue of their reuse. Declining membership and church attendance, a decrease in donations and, for the Roman Catholic Church, an acute shortage of parish priests are putting church authorities in a difficult position. Hence, church buildings – *a fortiori* listed buildings – are increasingly, in financial terms at least, a burden for their religious owners. Indeed, support measures developed in the Netherlands for the protection of built heritage are more or less based on the *entrepeneurship* of the monuments' owners. Listed religious buildings are – with some exceptions – owned by private parties, predominantly religious communities, and private law organizations for monument care, which are accordingly responsible themselves for the maintenance and restoration of their property. This responsibility goes hand in hand with the overall regime for church financing, which consists of self-financing, mitigated by tax benefits (Van Sasse van Ysselt 2013a, 2013b).

This chapter offers an overview of the type and importance of state support received by the religious communities still responsible for listed buildings (*Rijksmonumenten*). In a system of separation between church and state, one could argue that state efforts to support the preservation of religious built heritage is the equivalent of state support for religion.[5] Parliamentary debates on cultural heritage and monuments[6] reflect a lingering feeling of discomfort when support for religious buildings is on the agenda. Liberal MP De Liefde criticized his former

3 Even churches' sounds are very present in Dutch literary heritage: the Amsterdam Westerkerk carillon (the clock tower was visible from the attic of the Achterhuis) was frequently mentioned in Anne Frank's diary, and described by her as a source of comfort. So the heritage value of religious buildings does include *acoustic elements*. On church bells see Garrioch (2003: 10–13).

4 One of the elements giving rise to De Stuers' passionate *De Gids* essay in 1873 was the destruction of important elements of the thirteenth century Den Bosch Saint John cathedral interior (parts of the choir and high altar, sold to England).

5 See Fornerod (2010); see in general, on the financial aspects of church and state relations in the Netherlands: van Sasse van Ysselt (2013a, 2013b), van Bijsterveld (2010), Hirsch Ballin (1988).

6 Heritage protection legislation was reformed recently, as budgetary restraints also concern the cultural sector. Therefore the topic is present in parliamentary debate. See Modernization of Monument Care Act 2011 (*Wet van 6 juni 2011 tot wijziging van de Monumentenwet 1988 en de Wet algemene bepalingen omgevingsrecht in verband met de modernisering van de monumentenzorg*), *Staatsblad*, 2011, no. 330.

Christian democratic coalition partner for having a religious preference: 'they [the Christian democrats] literally want to protect their particular *taboo*.[7] They want to give churches a preferential position when it comes to the distribution of the budget for the preservation of monuments'.[8] The discussion suggests that protection of ancient religious buildings equals to state support for religion or is at least problematic in the context of the separation of church and state (Raats 2012: 96). At least, this supposes that listed religious buildings are, in principle, used for religious activities. However, a growing number of listed buildings, especially religious ones, are used for other purposes.

Indeed, the management of a church building with monument status is not without tension. For a religious community the consequence of monument status is a loss of economic value, especially when it limits alternative options for a building becoming redundant and/or too expensive, in a situation of decreasing membership and lower contributions by members.

Dutch Religious Heritage: an Overview

Legislation Applicable to Religious Heritage

In comparison to other European countries, Dutch State policies for the preservation of national cultural heritage started relatively late, in the last quarter of the nineteenth century,[9] with limited annual budgets and the creation of an Arts and Science Department (*Kunsten en Wetenschappen*) within the state administration.[10]

The relevant national legislation regarding listing and related state financing is the Monuments and Historic Buildings Act of 23 December 1988, amended by the Modernization of Monument Care Act in 2011 (*Monuments Act 1988*).[11] It replaced the first piece of comprehensive legislation for the protection and maintenance of national cultural heritage, drafted in 1961.[12] Before 1961 restoration of major historical buildings could be eligible for state grants on an *ad hoc* basis. The 1988

7 *Taboo* is in Dutch *heilige huisjes*, litterally 'sacred buildings'.

8 *Parl. Proceedings Tweede Kamer* (House of Representatives), 28 June 2012, no. 102–13, 60.

9 See de Stuers (1873).

10 This new agency was headed since 1875 by Victor de Stuers (1843–1916).

11 *Monuments Act 1988. Staatsblad* 1988, no. 638. For the publication of legislative changes in 2011, see *Staatsblad*, 2011, no. 330.

A translated (but non-official) version of the 1988 Act is available at: http://www.eui.eu/Projects/InternationalArtHeritageLaw/Documents/NationalLegislation/Netherlands/monumentshistoricbuildingsact.pdf (accessed 6 February 2014).

12 *Historic Buildings Act 1961, Staatsblad* 1961, no. 200. On the legislation and administration for monument protection in the Netherlands, see Stubbs and Makaš (2011: 1222–4). The Dutch legislator was relatively late with monument legislation, partially due to a reluctance to infringe on property rights (Lubina 2009: 10).

Act provides a definition of monuments, namely 'all objects constructed at least fifty years ago which are of public interest because of their beauty, scientific significance or cultural and historic value' (Article 1b).[13] Religious monuments (*kerkelijke monumenten*) constitute a separate subcategory, in that the Monuments Act 1988 defines them as 'immovable monuments which are the property of a particular denomination, congregation, parish or church organisation and which are used exclusively or mainly for worship' (Article 1e).

The national Cultural Heritage Agency (*Rijksdienst voor Cultureel Erfgoed*, RCE) has developed a set of five criteria in order to decide unambiguously the monumental value of buildings:

- the value of the building in a cultural historical perspective;
- the value of the building in an architectural or art-historical perspective;
- the situational or 'ensemble' value of the building;
- the undamaged character and identifiability of the building;
- the curiosity of the building.

As regards religious monuments, the relevant elements of the first criterium become visible by answering the following questions: does the building function as a house of prayer? Does it mirror the (changing) church–state relations? Does it represent a Roman Catholic architectural style (after 1853),[14] Protestant dissenting movements or post World War II architectural styles? (RCE 2012a: 11–21).

In general, the listed status of a building limits the room for change. If a place of worship is a monument, the requirements of the related legislation have to be met. Problems can arise when religious communities wish to adapt elements of the listed building for liturgical needs[15] or when they seek other functions for a church building, changing its original destination. In those cases an environment licence is needed (from national, provincial or municipal authorities, depending on the type of monument). However, the Monuments Act 1988 required with respect to a religious monument that 'the Burgomaster and Aldermen or Our Minister shall not take any decision [...] other than in agreement with the owner, insofar as decisions which are of vital significance to worship in the monument are concerned' (Article 18, old). Case law on this issue is very limited.[16] The provision on the 'agreement'

---

13 Since January 2012, the criterium related to the date of construction of the monument does not apply anymore. See *Modernization of Monument Care Act 2011*, Article 1a.

14 In 1853 (as a direct consequence of the liberal Constitution of 1848) the Roman Catholic Church was able to re-install a regular church organization in the Netherlands.

15 See Steensma (1981: 36–40).

16 See district court of Zutphen, 29 August 2006, LJN AY7098: objection by an association against the partial removal of church benches in the listed sixteenth century Protestant St Joris parish Church in Borculo; district court of Arnhem, 29 March 2011, LJN BQ0118: association for the protection of the interior of the church objecting against the

of religious authorities, giving weight to the specific religious needs (and thus to religious freedom rights of the religious communities concerned) was transferred from the specific Monuments Act to the General Provisions Environmental Act in 2012.[17] The provision facilitates in particular changes in the interior, but cannot be seen as an easy 'green light' for every religiously-inspired initiative affecting a listed church building.[18]

Composition of Religious Heritage

Dutch religious heritage is undeniably multireligious, reflecting the evolutions of church–state relations over past centuries. In addition, the ownership parameter is especially decisive in that it might go against the protection of cultural heritage logic and directly influence choices about maintenance.

A legacy of history: A heterogeneous and multireligious heritage

For historical reasons, religious heritage proves to vary in its composition from one denomination to another. Not all religions possess (and thus have to keep in a good state of repair) listed buildings. Two denominations have a big share of the whole category: the Protestant Church in the Netherlands[19] and the Roman Catholic Church.

Dutch religious history and the evolution of Dutch state-religion relations produced its own architectural variations, starting with a category of pre-Reformation church buildings that were converted in the sixteenth century into houses of worship for the state-favoured Reformed religion. In the seventeenth century the first new Reformed churches were built, but in the same period 'hidden churches' (*schuilkerken*) emerged, built by tolerated Protestant denominations

---

complete replacement for liturgical reasons of the *church interior* of the twelfth century listed St Martins Church in Doorn. See also Council of State, 5 November 2008, LJN BG3373; Council of State, 2 February 2011, LJN BP2812: case of the seventeenth century listed Reformed Church of Middenbeemster (situated in the Beemster *polder*, land created in the seventeenth century), where the congregation planned to build a 'community centre' close to the listed church. In this case, the interests of the religious owner and the interest of monument protection were eventually balanced. All cases available: at www.rechtspraak.nl (by introducing the LJN-codes).

17 *Wet algemene bepalingen omgevingsrecht* (*Wabo*). See Article 3-2a: 'In those cases where the decision touches at essential interests regarding the manifestation of religion in the building, the competent authority decides only if an agreement with the owner has been reached' [translation by the author]. See on the *Wabo*: Broekhuizen (2011: 105–8).

18 See the government's explanation in *Parliamentary documents, Eerste Kamer* (Senate), 2010–2011, 32433 no. C, 6–8.

19 The Protestant Church in the Netherlands (2004) is the merger of the *Dutch Reformed Church*, the *Reformed Churches in the Netherlands* and the *Lutheran Church*.

(Remonstrants and Mennonites) and by Roman Catholic communities.[20] The Jewish community obtained the right to build synagogues recognizable as such as early as 1670.[21]

When full religious freedom was constitutionally guaranteed in 1848, the 'restoration' of the Roman Catholic hierarchy in 1853 saw a tremendous outburst of Roman Catholic churchbuilding activity in nearly all Dutch provinces: this meant that the pillarised church (*zuilkerk*) succeeded the hidden church (*schuilkerk*) (Steensma 1981: 15). Full religious freedom ultimately meant the development of a striking number of Protestant divisions and subdivisions within Reformed Protestantism, resulting again in churchbuilding activities.[22] The last important building 'boom' occurred after a schism within Reformed Churches (*Gereformeerde Kerken*) in 1944. Then, building activities coincided with post-World War II reconstruction (*Wederopbouw*) and another one followed the Protestant Church unification process, leading to the Reformed-Lutheran Protestant Church in the Netherlands in 2004.[23]

Jewish communities, all with a longstanding presence in the Netherlands, also inherited a fairly high number of interesting listed religious buildings. Until World War II, the Jewish minority was deeply rooted in Dutch religious demographic landscape. For post-war Dutch Jewish communities (*Nederlands Israëlitisch Kerkgenootschap*, NIK), the *Shoah* meant that the huge number of synagogues was inherited by a tiny group of survivors.[24] A substantial number of abandoned synagogues, often listed monuments, were or had been in use by other religious denominations.[25] Today, Jewish listed buildings belong to various Jewish denominations or to private heritage organizations as well as other denominations too. Lastly, one should also mention the small number of listed temples of freemason lodges.[26]

---

20 Kaplan (2007: 172–97), Stiefel (2011: 119–27). Another category is the 'churches in barns' (*schuurkerken*): see Gielis (1998).

21 A famous example is the listed Amsterdam Portuguese synagogue, the largest synagogue in Europe at the time of its construction in 1675. See Vlaardingerbroek and Pekaar (2013), Stiefel (2011: 125–7).

22 This led to interesting case law on church property disputes between the 'heirs' of the pre-schism church buildings. See van Kooten and van der Ploeg (2004).

23 A segment of the former Dutch Reformed Church (*Nederlandse Hervormde Kerk*) did not join the unified Protestant Church and went apart in a Reformed Church Continuing (*Hersteld Hervormde Kerk*), a denomination of 119 local parishes.

24 In 1952 the NIK was reduced to 58 (of 139 pre-war) local religious communities (Brasz 1995: 364).

25 Inventory in Michman, Beem and Michman (1999). Available at: http://www.jhm.nl/cultuur-en-geschiedenis/Nederland (accessed 5 February 2014).

26 *Kampen*: freemason lodge 'Le Profond Silence' (1882); *Zaandam*: freemason lodge 'Anna Paulowna' (1858); *Alkmaar*: freemason lodge 'De Noordstar' (1924); *Hilversum*: building 'De Vereeniging' (freemason lodge 'De Gooische Broederschap') (1905).

Religious buildings with monumental status are primarily Christian churches, originating in a distant past – medieval pre-Reformation Catholic churches and chapels – and ending with the recent post-World War II architecture. The second largest religion in the Netherlands in demographic terms, Islam, is not (yet) present in the category of listed religious buildings, as a consequence of the recent phenomenon of mosque-building initiatives.[27] Five monumental buildings belong to Muslim communities although none of them was built as a mosque.[28] Other new minorities are not represented in this category (Hirsch Ballin 1988: 129).[29]

Religious Listed Buildings and Religious Heritage

Unlike what can be observed in many European countries, religious monuments constitute only a small part of Dutch immovable heritage. In 2013 approximately 60,000 national monuments were listed.[30] Almost 50 per cent belong to the category of 'private houses', 11 per cent are 'farms', while only 7 per cent (4,427 monuments) are categorized as 'religious buildings'.[31] Provinces and municipalities have their own monument regulations and selection criteria[32] for provincial and municipal monuments. In 2009, approximately 43,000 buildings were on municipal monuments' lists and only 760 on provincial lists. Religious buildings count for 2.3 per cent of municipal monuments (Stoelhorst consultancy e.a. 2009). Of 927 cases of 'surplus' church buildings researched in 2008,[33] only 106 had national monumental status (11 per cent) and 59 provincial or municipal monumental status (6 per cent).

However, from a religious community perspective, the situation is different. This small number of listed religious buildings represents a high proportion of all existing religious buildings. A full inventory of church buildings in the Netherlands is not available yet, but an important database available at the VU University Amsterdam contains information about 19,000 religious buildings built for local

27 See Fornerod (2010: 10).

28 One former Roman Catholic chapel, two former synagogues, two other non-religious buildings.

29 An exception is the First Church of Christ Scientist in The Hague (1927), *Rijksmonument*, built by the famous Dutch architect Berlage.

30 See http://monumentenregister.cultureelerfgoed.nl (accessed 6 February 2014).

31 Figures of 25,766 'private houses', 7,616 'farms', 4,427 'religious buildings' (Monumentenregister database). In the recent proposal for the listing of a selection of 1959–1965 architecture, the proportion of religious buildings is however proportionally high since it amounts to 18 per cent. See RCE (2013: 319–441).

32 The selection criteria are not always transparent. For a recommendation for objective criteria, to be inspired by the set of criteria used for the selection of *Rijksmonumenten*, see Belvedere (2008b: 12).

33 Belvedere (2008a). The research was undertaken in the two Roman Catholic dioceses Haarlem and Rotterdam, situated in the provinces North and South Holland.

religious communities, belonging to approximately 100 different denominations.[34] The estimated number of *remaining* religious buildings (8,000–9,000) leads us to conclude that approximately 40 per cent (4,427) are nowadays classified as *Rijksmonument*.[35] Only this 40 per cent are eligible for some sort of state support in the context of the protection of religious heritage.

Tensions between private ownership and heritage preservation

Only 3 per cent of the 60,000 listed buildings are state property.[36] Some ancient church towers are owned by municipalities and, due to the disappearance of many local Jewish communities, a number of synagogues have become municipal property too.[37] The vast majority of religious buildings – including listed buildings – are owned by religious communities. The mainly private ownership of Dutch religious heritage undoubtedly influences the protection of religious heritage, knowing that maintenance costs are borne by the owner. In addition, religious ownership is likely to be influenced by religious regulations and principles of the denomination concerned, namely deciding on the sacral status of a building, or regulating what church bodies should decide on the acceptable fate of redundant church buildings.[38] Ownership is regulated differently for religions with a strong hierarchical structure (such as Roman Catholic dioceses) compared to Protestant Churches (with sometimes absolute power at congregational level).

The Roman Catholic Church is an interesting example, combining a centralized church structure and a strong position on the sacral character of parish churches, with a relatively young building tradition that started in the nineteenth century. Demolition is easier to accept where the buildings concerned are relatively recent and where a substantial number of remaining buildings with the same style and from the same period are still in use. If the liberal 1848 Constitution is taken as a the starting point for the full religious freedom of the Roman Catholic Church in the Netherlands, the massive demolition of churches begins exactly there: 89 per cent of demolished churches were built since 1848 and approximately 46 per cent of these cases concern buildings built from 1941 to 1969 (Belvedere 2008a: 237).

---

34 See http://www.hdc.vu.nl/nl/online-informatie/ikgn/index.asp (accessed 6 February 2014). See also the inventory of pictures of the *Instituut voor Liturgiewetenschap, University Groningen*: http://www.kerkeninbeeld.nl (accessed 6 February 2014).

35 The numbers include listed buildings and listed *parts* of buildings (for instance: a church organ or a bell tower listed as a monument).

36 *Parl. Doc.* Tweede Kamer 2012–2013, 31490 – 32156, no. 105, 2. A small number of state owned monuments in the Netherlands, including two religious buildings, is however for sale: a fifteenth-century church tower in Goedereede and a fourteenth- or fifteenth-century church in Veere. See Breevaart (2013) and van der Kaaij (2013).

37 This was for instance the case for the synagogues in Borne, Delft, Deventer (since 2011), Emmen, Geertruidenberg, Groningen, Kampen, Leeuwarden, Lochem, Medemblik, Middelburg, Nieuweschans, Nijmegen, Tilburg and Weesp. See Michman, Beem and Michman (1999).

38 Meijers (2009, 2012); Hendriks (2013); Van Bijsterveld (2009).

In 2008 Roman Catholic bishop Punt (diocese of Haarlem) was very outspoken on his church's position, opposing the 'collectivisation' of private property churches:

> We notice that a lot of people spontaneously assume church buildings to be a sort of societal propriety and that every individual citizen has a right to be involved in the discussion on re-use. (…) But the buildings are owned by the Church and no one else. They are built, and for the greater part maintained, with money of the Church. The Church alone decides on their future.[39]

This is true as far as the sale or transfer of listed buildings is concerned, but *Rijksmonumental* status does limit the rights of the owner through the introduction of a number of prohibitions (Lubina 2009: 19–20).

Protestant denominations are influenced by their characteristic decentralized ownership structure. The Protestant Church in the Netherlands (that inherited the oldest religious buildings, owned by congregations of the former Dutch Reformed Church) limits this local autonomy on a regional level: for all legal acts of local church governors concerning 'drastic renovations, enlargements or restorations, sale (…) and demolishment of a church building or an organ with a cultural historical or architectural value', permission is needed from a supervising ecclesiastical body, the regional board for management affairs (*Regionaal college voor de behandeling van beheerszaken*).[40]

In some provinces, private law organizations for the preservation of built religious heritage own an important share of listed church buildings, but this phenomenon seems to be especially present in Protestant territories.[41] Indeed, a growing number of listed church buildings belong to non-profit organizations responsible for the exploitation and maintenance of these buildings, sometimes also renting them out to religious communities for worship purposes. This scheme was recently applied for a monumental synagogue in Amersfoort, built in 1727.

---

39 Punt (2009: 139). See on this aspect Raats (2012: 97), who pleads for open discussion and for proactive state policies: 'The fundamental question is if a church building is private property of a select group with a specific confession, or a building with a societal value.'

40 Ordinance 11, Article 8-3 Church order (*Kerkorde*) Protestant Church in the Netherlands (version 1 January 2013).

41 The private law foundation *Stichting Alde Fryske Tsjerken*, founded in 1970, acquired 42 church buildings and two campaniles in the province Friesland: see http://www.aldefrysketsjerken.nl/pag/kerken.php (accessed 7 February 2014). The *Stichting Oude Groninger Kerken*, founded in 1969, is responsible for 66 churches, 4 belfries and 34 cemeteries in the province Groningen: see http://www.groningerkerken.nl (accessed 7 February 2014). See Steensma (1981: 105–11). The religious buildings owned and maintained by other organizations (focusing on provinces Gelderland, Zeeland, the two Holland provinces) are also nearly exclusively Protestant (different denominations). The Brabant-based organization *Monumentenfonds Brabant* owns only four former Roman Catholic buildings.

The local religious community became too small to remain financially responsible for the maintenance of the complex.[42]

The costs of building maintenance and secularization

In December 2012, data from the Central Office for Statistics (*Centraal Bureau voor de Statistiek* – CBS) highlight the continuing process of secularization of the Netherlands (Schmeets 2012).[43] Only 55 per cent of the adult population claims to be religious. Furthermore, church attendance has declined significantly (Kregting 2011: 4). The changing religious demography, coinciding with a geographic demographic change (growth of agglomerations and depopulation of rural areas), leads to a large number of listed old churches being redundant.[44] In the years to come, this will be the case for approximately 30–40 per cent of all church buildings of the Protestant Church alone.[45] According to the Cultural Heritage Agency (RCE) approximately 1,000 church buildings will have to close their doors in the next 10 years.[46] The situation of monasteries is even worse.[47] The RCE's forecast is that in the near future between 120 and 175 of these complexes will become redundant, most of them in the Southern – predominantly Roman Catholic – provinces of Brabant and Limburg (RCE 2013a: 33).

This development, combined with high maintenance and restoration costs, put the owners of listed church buildings in a difficult position. Being responsible for monumental buildings is a growing problem for the religious communities involved which are the two traditional Christian denominations: the Protestant Church in the Netherlands and, for historical reasons but to a lesser extent, the Roman Catholic Church.[48] Regardless of the status (listed/non-listed) of buildings,

---

42 Since 12 December 2012 the Amersfoort synagogue complex is the property of *Stadsherstel Midden-Nederland*. This organization for monument care also owns the former seminary complex of the Old Catholic Church in Amersfoort, including a listed former 'hidden church' (*schuilkerk*).

43 See also, for long-term trends, Velthuis and Spennemann (2007: 48–50) and de Vries (1990: 18–19).

44 This is with an exception for rural communities in the Dutch (orthodox Protestant) so-called 'Bible belt'. See, on the geographical variation, Knippenberg and de Vos (1989) and Knippenberg (1998). Redundancy of churches in rural areas is an older problem, existing already in the Reformation period: see Steensma (1981: 90–91).

45 Predicted by P.A. de Lange, president of the umbrella organization for Protestant churchwardens (VKB), in Mulder (2012).

46 Since 1975 already 1,340 church buildings have been closed, partly as a consequence of the merger of local congregations. In 2008, 8,323 churches were still in use. In the period 2012–2020 a number of 600–700 Protestant churches and 400 to 500 Roman Catholic churches are expected to lose their function. RCE (2012a: 7).

47 In 2013 special attention was given to this category of religious heritage: see RCE (2013a).

48 In 1990 the then *Dutch Reformed Church* (2.5 million members) owned over 900

their maintenance costs have become a heavy burden in light of decreasing financial resources.[49] In this regime of self-financing, church boards have to make difficult choices on a daily basis. The budgets of the seven Roman Catholic dioceses in the Netherlands are dominated by the maintenance costs of church buildings: in 2011 70.8 million euros (39 per cent of the budget) were spent for this purpose, compared to 63.6 million euros for personnel (35 per cent of the budget).[50] Monument status carries additional costs, such as growing investment in security measures.

As far as *listed* church buildings are concerned, the financial burden for Roman Catholic parishes is estimated at 13 million euros per year (Bernts and Kregting 2010: 27). High maintenance costs and limited funds leave church organizations faced with another difficult choice, namely between modern and right-sized buildings or old and expensive listed places of worship.[51] High costs compel traditional denominations to close redundant churches and to find solutions such as alternative use, sale of the building or even demolition (see below).

Direct and Indirect Funding of Religious Heritage

State support for the maintenance and restoration of listed religious buildings can be divided into direct – but partial – public support in the context of the granting system of the Monuments Act 1988, and indirect support which comes from the funding regime for religious organizations.

Direct State Support for Listed Religious Monuments

Support by local authorities exists, but is not important in financial terms compared with funding opportunities at the national level. In 2010 the provinces' own budgets for monument care subsidies amounted to approximately three million euros (Schellevis 2011: 19). Within the decentralized system, provinces are made responsible for granting national subsidies. Therefore, the focus will be here on central state support mechanisms.

The relevant legislation regarding *subsidies* for monumental buildings is the Monuments Act 1988, which underwent important changes in 2012 (*Evaluatie*

---

listed buildings, the *Roman Catholic Church* (5.6 million members) over 300 (de Vries 1990: 18).

49 For the Protestant Church the 2012 data on the national donation campaign show a decrease of 2 per cent from an estimated total of 189 million euros. Source: Raad voor de plaatselijke geldwerving (RPG) (2012).

50 Press information Roman Catholic Church (Kerkbalans 2013).

51 Velthuis and Spennemann (2007: 51) and Raats (2012: 93). See also the declaration of an adviser of the Protestant Church of Deventer about the choice between the listed fifteenth century Lebuïnus Church and a 1970s church complex, in Nationaal Programma Herbestemming (2011: 4).

Brim 2011; Elbers and Verfürden 2012). Article 34 provides a legal basis for subsidies for the *maintenance* of monuments. The focus on maintenance and not on restoration efforts is relatively new.[52] Regulation is delegated to the government (Ministry of Education, Culture and Science, OCW), responsible for the fixation of the conditions for subsidiation. The government regulation in force is laid down in a decree on the subsidiation for the maintenance of monuments (*Besluit rijkssubsidiëring instandhouding monumenten* 2013, *Brim* 2013)[53] and in the ministerial regulation for the maintenance of monuments (*Subsidieregeling instandhouding monumenten, SIM*).[54] The new subsidy policy comes down to the principle of 'going Dutch' or 'Dutch treat', which means 'paying one's own expenses'.[55] According to the *Brim* 2013 regulations (and the former regulations), church buildings are eligible for a subsidy with regard to maintenance, provided they have national monument status. The maximum of this subsidy for the category of listed religious buildings under the old regulation used to be 65 per cent of the subsidisable maintenance costs,[56] but since 2013 this percentage dropped to 50 per cent. The maximum grant will be 3 per cent of the reconstruction value of the building, namely the investment needed to rebuild a listed monument with the same construction materials and details (Article 1 *SIM 2012*). This new maximum for subsidisable costs compels the religious communities concerned to fill the gap with additional private funding (50 per cent instead of 35 per cent) in order to match government grants.

A more prominent position is given to professional organizations for the preservation of monuments (*professionele organisatie voor monumentenbehoud*), on the condition that they own at least 20 monuments (Articles 30–35 and 30–32 *SIM 2012*). This category has a preferential position when it comes to the allocation of grants in that they take precedence over all other applications.[57] This means that a local parish, owning one (or even a handful) church building(s) will be in a less favourable position when applications for subsidy exceed the upper limit. However, religious communities can also act as a professional organization for the preservation of monuments. This means, however, a change in the community structure for those denominations where church buildings are, in principle, owned by the local parish or congregation.

---

52 Until the end of the twentieth century the focus was primarily on *restoration* activities. See Hirsch Ballin (1988: 130–31), de Boer (2010: 127 and 132).

53 *Besluit rijkssubsidiëring instandhouding monumenten* 2013 – Brim 2013, *Staatsblad* 2012, no. 438.

54 Regulation of the Minister of Education, Culture and Science of 19 September 2012, no. WJZ/387165 (10152), *Staatscourant* 2012, no. 20420 (*Subsidieregeling instandhouding monumenten* 2012, *SIM* 2012).

55 See *Beleidsbrief Brim* 2013 (2012: 2).

56 Only a selection of the costs related to the maintenance of the *Rijksmonument* are eligible for subsidy (Article 4 and Annexe of *SIM 2012*).

57 See the granting priorities in Article 14-1 *SIM 2012*.

In 2011 – under the old regulations – the Cultural Heritage Agency invested approximately 58 million euros for the maintenance of 500 monumental assets, mainly buildings, out of which 31 million euros were spent on 230 religious buildings, for maintenance projects and for 'reuse' activities if listed buildings are selected for a new function (RCE 2012b). In 2012 grants were received for approximately 630 windmills, 550 church buildings and 460 other monuments. Out of a total budget of 49.1 millions euros, 9.2 million euros were made available for grants for the maintenance of 347 church buildings of the Protestant Church in the Netherlands.[58] From 2013, the budget for *Brim* grants amounts to 48.5 million euros per year.[59]

Although the regime focuses on the *maintenance* of listed buildings, it is complemented by additional regular *restoration* budget amounting to 37 millions euros a year (data 2013).[60] Every year 20 million euros of this regular budget is given to restoration grants awarded by provincial authorities, for the restoration of windmills, castles and churches. In September 2012, a special *incidental investment programme* for listed buildings was announced. Its aim is primarily economic in nature: fighting the recession, which has a negative impact on the restoration sector, through an investment of 47.2 million euros. An amount of 27.2 million euros is dedicated to six restoration projects, all but one concerning religious buildings (three Roman Catholic and two Protestant churches).[61]

With these diverse government policies, the Dutch State complies with its obligations under Article 6 of the Granada Convention 1985 'to provide financial support by the public authorities for maintaining and restoring the architectural heritage on its territory, (…) to resort (…) to fiscal measures to facilitate the conservation of this heritage' and 'to encourage private initiatives for maintaining and restoring the architectural heritage'.[62]

In 1986 the Interecclesiastical Contact in State-affairs (*Interkerkelijk Contact in Overheidszaken*), an umbrella organization representing Christian and Jewish denominations, and the state agency responsible for monument care (*Rijksdienst voor de Monumentenzorg*) suggested the creation of a special, separate regime for religious buildings, including a separate budget, a structural platform for dialogue and advice and the creation of a government agency for this special subcategory

58 See the data in 'Monumentensubsidie voor 347 PKN-kerken' (2012), available at: http://www.kerkrentmeester.nl/site/index.php/artikelen/gebouwen/gebouwen_kerken/Monumentaal/monumentensubsidie_voor_347_pkn-kerken (accessed 8 February 2014).

59 Government letter 16 November 2011, *Parl. Doc.* Tweede Kamer 2010–2011, 32156, no. 31, 6.

60 Government letter 16 November 2011, *Parl. Doc.* Tweede Kamer 2010–2011, 32156, no. 31, 1–6.

61 Government letter 6 September 2012, *Parl. Doc.* Tweede Kamer 2012–2013, 32156, no. 42, 3.

62 Article 6 of the *Convention for the Protection of the Architectural Heritage of Europe* (Granada Convention 1985). The Netherlands ratified this convention in 1994.

(*kerkelijke gebouwendienst*).[63] Two years later the issue was addressed in an expert report for the Dutch government. The experts recommended increasing state support for the maintenance of listed religious buildings to 80 per cent of the eligible costs, instead of 40 per cent (for restoration the grants amounted to 50 per cent of the costs) (Hirsch Ballin 1988: 136 and 126–7).[64]

In 2013, grants by central public authorities for the maintenance of listed religious buildings underwent a significant decrease per selected project. This is the result of changes in the granting system as such,[65] but this new regulation, limiting maintenance grants for *all categories* at 50 per cent, puts the subcategory of monumental religious buildings in a less advantageous position in the long term. Under the old regulations criteria, a very high share of the global budget for maintenance grants went to the subcategory of religious buildings.[66] Nevertheless, in financial terms owners of religious buildings will still keep a proportionally strong position under the new granting regime. Given that direct support for listed buildings remains partial, namely limited to a proportion of subsidisable costs, indirect state support for religious communities granted on religious grounds can be important too.

Indirect State Support for Religious Communities: Tax Instruments

The Dutch regime of separation of state and religion includes the principle that religious activities are to be covered by religious communities themselves. However, they benefit from indirect state support, mainly through tax facilities (exemption and deductibility), related to – substantial – support from believers or private companies and funds on a national level (Van Sasse van Ysselt 2013a; 2013b).

The Institution for General Benefit status (ANBI)

Dutch tax legislation offers instruments to stimulate the self-financing capacity of churches *via* the regime of ANBI's (*Algemeen Nut Beogende Instellingen*, Institutions for General Benefit), a regime that allows churches to get ANBI-status. The tax deductibility regime for donations to ANBIs amounts to indirect state support.

---

63 See the text in Hirsch Ballin (1988: 250–53).

64 See Hirsch Ballin (1988: 135), pleading for a *national agency for religious buildings* and Jelsma (2008: 29), pleading for a *national organization for religious heritage* and a *national fund*. In August 1987 the minister announced plans for a National Fund for the maintenance of prominent (voluminous) monumental churches (*grote kerken*) (Hirsch Ballin 1988: 135).

65 A change partially based on the advisory report of Elbers and Verfürden (2012).

66 Policy letter 9 July 2009, *Parl. Doc.* Tweede Kamer 2008–2009, 31700 VIII, no. 212.

The two religious groups most involved in the issue of heritage preservation, Protestant and Roman Catholic parishes, are in a very different situation when it comes to the financial behaviour of their members (*offerbereidheid* – willingness to pay for the church) as is shown in recent figures (Kregting 2013: 3). While the Roman Catholic Church, in 2009, benefited from an average contribution per member and per year of 14 euros, the Protestant Church in the Netherlands received 91 euros. One understands that the average Protestant parish gets presumably more indirect state support via tax benefits than a Roman Catholic parish, due to the higher level of contributions, in combination with the fact that tax deductability is not available for all contributions to churches (or cultural and other organizations) but only starts from a minimum donation level (1 per cent of the taxable income and a minimum of donations of 60 euros). Tax deductability regulations are formally equal for the contributions to all religious groups (and for other non-religious ANBIs as well), but it appears that the outcome is probably unequal while tax deductions are proportionally higher for donations by persons with a higher income.[67]

A new category for tax deductibility: the 'Cultural ANBI'[68]

A recent change in tax policies is relevant here. Since 2012 a higher tax deductability is applicable to donations in the cultural sphere by introducing a 'multiplyer' of 125 per cent for personal donations and 150 per cent for donations by companies for tax deductibility,[69] a tax base reduction accepted by the European Commission.[70] The 'multiplyer' should stimulate the cultural sector to become less dependent on government subsidies and to raise more funds from private sources. For this purpose a new subcategory, the *Cultural ANBI*, was introduced.

Organizations for monument care are included in this new category. The national tax service website warns that 'churches and religious organizations are not eligible for the Cultural ANBI status'.[71] Therefore donations to the *Stichting Oude Groninger Kerken* and de *Stichting Oude Friese Kerken*, heritage organizations entirely focused on the maintenance of religious buildings[72] (but no church or religious organizations themselves), are 'matched' by the state on

67 Tax level amounts to 52 per cent for the segment of taxable income starting from 55,991 euros per year.

68 See on this topic Vrieling and Bruggink (2012), Bruggink and Hopman (2012).

69 Article 6-39a *Wet inkomstenbelasting 2001* [Personal Income Tax Act 2001] and Article 16-3 *Wet op de vennootschapsbelasting 1969* [Corporate Income Tax Act 1969]. The tax measure ends on 31 December 2016, but will probably be prolonged.

70 Decision 20 March 2013, C(2013) 1502 final, http://ec.europa.eu/competition/state_aid/cases/246177/246177_1418793_56_2.pdf (accessed 10 February 2014).

71 Detailed information on: http://www.belastingdienst.nl/wps/wcm/connect/bldcontentnl/belastingdienst/prive/relatie_familie_en_gezondheid/schenken/giften_aan_goede_doelen/culturele_anbi/ (accessed 10 February 2014).

72 See the section *Tensions between private ownership and heritage preservation* above.

the new 125 per cent deductibility level for Cultural ANBIs, while donations to religious communities who remain themselves responsible for the maintenance of a higher number of monumental churches are qualified as donations for regular ANBI's (100 per cent tax deductibility).[73]

Here a distinction, based on the religious character of the organization and not related to its cultural activity or value, is suggested between religious owners of religious buildings with monument status and non-religious monument care organizations owning and/or maintaining religious buildings. This difference in treatment is only superficial. Many religious communities already established separate legal persons focusing on the maintenance and exploitation of their historical churches long before the introduction of the Cultural ANBI. These legal persons are also eligible for the cultural ANBI-status (and thus for the related tax benefits). A quick survey[74] suggests that the size of the denomination determines the use made of this new tax benefit. Cultural ANBI's for Protestant churches predominantly belong to the Protestant Church in the Netherlands while the smaller Protestant denominations are quasi absent.[75]

Monitoring the fiscal effects of financial efforts made by religious communities themselves makes sense. Direct state support for heritage protection is, after all, to be matched by these private efforts. Since 1 January 2013, applying for direct state support (the *Brim*-subsidy) means an increase (of 43 per cent) of this 'matching' level for religious owners of monumental churches. In this context a (higher) tax benefit stimulating private support for religious monumental buildings can fill part of the gap created between the old (65 per cent) and the new (50 per cent) *Brim* subsidy level.

However, such an improvement does not make other ways – such as alternative uses – of seeking the good maintenance of religious heritage useless.

73 As an example, for 1,000 euros donated for a regular ANBI, the taxpayer will pay 480 euros (and the state 520 euros), while the same taxpayer will have to pay only 220 euros (and the state 780 euros) within the scheme of the Cultural ANBI.

74 See the Dutch Tax and Customs Administration's ANBI-database: http://www.belastingdienst.nl/wps/wcm/connect/bldcontentnl/themaoverstijgend/rekenhulpen/programma_anbi_opzoeken (accessed 10 February 2014).

75 Remonstrant Brotherhood, Mennonite Church, Old-Catholic Church, Christian Reformed Churches (a small Reformed denomination, owning a handful listed buildings) did not or only in a few cases, apply yet for the cultural ANBI status. The same goes for the Reformed Churches in the Netherlands.

Salvation through Alternative Uses? Is there a Future for Alternative Uses?

On Solutions for Redundant Buildings

Regarding the issue of alternative use, the policy regarding cultural built heritage focuses on the prevention of a situation where redundant buildings remain vacant, a situation for approximately 1,000 monumental buildings in the Netherlands in 2008 (Strolenberg 2011: 14). This means that all possible alternative new functions have to be looked at when a religious community decides to terminate regular religious services in a monumental building. State support for the preservation of listed religious buildings is not in place for *religious reasons*. The focus on preventing monuments being vacant is not the equivalent of policies stimulating religious use, but primarily aims at stimulating the research on all possible options for alternative use.

This tendency consisting in the preservation of religious buildings beyond their primary use has already been displayed 25 years ago by the Council of Europe Parliamentary Assembly, recommending member states to:

> (11.5.) promot[e] projects for reuse and readaptation which are not incompatible with the original function of the building and do not cause irreversible alteration to the original fabric;
> (11.6.) provid[e] funds or tax benefits for the restoration, repair and maintenance of religious buildings, whether in use or redundant, in order to ensure they are not abandoned;
> (11.7.) encourag[e] a more imaginative use of existing religious buildings;[76]

The recommendations of the Council of Europe, including the third one, were followed,[77] albeit with some reluctance. It is true that where religious buildings are transformed, especially for non-religious use, most of their *interior* loses its function or is even considered to be an obstacle for the new function.[78] The 're-adaptation' or even 'recycling' of listed religious buildings has its limits, given the growing number of these redundant religious buildings and the accompanying architectural and sometimes ecclesiastical constraints (Meijers 2009: 72–8; Hendriks 2013). Furthermore, ecclesiastical views on the religious value or even the sacral status of a church building differ according to the denominations involved,[79] as do their organizational structures, and thus have consequences for the choices to be made.

---

76 Council of Europe, Parliamentary Assembly (1989).

77 Reuse-solutions are a cornerstone for the modernization of government policies regarding built cultural heritage: see *Beleidsbrief Modernisering Monumentenzorg* (2009).

78 See examples in de Vries (1990: 23) and Kroesen (2013).

79 On the different viewpoints in ecclesiastical terms: for Protestantism, van der

In 2012 the government introduced a *Strategy for Churches* in order to find a solution for listed churches likely to be funded with government grants but which are not in use for religious purpose anymore (*Beleidsbrief Brim 2013* 2012: 4–5). Since 2013, grants for maintenance are only available if the owner, the religious community, provides a 'Declaration of permanent use' (for six years) (Article 8-2, h, *SIM 2012*). This permanent use does not have to be a religious use. The accessibility of a building by the public is not a condition for state funding. The state's obligation under the Granada Convention 1985 to ensure 'reasonable access' to a part of its cultural heritage (Article 5) does not imply a *right* of the public to have access to heritage. Subsidiation is not conditional on the accessibility of the building for cultural use. In 1986 the Interecclesiastical Contact in state-affairs already supported the idea (for cultural reasons and the museal function of many listed churches) to open church buildings to visitors, on the condition that the government supports this policy and guarantees advice, guidance, security and publicity (Hirsch Ballin 1988: 251). It is considered to be an acceptable form of 'multifunctional use' for religious buildings (Hirsch Ballin 1988: 253).

More generally, various solutions were found for the surplus of religious buildings, especially when they have monumental status.

From Adaptive Reuse to Demolition

The Netherlands is densely populated and needs a careful land use policy. Therefore one option that was never envisaged was to leave buildings for degradation on purpose (by creating ruins). Adaptive reuse as a strategy for the preservation of built cultural heritage is integrated into national state policies and has its own granting-system. This strategy corresponds to an *entrepreneurial spirit*, that does not allow buildings to remain unused and unprofitable (de Vries 1990: 19). Private ownership not only means private responsibility for the maintenance of the building, but it also means that the religious owner has a certain freedom to act when a religious building becomes redundant (Punt 2009).

Religious recycling

What we see happening – for a long time already – are policies where religious owners are trying to find new religious users for their property, enabling them to maintain the original function of the building. The phenomenon is not new, but the religious pluralization fosters such religious recycling. In the recent past, numerous church buildings have been sold to other new religious groups, sometimes immigrant communities. In some cases the buildings have monumental status. New religious communities are therefore also eligible for state support for the maintenance of these buildings. The Belvédère research project gives a good picture of this policy of 'religious recycling': out of approximately 170 places

---

Lingen and Uytenboogaart (2008); for Roman Catholicism, Meijers (2009), (2012) and Hendriks (2013).

of worship (128 Protestant and 39 Roman Catholic buildings), 20 have been transformed into mosques, two into synagogues, six into Orthodox churches, and over 100 are now in use by other Christian denominations (Belvedere 2008a: 223–4). The data suggest that Protestant communities (25 per cent of the reported cases) use this solution more frequently than the Roman Catholic Church (11 per cent of reported cases).[80] In Amsterdam, Roman Catholic parishes were transferred to Syrian Orthodox[81] and Russian Orthodox parishes.[82] In 1979 the former Hoogduytsche synagogue in The Hague was transformed into a Turkish mosque.[83] Accommodating the special needs of religious newcomers is however not taken for granted (and this for religious reasons) when a non Christian religion, especially Islam, is the potential candidate (Jelsma 2008: 30; Hendriks 2013: 28).

Organizations specialized in the management of listed heritage buildings are in some cases prepared to become the owner of religious buildings without radical changes for the religious communities where the religious use of the building is concerned.[84]

Recycling – non-religious functions

A large number of religious buildings are reused for different non-religious functions. The Belvédère research project again gives an indication of possible subcategories (Belvedere 2008a: 224–8). Apparently in all these subcategories (except buildings converted into health care and social services places) church buildings of Protestant denominations are dominant. A majority of these buildings now serve for housing. Hence, the variety of recycling solutions is striking, ranging from office buildings, restaurants, theatres or industrial uses. Here we see (be it for Protestant and Catholic churches in only two dioceses), on a large scale, the implementation of what the Council of Europe Parliamentary Assembly advised in 1989, namely the 'more imaginative use of existing religious buildings' (Council of Europe, Parliamentary Assembly 1989). Yet, in 1961 already the University of Amsterdam rented, on weekdays, the Old Lutheran Church and made it her central promotion hall.[85] The Amsterdam New Lutheran Church became – after closure in 1935 – a showroom for tents and finally, in 1975, a congress hall for a hotel.[86] In Dordrecht, after closure in 1960, the sixteenth century Nieuwkerk was transformed in the 1970s into a supermarket and, finally, a kitchen showroom (de

80 The considerable number of Protestant denominations in this market of redundant/wanted religious buildings causes many intra-Protestant transactions.

81 This is the case of the listed Syrian Orthodox church in Amsterdam. The church is also in use by a local Opus Dei community and the Surinam Roman Catholic community.

82 Amsterdam, Russian Orthodox St Nicolas from Myra Church, former Roman Catholic Capucine church (municipal monument).

83 The Hague, Mescidi Aksa mosque, *Rijksmonument*, except for the added minarets.

84 For monumental church buildings, the lack of expertise on the owners' level is a problem in itself. See Hirsch Ballin (1988: 131).

85 Amsterdam, Oude Lutherse Kerk (1633), *Rijksmonument.*

86 Amsterdam, Nieuwe Lutherse Kerk (1671), *Rijksmonument.*

Vries 1990: 25) Already since 1984, the famous Speelklok museum in Utrecht, an internationally renowned array of self-playing mechanical musical instruments, is housed in the fourteenth century Buurkerk.[87] This type of (sometimes involuntary and chilling) change in functions has a long tradition and at least prevents church buildings from demolition (Steensma 1981: 96–7; Kroesen 2012: 95 *et seq.*).

Imaginative power is still present, where new solutions for redundant religious buildings have to be found. In 2013 a new type of reuse was introduced: the listed nineteenth century Roman Catholic St John the Baptist Church in Arnhem was partially transformed in a *memorarium* (columbarium) (Vermeulen 2013). Since 2012 a listed nineteenth-century Reformed church is reused as a liquor distillery.[88] At the same time the consequences of this type of creativity also causes feelings of discomfort, as shown by the discussion following the decision of a commercial owner of a listed seventeenth century monumental Reformed church to transform it into a sushi restaurant[89] or the choice to set up a day nursery in a monumental former Roman Catholic parish church.[90] These controversial cases illustrate a problem that will arise when the monumental value of the religious building concerns not only the architectural structure but also the church interior (de Vries 1990). The choice of a non-religious reuse leaves the possibility of a renewed religious use at a later stage. The listed former Roman Catholic St Boniface Church in Dordrecht was reused as a pop concert hall until 2013,[91] but now the municipality, which owns the church, rents it out for religious purposes again, seemingly meeting the support of the surrounding inhabitants (Bijl 2013). In 2013, the listed eighteenth century Uilenburger synagogue, property of the Amsterdam municipality, was handed over to a Jewish foundation.[92]

Demolition

Finally this – irreversible – solution was chosen for a quarter (257) of all reported cases in the Belvédère research project. Listing status does not exclude demolition. This argument plays a role in upholding listing decisions against the opposition by religious owners. Regarding the decision of the municipal authorities of Oss to list a closed parish church as a municipal monument, the Council of State recently

87 Utrecht, Buurkerk, *Rijksmonument*. Reformed church in 1579, closed for religious services in 1975.

88 See www.hoofdvaartkerk.nl (accessed 10 February 2014).

89 Zwolle, Reformed Bethlehemkerk (1309), *Rijksmonument*, closed for religious services in 1998. See 'Zorgen om orgel Bethlehemse "sushi-kerk"', (daily newspaper) *De Stentor*, 21 March 2013.

90 Hilversum, Clemenskerk (1914), *Rijksmonument*. See 'Hilversum: commotie rond Clemenskerk', (daily newspaper) *Gooi- en Eemlander*, 11 March 2013.

91 See de Vries (1990: 23), who criticizes the consequences for the valuable interior of this church.

92 Since 1997 the synagogue is in use by a modern-progressive Jewish community, Beit Ha'Chidush (see: http://www.beithachidush.nl/english (accessed 12 November 2014).

held that 'the listing decision does in itself not stand in the way of demolition [...] of the church building'.[93]

In addition ecclesiology has its influence on the possible solutions: this is visible for the Roman Catholic Church (Meijers 2009: 78; Hendriks 2013). The Protestant Church also prefers, like the Roman Catholic Church does, demolition where acceptable forms of profane reuse are absent (Van der Lingen 2009: 98), but there is obviously a difference in practice between the two denominations. The Belvedere research project revealed 51 demolition cases out of a number of 511 Protestant redundant churches and 206 demolished Roman Catholic churches out of 366 cases (Belvedere 2008a: 224). However, budgetary arguments are of some weight too (Raats 2012: 94–5). Geographically many churches have a prominent and central location, making the property a top price building land after demolition (Steensma 1981: 96). Evidently, this aspect will be taken into account when a choice has to be made between reuse and demolition, especially where local church finances are under pressure. A future monument status is, in this context, a serious threat: demolition will be more problematic and the perspective for the church community will be the reverse: funds will have to be diverted away from religious uses to pay for the maintenance of the monumental church building. Monumental status 'often proves more of a handicap than an honor' (Homer 1996: 327; Raats 2012: 97). The demolition of a large proportion of post-World War II church buildings is a growing concern.[94]

Church demolition is a painful process for the broader community in general, but for religious congregations and church authorities in particular, and often a source of conflict between these stakeholders (Velthuis and Spennemann 2007: 53). Several conflicts on licences for demolition (and on refusal of licences) ended through adjudication by courts.[95]

*Multi-functional use (*nevenfunctie*): less radical, but attractive*

In 1988 – at the request of the Dutch government – the possibility of multifunctional use was studied by the expert-commission Hirsch Ballin (Hirsch Ballin 1988: 131–13). Multifunctional use introduces a solution not affecting the original religious function of the building. By new functions, the commission mainly meant 'non religious meetings and activities' such as 'concerts, expositions, lectures, tourist visits' (Hirsch Ballin 1988: 131–3). They are added to the original function

93 Council of State, 22 May 2013, LJN CA0688, *Roman Catholic parish Oss v. Municipality of Oss*.

94 See Kroesen (2008), Vervat and Wesselink (2010) and Wesselink (2013).

95 Council of State, 8 September 2004, LJN AQ9966 (regarding the listed Roman Catholic Sacred Heart of Jesus Church in Breda), *Administratiefrechtelijke Beslissingen*, 2005, 290. District court of Almelo, 19 September 2003, LJN AK8277 (organization for the protection of monumental buildings unsuccessfully opposing the demolition of the twentieth century Roman Catholic Thomas van Aquino Church and school-complex in the Amsterdamese School-style).

in order to guarantee the maintenance of the building with a long-term perspective, depending on the possibilities offered by the building (such as the space available or the facilities needed, like a pantry, toilets and so on) and will have to be in harmony with the demands for the continued religious function or the sacrality of the building (Hirsch Ballin 1988: 131–3).[96]

The Belvédère research project has made an inventory of the use made of this solution: only a small number of 20 church buildings (65 per cent Protestant, 35 per cent Roman Catholic) did get additional functions. The Belvédère data are however not representative of the situation of the category of listed buildings. For a number of Jewish prayer houses that have been reused for decades in non-religious functions (or for religious use as a Christian house of worship), a return to the original function was made possible thanks to a combination of activities: this is for instance the case of the eighteenth century Uilenburg synagogue in Amsterdam.

The Belvédère research included a recommendation stating that preference should be given to this solution of religious use with new functions or transformation to a new function including the opportunity for a continuation of religious activities (Belvedere 2008b: 13). At the same time, decreased religious use exposes the religious community to financial risks, since some tax reductions are linked to the building being used for religious purposes for at least 70 per cent of its activities. Indeed, places of worship 'are exempted from property tax under a local government law, provided the building is used for religious worship at least 70 per cent of the time. The legal base for this tax is Article 132, section 6 of the Constitution and article 219 of the Municipality Act' (van Sasse van Ysselt 2014).

In his 2013 annual address, the president of the Protestant Society of Churchwardens (VKB) also pleaded for multifunctional use as a solution for the revitalization of church buildings, stressing that multifunctional use of church buildings was – especially in the Middle Age – the rule, not the exception (de Lange 2013: 3).

*Funding Reuse Possibilities and Minimum Protection (*winddicht maken*)*

The multi-function solution requires investments different from usual maintenance and restoration activities. In order to allow church building owners to adapt them for new additional functions while maintaining the religious use, a low renting loan of maximum 50,000 euros was introduced in 2009 (*Kerken Nevenfunctie-lening*). It is made available under the auspices of the *Nationaal Restauratiefonds*.[97]

---

96 See, on the limitations based on the sacral character of Roman Catholic church buildings: Meijers (2009: 71–3) and Hendriks (2013: 28–9). In spite of the potential financial attractivenesss, this solution is problematic for the potential risks for valuable church interiors: see Kroesen (2013) and Hirsch Ballin (1988: 132).

97 See: http://www.restauratiefonds.nl/restaureren/kerken/Kerkennevenfunctielening (accessed 12 February 2014).

A new – but small – subsidy product introduced by the Agency for Cultural Heritage (*RCE*) on 1 November 2011 supports policies that favour reuse in a new function for listed and non-listed buildings.[98] The maximum grant amounts to 17,500 euros and the applicant has to match the subsidy (or to find additional funds) for 30 per cent of the research costs (Article 8 *Subsidieregeling stimulering herbestemming monumenten 2011*). Owners and other stakeholders (Article 6-1, b) involved in a reuse-project can apply for this subsidy, available for research on the feasibility of a multi-functional use of the building (*haalbaarheidsstudies*). The budget for all subsidies was 4.6 million euros for the first year (2012–13) and 1.7 million euros for each following year (Article 7-1). Sometimes, and this is often the case for redundant churches, it will not be easy to find a new function for the building in the short term. In order to prevent demolition, long term vacancy (and pending a reuse solution), the *Wind en waterdichtregeling* offers small grants[99] to keep the building free from deterioration and collapse from, for instance, water damage.[100] Here emergency measures are envisaged, such as making broken windows weather-resistant, provisional repairing of worn-out roofing, or to shore unstable constructions. The budget for *wind en waterdicht*-grants was 1.6 million euros for the first year (2012–13) and 0.7 million euros for each following year.[101]

In this light a changed ownership structure seems to offer some advantages. Church communities selling their church building to a private partner negotiate future *religious use* (parallel to *cultural activities*) for a building now owned by a heritage foundation being in a better position to keeping up a monumental building.

Conclusion – Religious Heritage: A Future of Shared Responsibilities

The fate of religious buildings (all categories: listed, not yet listed, non-listed) depends heavily on the 'market' for alternative use. Heritage policies are framed until now in one simple formula, when it comes to the maintenance of buildings: the owner's (financial) self-responsibility combined with tightly measured state support. As a consequence of the weakening position of religious owners (both in demographical and financial terms) this burden is felt to be disproportionately heavy, especially where they do not apply for listed status for their buildings. The growing problems confronting the traditional churches will inevitably lead to a deterioration of the physical condition of important segments of Dutch religious built heritage.

---

98 Regulation of 12 October 2011, no. WJZ/337681 (8299), *Staatscourant* (State Gazette) 2011, no. 19007 (*Subsidieregeling stimulering herbestemming monumenten 2011*).

99 A maximum grant of 35,000 euros for 70 per cent of the subsidiable costs (Article 22 *Subsidieregeling stimulering herbestemming monumenten 2011*.

100 Article 17-1 *Subsidieregeling stimulering herbestemming monumenten 2011*.

101 Article 19-1 *Subsidieregeling stimulering herbestemming monumenten 2011*.

The new financial regime for monument care, focusing on maintenance costs for listed buildings, ended the differentiation in the amount of subsidies awarded to the different categories of *Rijksmonumenten*, a system that had beneficial effects for the category of religious buildings. This brings about an important reduction of state support for the maintenance of a listed religious building and – as a consequence – an important pressure on the religious community to raise the higher sums needed in order to fulfil the obligation to match state subsidies with 50 per cent of its own financial means. It is very uncertain that religious denominations responsible for the bulk of this category (especially the Protestant Church) and the smaller religious denominations with a proportionally high number of monumental church buildings or synagogues will be able in the long run to cope with this challenge. Here an improvement of the existing regime of partial state support is needed.

But a more intensive state financing will not come without cost. The substantial share of the subsidies spent on the maintenance (and restauration) of religious monuments inspired the liberal MP Van der Ham in 2012 to plead for a stronger 'return' to society. He suggested developing new decentralizing policies, supporting local authorities:

> In a country of "dominees" (reverends, protestant pastors) there is of course no shortage in church buildings, but often they do not have a religious function anymore. Churches even consider the demolition of the surplus. [...] We suggest other types of support, for instance through the *Rijksgebouwendienst* (national agency for state-owned buildings), to the local authorities.[102]

Traditional Christian denominations – experiencing high levels of church redundancy – are asking for a fair redistribution of responsibilities: 'if Dutch society wants these buildings saved in a good condition for the coming generations, the state has to take its responsibility.'[103] In 2008, the Belvédère research project suggested a close cooperation (and the development of a common policy) between public authorities and churches, including a structural financial involvement (subsidies, tax measures) of public authorities for religious buildings listed as municipal or provincial monuments (Belvedere 2008b). That same year the Protestant Church in the Netherlands and the Roman Catholic Church, in a joint declaration, stressed the fact that they alone bear the responsibility for 80 per cent of Dutch built religious heritage. They defend the idea of a stronger financial effort of the state, based on the national and cultural value of this category and pointed, when they compare the national policies with 'nearly all European countries', to

102 Proceedings parliamentary commission, 23 May 2012, *Parl. Doc.* Tweede Kamer 2011–2012, 32156, no. 34, 8.

103 Position of the Protestant Church of the Netherlands Kroesen (2008: 71). For a Roman Catholic point of view see Punt (2009).

the exceptional low level of Dutch state support.[104] This idea of increased state responsibility in a well-coordinated cooperation with all the other interested parties is also advocated by (church) art and architecture historians[105] and legal experts.[106] Here the societal value of built religious heritage (Raats 2012: 97) – and not a purely religious interest – is undoubtedly seen as a key argument for shared responsibilities. A stronger position of state authorities would also be in conformity with Dutch state obligations under the Granada Convention 1985 (Article 4).

References

Books and Articles

Ashworth, G.J. (2002), 'The conservation of the built environment in the Netherlands', in Phelps, A., Ashworth, G.J. and Johansson, B.O.H. (eds), 45–54.

Bijl, A. (2013), 'Sint Bonifatiuskerk wordt weer kerk' (daily newspaper), *Reformatorisch Dagblad*, 6 March.

van Bijsterveld, S.C. (2008), 'Religieus cultureel erfgoed: Gezamenlijke verantwoordelijkheid van kerk, overheid en samenleving', *Kerkbeheer*, 8(6), 177–82.

van Bijsterveld, S.C. (2010), 'Religion and the secular state in the Netherlands', in Durham, W.C. and Martinez-Torrón, J. (eds), 523–48.

Bisseling, H., de Roest, H. and Valstar, P. (eds) (2011), *Meer dan hout en steen – Handboek voor sluiting en herbestemming van kerkgebouwen* (Zoetermeer: Boekencentrum).

Blom, J.C.H., Fuks-Mansfeld, R.G. and Schöffer, I. (eds) (1995), *Geschiedenis van de Joden in Nederland* (Amsterdam: Balans).

Broekhuizen, J. (2011), 'Regelgeving en praktijk van overheden – beschrijving en praktijk', in Bisseling, H., de Roest, H. and Valstar, P. (eds), 95–110.

Boelens, O. and Meijers, T. (eds) (2009), *Het kerkgebouw als religieus erfgoed* (Bergambacht: Uitgeverij 2VM).

de Boer, S. (2010), *Traces of change. Dynamics in cultural heritage preservation arrangements in Norway, Arizona and the Netherlands*, PhD thesis, Radboud Universiteit Nijmegen.

Brasz, F.C. (1995), 'Na de tweede wereldoorlog: van kerkgenootschap naar culturele minderheid', in Blom, J.C.H., Fuks-Mansfeld, R.G. and Schöffer, I. (eds), 351–403.

104 Joint press release by the Roman Catholic Church and the Protestant Church in the Netherlands, 11 December 2008, reproduced in Boelens and Meijers (2009: 149–51).

105 Jelsma (2008: 30), Vervat and Wesselink (2010), Raets (2012: 97), Kroesen (2013), Wesselink (2013) and Velthuis and Spennemann (2007: 64).

106 Van Bijsterveld (2008: 179–81) and Stasssen (2009: 131).

Bruggink, H.P. and Hopman, J.P. (2012), 'Wijziging monumentenaftrek per 2012', *Weekblad voor Privaatrecht, Notariaat en Registratie*, no. 6917, 111–15.
Doevendans, K. and van der Harst, G. (eds) (2004), *Het kerkgebouw in het postindustriële landschap*, Zoetermeer, Boekencentrum.
Doevendans, K., Schram, A., Kvan Velzel and van Velzel, W. (eds) (2007), *Kansen voor kerkgebouwen: vragen en uitdagingen bij hergebruik en herbestemming* (Utrecht: Libertas – Protestantse Kerk in Nederland).
van Drimmelen, L.C. and van der Ploeg, T.J. (eds) (2004), *Kerk en Recht* (Utrecht: Lemma).
von der Dunk, Th.H. (1996), 'De Bataafse omwenteling en de bouwkunst. De betekenis van het jaar 1795 voor de Nederlandse architectuur. Een eerste balans', *BMGN – Low Countries Historical Review*, 111: 3, 314–43.
Durham, W.C. and Martinez-Torrón, J. (eds) (2010), *Religion and the Secular State: Interim National Reports* (Provo: The International Center for Law and Religion Studies – Brigham Young University).
Fornerod, A. (2010), 'Funding religious heritage', RELIGARE Working Paper no. 5, available at: http://www.religareproject.eu/system/files/Religare%20WP6%20Fornerod%20on%20Funding%20Religious%20Heritage%2028%20June-1.pdf (accessed 5 February 2014).
Garrioch, D. (2003), 'Sounds of the city: the soundscape of early modern European towns', *Urban History*, 30: 1, 5–25.
Gielis, M. (1998), 'Reformatie na de Contrareformatie: de betekenis van de vrede van Münster (1648) voor de geloofsbeleving van de katholieken in de bisdommen Antwerpen en 's-Hertogenbosch', in van Royen, H. and Müller, R. (eds), 26–42.
Hendriks, J. (2013), 'Een katholieke kerk onttrekken aan de eredienst', *Tijdschrift voor Religie, Recht en Beleid*, 4: 2, 23–33.
Hirsch Ballin, E.M.H. (Commission) (1988), *Overheid, godsdienst en levensovertuiging. Eindrapport criteria voor steunverlening aan kerkgenootschappen en andere genootschappen op geestelijke grondslag* (Den Haag: Staatsuitgeverij).
Homer, M.E. (1996), 'Landmarking religious institutions: The burden of rehabilitation and the loss of religious freedom', *The Urban Lawyer*, 28: 2, 327–47.
Jelsma, D. (2008), 'Hoe verder met de Godshuizen in Nederland', *Vitruvius*, 5, 26–31.
Jelsma, D. (2011), 'Van traditioneel gebruik tot herbestemming - Transformatie als kans voor kerk en samenleving', in Bisseling, H., de Roest, H. and Valstar, P. (eds), 111–50.
van der Kaaij, M. (2013), 'Monument overnemen? Alleen met bruidsschat' (daily newspaper), *Trouw*, 25 February.
Kaplan, B.J. (2007), *Divided by Faith. Religious Conflict and the Practice of Toleration in Early Modern Europe* (Cambridge: Belknap Press of Harvard University Press).

Kennedy, J.C. and Zwemer, J. (2010), 'Religion in the modern Netherlands and the problems of pluralism', *BMGN – Low Countries Historical Review*, 125: 2–3, 237–68.

Knippenberg, H. (1998), 'Secularization in the Netherlands in its historical and geographical dimensions', *GeoJournal*, 45, 209–20.

Knippenberg, H. and de Vos, S. (1989), 'Spatial structural effects on Dutch church attendance', *Tijdschrift voor economische en sociale geografie*, 80: 3, 164–70.

Kregting, J. (2011), *Kerncijfers van de kerkgenootschappen die deelnemen aan de actie 'Kerkbalans 2011'* (Nijmegen: KASKI).

Kregting, J. (2013), *Kerncijfers van de kerkgenootschappen die deelnemen aan de actie 'Kerkbalans 2013'* (Nijmegen: KASKI).

Kroesen, J.E.A., Luthe, J.R. and Molendijk, A.L. (eds) (2002), *Religieuze ruimte. Kerkbouw, kerkinrichting en religieuze kunst: Feestbundel voor Regnerus Steensma bij zijn vijfenzestigste verjaardag* (Zoetermeer: Boekencentrum).

Kroesen, J.E.A. (2008), 'Tussen God en de Mammon. Het lot van te duur of overtollig geworden kerkgebouwen in Nederland', *Jaarboek voor Liturgie-onderzoek*, 24, 69–94.

Kroesen, J.E.A (2013), 'Wees zuinig op kerkinterieur' (opinion article, daily newspaper), *Nederlands Dagblad*, 8 April.

Kuipers, M. (2011), 'Saxa loquuntur? Spankracht en draagkracht van eeuwenoude stadskerken', *Bulletin KNOB*, 110: 5, 174–82.

Kuipers, M. (2012), 'Culturele grondslagen van de Monumentenwet', *Bulletin KNOB*, 111: 1, 10–25.

de Lange, P.A. (2013), 'Meer dan steen – over beleid en beheer van kerkgebouwen', presidential address 6 April 2013, Vereniging Kerkelijk Beheer, available at: http://kerkrentmeester.a-i4.nl/site/media/vkbdocs/Jaarrede 2013.pdf (accessed 13 November 2014).

van der Lingen, A. and Uytenboogaart, J.H. (2008), *Een protestantse visie op het kerkgebouw. Discussienota van de Protestantse Kerk in Nederland* (PKN).

Lubina, K. (2009), 'Protection and Preservation of Cultural Heritage in the Netherlands in the 21st Century', *Electronic Journal of Comparative Law*, 13: 2, available at: http://www.ejcl.org/132/art132-4.pdf (accessed 14 November 2014).

Meijers, A.P.H. (2009), 'Sacrum sacre tractandum. Over de canoniekrechtelijke aspeecten van de bestemming van kerkgebouwen en herbestemming van voormalige kerkgebouwen', in Boelens, O. and Meijers, T. (eds), 59–78.

Meijers, A.P.H. (2012), 'Over de bestemming en herbestemming van katholieke kerkgebouwen', *Nederlands Tijdschrift voor Kerk en Recht*, 6, 4–20, available at: http://www.ntkr.nl/bestanden/NTKR%206%20(2012)/NTKR%20(2012)4-20.pdf (accessed 14 November 2014).

Messner, F. (ed.) (2015), *Funding Religions in Europe* (Farnham: Ashgate).

Michman, J., Beem, H. and Michman, D. (eds) (1999), *Pinkas. Geschiedenis van de joodse gemeenschap in Nederland* (Amsterdam: Contact).

Mulder, E. (2012), 'Massaal kerkgebouwen dicht' (daily newspaper), *Trouw*, 2 January.
Onderwater, L.Q. (2006), 'Slopen? Een lege kerk is een weldaad!' (opinion article, daily newspaper), *Trouw*, 3 May.
Phelps, A., Ashworth, G.J. and Johansson, B.O.H. (eds) (2002), *The Construction of Built Heritage. A North European Perspective on Policies, Practices and Outcomes* (Farnham: Ashgate).
van der Ploeg, T.J. (2004), 'De kerken in het privaatrecht', in van Drimmelen, L.C. and van der Ploeg, T.J. (eds), 123–36.
Punt, J.M. (2009), 'Religieus erfgoed als gemeenschappelijke verantwoordelijkheid', in Boelens, O. and Meijers, T. (eds), 133–40.
Raats, K. (2012), 'Lege kerkgebouwen: slopen of omdopen', *Rooilijn*, 45: 2, 92–7.
van Royen, H. and Müller, R. (eds) (1998), *De vrede van Münster, 1648: scheiding binnen de Nederlanden & Staats-Brabant en de bronnen* (Gooik: Ballet).
van Sasse van Ysselt, P. (2013), 'Financiële verhoudingen tussen overheid, kerk en religieuze organisaties', *Tijdschrift voor Religie, Recht en Beleid*, 4: 1, 65–86.
van Sasse van Ysselt, P. (2015), 'Public funding of religious organizations in the Netherlands', in Messner, F. (ed.).
Stassen, P. (2009), 'Herbestemmen, of toch maar niet?' in Boelens, O. and Meijers, T. (eds), 125–131.
Steensma, R. (1981), *Kerken, wat doe je ermee?* (Baarn: Bosch & Keuning).
Steensma, R. and van Swigchem, C.A. (eds) (1986), *Honderdvijftig jaar gereformeerde kerkbouw* (Kampen: Kok).
Stiefel, B. (2011), 'The architectural origins of the great Early Modern urban synagogue', *Leo Baeck Institute Year Book*, 56, 105–34.
Stubbs, J.H. and Makaš, E.G. (eds) (2011), *Architectural Conservation in Europe and the Americas. National Experiences and Practice* (Hoboken: John Wiley & Sons, Inc.).
Strolenberg, F. (2011), 'Leeg!. Internationale biënnale leegstand & herbestemming', *Tijdschrift van de Rijksdienst voor het Cultureel erfgoed*, 4, 14–15.
de Stuers, V. (1873), 'Holland op zijn smalst', *De Gids*, 320–403.
Tillema, J.A.C. (1975), *Schetsen uit de geschiedenis van de Monumentenzorg in Nederland* (Den Haag: Staatsuitgeverij).
Velthuis, K. and Spennemann, D.H.R. (2007), 'The future of defunct religious buildings: Dutch approaches to their adaptive reuse', *Cultural Trends*, 16:1, 43–66.
Vermeulen, M. (2013), 'Memorarium in oude kerk bewaarplaats voor urnen' (daily newspaper), *Nederlands Dagblad*, 16 May.
Verplanke, C.J. (1963), *Subsidiëring van de kerkenbouw* (Arnhem: Vuga).
Vervat, N. and Wesselink, H. (2010), 'Nog even en de wederopbouwkerk is uit ons landschap verdwenen' (opinion article, daily newspaper) *De Volkskrant*, 25 June.

Vlaardingerbroek, P. and Pekaar, R. (2013), 'De Portugese Synagoge in Amsterdam. Een schatkamer van eeuwen geloof', *Tijdschrift van de Rijksdienst voor het Cultureel erfgoed*, 2, 12–13.

Vrieling, C. and Bruggink, H.R. (2012), 'Culturele instellingen', *Weekblad voor Privaatrecht, Notariaat en Registratie*, 6917, 105–10.

de Vries, A. (1990), 'Kerken maken schoon schip; hergebruik een zegen?', *Jaarboek voor de Monumentenzorg 1990*, 17–29, available at: http://www.dbnl.org/tekst/_jaa030199001_01/_jaa030199001_01_0004.php (accessed 14 November 2014).

de Vries, B. (2009), 'Reuse of religious heritage in the Netherlands', paper delivered at European Heritage Heads Forum, Vienna and Bratislava, May 2009, available at: http://ehhf.english-heritage.org.uk/upload/pdf/Vries.pdf?1391592074 (accessed 14 November 2014).

Wesselink, H. (2013), 'Herbestemming kerken vraagt gezamenlijke aanpak' (opinion article, daily newspaper), *Reformatorisch Dagblad*, 22 February.

Reports – Documents

Beleidsbrief Modernisering Monumentenzorg (2009) (governmental policy letter), annex *Parl. Documents* Tweede Kamer 2009-2010, 32156, no. 13.

Beleidsbrief Brim 2013 (governmental policy letter on BRIM 2013) (2012), *Parl. Documents* Tweede Kamer 2011/12, 33 000 VIII, no. 181.

Belvedere (2008a), *Onderzoek herbestemming kerken en kerklocaties. Een inventarisatie vanaf 1970* (diocese Haarlem, diocese Rotterdam and projectbureau Belvedere), available at: http://www.belvedere.nu/download/1239262995Onderzoek%20herbestemming%20kerken.pdf (accessed 14 November 2014).

Belvedere (2008b), *Aanbevelingen herbestemming kerken en kerklocaties aan lokale overheden en kerkelijke bestuurders* (diocese Haarlem, diocese Rotterdam and projectbureau Belvedere), available at: http://www.belvedere.nu/download/1239262995Aanbevelingen%20herbestemming%20kerken%20en%20kerklocaties.pdf (accessed 6 February 2014).

Bernts, T. and Kregting, J. (2010), *De kerk telt. De maatschappelijke waarde van parochies en gemeenten*, Rapport no. 594 (Nijmegen: Kaski), available at: http://www.ru.nl/kaski/onderzoek/publicaties/2010-0/ (accessed 6 February 2014).

Council of Europe, Parliamentary Assembly (1989), *Redundant religious buildings*, Resolution 916 (1989), 9 May.

Elbers, A. and Verfürden, H. (2012), *Advies aan OCW over een effectieve subsidieregeling voor onderhoud van rijksmonumenten* (Bodegraven: Arcadis), available at: http://www.eerstekamer.nl/overig/20120130/advies_aan_ocw_over_een_effectieve/document (accessed 6 February 2014).

Evaluatie Brim 2011 (research report 26 July 2011), annex *Parl. Documents* Tweede Kamer, 2011/12, 33 000 VIII, no. 170.

Nationaal Programma Herbestemming (2011), *Onderweg van Hemel naar Aarde. Leegstaande kerken: van incidenten-politiek naar clusteraanpak*

(Amersfoort: Nationaal Programma Herbestemming), available at: http://www.herbestemming.nu/sites/default/files/NPH-bijeenkomstverslag-kerkenplannen.pdf (accessed 6 February 2014).

Nationaal Restauratiefonds (2007), *Investeren in Monumenten 2010*, Hoevelaken.

Raad voor de plaatselijke geldwerving (RPG) (2012), *Verslag Actie Kerkbalans 2012 Raad voor de plaatselijke geldwerving (RPG)*, available at http://www.pkn.nl/Lists/PKN-Bibliotheek/Kerkbalans-verslag-actie-Kerkbalans-2012-Raad-voor-de-plaatselijke-geldwerving.pdf (accessed 8 February 2014).

RCE (2012a), *Een toekomst voor kerken. Handreiking voor het aanpassen van kerkgebouwen in religieus gebruik*, Amersfoort, Rijksdienst voor Cultureel Erfgoed, available at: http://www.cultureelerfgoed.nl/sites/default/files/u6/kerken2012.pdf (accessed 6 February 2014).

RCE (2012b), '50 miljoen euro toegekend voor instandhouding monumenten', available at: http://www.cultureelerfgoed.nl/actueel/persberichten/50-miljoen-euro-toegekend-voor-instandhouding-monumenten (accessed 8 February 2014).

RCE (2013a), *Een toekomst voor kloosters. Handreiking voor het herbestemmen van kloostercomplexen*, Amersfoort, Rijksdienst voor Cultureel Erfgoed, available at: http://www.cultureelerfgoed.nl/sites/default/files/u4/Toekomst_kloosters.pdf (accessed 6 February 2014).

RCE (2013b), *Monumenten van de prille welvaartsstaat. Selectievoorstel Beschermingsprogramma Wederopbouw 1959 – 1965. Adviesaanvraag door de minister van OCW aan de Raad voor Cultuur 2013* (Amersfoort: Rijksdienst voor Cultureel Ergoed).

Rijksoverheid (2011), *Kiezen voor karakter. Visie erfgoed en ruimte* (Den Haag), available at: http://www.rijksoverheid.nl/documenten-en-publicaties/kamerstukken/2011/06/15/beleidsvisie-kiezen-voor-karakter-visie-erfgoed-en-ruimte.html (accessed 6 February 2014).

Schellevis, H. (2011), *Restauratie en onderhoud van monumenten. Marktverkenning tot 2015*, research report for Vakgroep Restauratie, RCE and Nationaal Restauratiefonds, available at: http://www.vakgroeprestauratie.nl/doc/Restauratiemarktverkenning%20EIB%20tot%202015.pdf (accessed 6 February 2014).

Schmeets, H. (CBS) (2012), 'One in six go to church or mosque on a regular basis', *CBS Web magazine*, 21 December 2012, available at: http://www.cbs.nl/en-GB/menu/themas/vrije-tijd-cultuur/publicaties/artikelen/archief/2012/2012-3759-wm.htm?RefererType=RSSItem (accessed 6 February 2014).

Stoelhorst consultancy e.a. (2009), *Jaarboek Monumenten, Archeologie en Cultuurlandschap 2009* (Erfgoed Nederland).

VKB (2012), *Resultaten enquête: afstoting van kerkgebouwen*, Vereniging voor Kerkrentmeesterlijk Beheer (VKB), available at: http://www.kerkrentmeester.nl/site/media/vkbdocs/Afstoting%20kerkgebouwen.pdf (accessed 6 February 2014).

Chapter 12
Managing and Enhancing the Religious Heritage of Quebec

Solange Lefebvre

Quebec is unique in North America for its religious heritage. Eastern Canada is one of the oldest colonized areas, birthplace of Roman Catholicism, followed by an important settlement for Protestantism and Anglicanism. This province also stands out from Canada by its important movable and immovable religious heritage. In 2004, 2,751 places of worship built before 1975 or recently closed were listed in the inventory of places of worship in Quebec maintained by the Council for Religious Heritage (Committee on Culture 2006). Among these buildings are 2,023 Catholic places of worship (including churches, conventual chapels, oratories, sanctuaries and places of pilgrimage), 238 Anglican buildings, 181 belonging to the United Church of Canada, 25 synagogues, 49 Presbyterian churches and some buildings belonging to various other Protestant traditions (with Buddhists counting in this 2004 inventory only two recent pagodas and two Sikh gurdwaras).[1] Hence, this chapter presents aspects of public policies relating to religious heritage and its funding in Quebec. First, Quebec's specificity will need to be examined in the light of the importance of heritage in North America, as well as its policies with respect to religion. Secondly, developments over the last 15 years and some legal aspects will be addressed. A third point will cover the effects of classification and funding granted during this period, as well as places of worship undergoing transformation, following a recent survey by the Quebec Council for Religious Heritage (*Conseil du Patrimoine Religieux du Québec*, CPRQ). A brief summary of the main criticisms in the debate and a few illustrative examples will follow.

The Specificity of Quebec

To comment briefly on the system of state-religion relations, neither in Canada nor in Quebec do we find an official statement of separation from, or collaboration with, churches, but instead various measures and conditions for separation and recognition all at once. The charters of rights give rise to policies of neutrality, following rich and complex case law. On the one hand, there is the Charter of

---

1 For one example of the heritage of the First Nations, see Bousquet and Morissette (2008).

Rights adopted in Quebec in 1975, and 'some of the rights it enacts may not be contravened by any other Act; these include fundamental rights, political rights, judicial rights and equality rights'.[2] As for the Canadian Charter, it was included in the Canadian Constitution of 1982 and refers to God in its preamble. The Constitution of 1867, still in force, contains an article protecting the rights of Catholics and Protestants to a religious education provided by the state (repealed since in some provinces, including Quebec). Having acted as substitutes for the state in matters of education, health and social services, churches and religious congregations retain various links with communities. However, since the 1960s in particular, these services have been broadly secularized and brought under state control, but historical links and collaborations remain here and there. The concept of open secularity (*laïcité ouverte*) has been heavily debated since the secularization of schools that took place between 1998 and 2008, but it is not the subject of policy statements or official constitutional declarations (Proulx 1999). It should be noted that the final report by the Commission on Religious Heritage, held between 2004 and 2006, itself mentions positive secularity (*laïcité positive*) (Committee on Culture 2006: 11; Lefebvre 2012).

As regards more specifically the legal – and financial – framework applicable to religious goods, let us mention several Acts proven to be, on these aspects, fundamental. Briefly and first of all, the Act respecting municipal taxation (R.S.Q., chapter F-2.1) provides, *inter alia*, exemptions from municipal and school taxes (section 204) for properties of a religious nature, as follows:

> 8° an immovable included in a unit of assessment entered on the roll in the name of an episcopal corporation, a *fabrique*, a religious institution or a Church constituted as a legal person, and principally used for the exercise of public worship, either as an episcopal palace or as a presbytery, to the extent of only one for each church, and its immediate dependencies used for the same purposes;
> 9° an immovable used as a cemetery for human beings, unless it is operated for pecuniary gain.[3]

As the Roman Catholic Church owns the vast majority of places of worship, let us turn next to the Act respecting *fabriques* (R.S.Q., chapter F-1). This Act includes several elements on managing the *fabrique*. The following aspects are worthy of note:

> A "*fabrique*" means 'a legal person constituted under this Act and consisting of the chairman, the pastor of a parish or the ministering cleric of a chapelry and

2 http://www2.publicationsduquebec.gouv.qc.ca/dynamicSearch/telecharge.php?type=2&file=/C_12/C12.HTM (accessed 17 January 2014). The Human Rights and Youth Rights Commission is an independent body which works to promote and respect the rights set out in this charter.

3 http://canlii.ca/t/xf2 (accessed 17 January 2014).

the churchwardens *(parishioners elected annually by parishioners at a general assembly)* of such parish or chapelry' (section 1.1.g);
A *fabrique* is an ecclesiastical corporation whose object is to acquire, possess, hold and administer property for the practice of the Roman Catholic religion in the parish or chapelry for which it is constituted (3.13);
Among the powers of the *fabrique* are those to 'acquire, establish, erect, possess, maintain, administer and manage churches, chapels, parsonages, cemeteries, columbariums, burial vaults and other buildings' (4.18.c); it can similarly "acquire, possess, lease, hold, administer and alienate property, by any legal means and by any title, without being subject to the Act respecting lands of religious congregations" (4.18.m);
In the case of dissolution, the property of the *fabrique*, after payment of its obligations, shall revert to the bishop who shall convey it to one or more *fabriques* in his diocese (3.16).[4]

Managing the sales of Catholic churches therefore implies that the money is returned to the *fabriques* themselves, being variably distributed. In some cases, the bishop hands over the majority of the money to merged or consolidated parishes and keeps a share for distribution to the poorest parishes. Managing the property is therefore shared between the parish and the diocese.

Several other religious groups are governed by the Canada Not-for-profit Corporations Act (S.C. 2009: ch. 23) and, in Quebec, the Act concerning any 'non-profit entity or body (*Organisme Sans But Lucratif*, OSBL)'. They are also governed by the Act respecting lands of religious congregations. This means in particular that there is exemption from land value taxes, which represents a considerable fiscal advantage. The various religious groups buy or rent a place to facilitate worship. As we have seen, a place of worship exempted from land value taxes cannot perform activities for profit. This means that the body cannot seek financial gain. However, it can impose usage fees in order to maintain a balanced budget. This aspect is part of the mission of *fabrique* administrators or of anyone in charge of places of worship. Churches can rent a space for a cultural or social activity. If the place is exempt from land value taxes, any rent or charges received for its use are taxable.

Public Policies on Religious Heritage

As regards religious heritage, the last 20 years have been rich in public policy developments. The government has adopted several measures to ensure the protection and restoration of property belonging to the various religious traditions. In 1995, it created the Foundation for the Religious Heritage of Quebec (*Fondation*

4 http://www2.publicationsduquebec.gouv.qc.ca/dynamicSearch/telecharge.php?type=2&file=/F_1/F1_A.html (accessed 17 January 2014).

du patrimoine religieux du Québec), which became in 2007 the Quebec Council for Religious Heritage (*Conseil du Patrimoine Religieux du Québec*, CPRQ), tasked with administering grants for the restoration and conservation of buildings and generally stimulating interest in religious heritage.[5] Note that the institution *Musées de la civilisation* in Quebec is responsible for the conservation of movable heritage. Between 1995 and May 2012, the state invested 257 million dollars, to which must be added contributions from private partners, giving a total of 379 million dollars.[6] The CPRQ's private partners include, notably, the Roman Catholic *fabriques* of beneficiary places of worship, who must collect several types of donations, and other official corporation in charge of a religious group's administration and heritage. These consist of contributions from patrons, individuals and public or private companies associated with the restoration of the premises in one of many ways.

In addition, in 2004–2006 the Government of Quebec held a parliamentary commission on the issue. After substantial consultation, this commission resulted in the publication of the report *Croire au patrimoine religieux du Québec* (Believing in Quebec's religious heritage) (Commission de la culture 2006). Unlike other commissions with a religious remit – that of 1999 on religion at school (Proulx 1999) and that of 2007–2008 on reasonable accommodation (Bouchard and Taylor 2008), which were very controversial – this commission gave rise to very broad consensus around the need to do everything possible to safeguard Quebec's religious heritage. It should be noted that there was some urgency, given the combination of several factors: accelerated secularization, downsizing of religious personnel, confirmed negligence in several cases of heritage management, the unmanageable nature of heritage for several religious communities (congregations and parishes). The report addresses all aspects of religious heritage, including movable and immovable heritage, cemeteries, archives and intangible heritage.[7]

Over the years, the CPRQ has developed large consultation and mobilization networks. It now includes 12 regional round tables – bodies bringing together experts, architects, historians, managers from municipalities, cultural and rural officials, representatives from religious groups and from government. It has also established committees specialized in movable property and works of art,

5 Its website is very extensive, including several publications as well as an inventory. See http://www.patrimoine-religieux.qc.ca (accessed 17 January 2014).

6 This figure is valid for May 2012. Frequent, successive announcements about religious heritage grants are made, notably via CPRQ press releases.

7 We might add that Laurier Turgeon, holder of a Canadian Research Chair in Heritage and Professor in the Department of History at Laval University, was subsequently responsible for directing a vast project to gather together and inventory intangible heritage, the results of which are available online. See http://www.ipir.ulaval.ca (accessed 17 January 2014).

organs and archives.[8] It inspires, stimulates and acknowledges the efforts made by communities contributing to its objectives and the enhancement of heritage. Above all, it has created a detailed inventory of places of worship and conventual buildings that is accessible on the Internet.[9]

The main problem in recent years has been the growing number of buildings no longer used for worship, making it necessary to contemplate their sale or transfer, or else a lack of money to properly maintain temples still in use by practicing communities. The State of Quebec has never owned them. No level of government, whether federal, provincial or municipal, includes a department responsible for faiths. Religious heritage is partly recognized and supported, depending on the value that the state sees in it on these different levels.

Classification and Funding: An Initial Assessment

Religious heritage enjoys several types of legal protection. At provincial level, it is governed by the Cultural Heritage Act.[10] Several levels of classification exist. According to the law, at provincial level, the Government of Quebec may undertake a 'declaration of heritage sites' and a 'designation of cultural heritage landscapes'. The Minister of Culture may carry out a 'classification of documents, buildings, objects and heritage sites', as well as 'designation of intangible heritage, historical characters, events and places'. A municipality may decide on 'citation of documents, buildings, objects and heritage sites', as well as 'identification of intangible heritage, historical characters, events and sites'. These classifications are a recognition of the value of heritage, as well as a commitment to protect assets and to ensure transmission to future generations.

The legislative and explanatory documents do not suggest a list of precise evaluation criteria, but identify broad categories according to the 'heritage value' – whether archaeological, architectural, artistic, emblematic, ethnological, historical, landscape, scientific or technological – of a patrimonial asset. However, among the elements which it is recommended should be documented in order to enable recognition of an asset, are included aspects that suggest criteria: the age of the asset (as dates of design and construction must be documented), the artists or craftsmen who participated in its design or construction, the owners, its physical characteristics (aesthetics, artistic value and so on), characters and events related to the asset and the socio-political and religious context (Ministry of Culture 2012).

---

8 http://www.patrimoine-religieux.qc.ca/fichiers/FIC121106122001_2011-2012_cprq_rapport-annuel.pdf (accessed 17 January 2014).

9 http://www.lieuxdeculte.qc.ca (accessed 17 January 2014).

10 The Cultural Heritage Act (LPC) replaced the Cultural Property Act (LBC) on 19 October 2012. R.S.Q. P-9.002.

One example will serve to illustrate this: the set of properties designated as the Church of *Sainte-Famille de Boucherville*, including the church, the old rectory dating from 1896 and converted into a cultural and community centre, as well as the former convent of *Les Dames de la Congregation de Notre-Dame* (1890) – now a residence for the elderly – all on a magnificent site beside a river and facing the Boucherville Islands. At provincial level, it enjoys the following recognitions: classification by the minister as a 'historic monument' (1964) and 'work of art' (1964) and as a 'protected area' by ministerial decree (1976). At municipal level, it is a 'Heritage Site' (1989). Moreover, the whole square was designated a patrimonial treasure of the town of Longueuil in the spring of 2003 (south of Montreal). The CPRQ has its own classification and gives the church grade A (on a scale from A to E). This assessment relates to two aspects: the value of art and architecture and the regional assessment. The argument highlighted on the technical report is as follows: with regard to the value of art and architecture, the CPRQ considers that:

> The church contains numerous historical jewels, such as the carved decoration by Louis-Thomas Berlinguet, the works of Gilles Bolvin (high altar, tabernacle), of Louis Quévillon (pulpit), Nicolas Manny (baptismal fonts), Jean-Baptiste Roy-Audy (three paintings) and many objects of worship (that too are classified), including the Paschal candlestick (1846). The pulpit and balustrade were preserved, the chandeliers and the vault are quite exceptional.

As for the 'A' regional assessment, it refers to the fact that 'the church beautifully reflects all the historical stages of Quebec's religious architecture' (CPRQ 2003).

In respect of the funding issue, the question of classification is crucial, because it implies the possibility of government funding for up to 70 per cent of restoration and repair costs for places of worship, via the CPRQ. It is important to note that until 2014, only active places of worship, that is, those still being used for worship, had access to this funding. The government decided to eliminate the criteria of religious usage, and gave access to funding to private owners and non-profit organizations.[11] The Council may assign five types of rating for heritage interest, from A to E (for buildings built before 1945). However, only property with an A, B or C rating is eligible for grants to aid with restoration.

---

11 Since 2011, the owners of places of worship as well as municipalities could benefit from subsidies. Since then, the CPRQ has extended this possibility by including not only places no longer used for worship, but also other owners, such as non-profit organizations and private owners. The CPRQ can now fund alteration projects which meet heritage conservation criteria. It should still be for monuments built before 1945, although the CPRQ intends to modify this criterion in order to include more recent buildings. Information available at: http://www.patrimoine-religieux.qc.ca/fichiers/FIC140214114350_2014_02_14_cprq_communique_budget_2013_2015.pdf (accessed 10 April 2014).

A 2012 study by the CPRQ on 'transformations' in recent years is very instructive in this regard, showing how a favourable grading is important for the continued existence of the place. In April 2012, the CPRQ unveiled the first research findings into the situation of places of worship in Quebec, on closures, sales and transformations of churches and chapels since the inventory of 2003 (CPRQ 2012).[12] The highlights are as follows:

> 1. 10 per cent (270) of the total of sites listed have undergone such transformation;
> 2. In 20 per cent of cases, municipalities took charge of them, turning them into multipurpose and community rooms;[13]
> 3. Of the 270 sites concerned, 34 (12 per cent) had been destroyed (9 by fire, 25 demolitions). Of 66 places of worship that have closed since 2003, 24 are waiting for a new purchaser and 42 have been sold without having been totally transformed for the moment, most to private interests.
> 4. Undergoing transformation: 33 buildings built before 1900, 91 built between 1900 and 1945, 146 churches and chapels built between 1945 and 1975.
> 5. The attribution of heritage interest ratings is proving crucial, those of the CPRQ (A, B, C, D or E) as well as classification under the Cultural Heritage Act. Indeed, most of the buildings being transformed have lower grades D or E or were built after 1945 (227 in total). Only 43 benefiting from an A to C rating are being transformed. Only 14 sites classified according to the Act on Cultural Property are being transformed. The financial support from the CPRQ (70 per cent) for the restoration of religious heritage, eligible only for places of worship rated A, B or C or classified according to the law, appears to have been decisive.

In the case of sales, the new owners are often municipalities (46 cases) and some places retain their religious function by combining it with a community function. Forty-six locations were sold to other religious traditions (29 cases in Montreal), most to Adventist or Evangelical Christian groups and to ethnic Catholic or Eastern rite communities.[14] The private sector bought 93 churches or chapels, 'for commercial use (columbarium, offices, restaurant), but primarily residential use (multiple homes, residences for the elderly)' (CPRQ 2012: 3). In 35 cases, multipurpose projects were developed, which may include, in addition to space for worship, a community space and various rooms. Sixteen sites are now community-oriented, 22 culturally-oriented, 9 sports-oriented. We may note

---

12 http://www.patrimoine-religieux.qc.ca/fichiers/FIC120404170603_2012-04-04_cahier-1_etat-patrimoine-religieux.pdf (accessed 17 January 2014).

13 Non-profit use by the community. The space can thus be funded in part by one or other level of government.

14 The website of the Diocese of Montreal details various types of transfers: http://www.diocesemontreal.org/leglise-a-montreal/nos-lieux-de-culte/eglises-vendues.html (accessed 17 January 2014).

that this assessment dates from spring 2012 and can change rapidly, with many communities thinking about the future use of their place of worship.

Critical Aspects

At the heart of the very lively debates during these years rich in developments, we can identify four critical issues. For some, the expropriation of places of worship would be necessary in order to protect them better. Secondly, faced with the proliferation of new places of worship in the wake of immigration, people here and there are calling for an end to tax privileges. Thirdly, the protected places that can rely on government funding for their restoration have two conditions that may be challenged: being constructed before 1945 and having heritage value, determined according to several criteria. Fourthly, given the various rules governing the destruction of a place of worship, unique stories may surface.

Debate on Ownership

The ownership of places of worship was the subject of an important debate before the parliamentary commission set up in 2004. Researchers Luc Noppen and Lucie Morisset have campaigned for the expropriation of ecclesiastical assets in order that the state can retake control. In 2004, they painted a catastrophic picture of the current situation, recalling that less than 200 places of worship were protected at federal, provincial and municipal levels (Noppen and Morisset 2005a, 2005b). Although it is difficult to check these facts that they put forward, 135 parishes had apparently been abolished between 1995 and 2003, together with 453 disused churches and public chapels. Combining a very low rate of religious practice with funding problems, the Catholic Church in particular did not seem capable of managing these places of worship:

> Discussing the future of the churches with its members confines the questioning to representatives of less than 5% of the population (churchgoers and not the large numbers of affiliates), while it would be fair and much easier to invite the 95% who do not practice by virtue of historical traditions to participate in the reflection. (Noppen and Morrisset 2005a: 78)

Noppen challenges not only the fact that CPRQ grants are paid to religious groups, but also their very ownership rights, taking issue with, for example, the fact that *fabriques* are historically legitimate owners. As the community paid for the churches, they should be returned into the public domain.

The Commission on Religious Heritage of 2004–2007 did not retain this proposal, admittedly very complex legally, but decided to build instead on collective and multi-disciplinary mobilization around heritage. Beyond the issue of ownership, the central issue is that of the resources available to ensure the transmission of heritage to future generations. As has already been seen, hundreds of places are involved, and the state is seeking to maintain the balance between its own financial investment and that of the community. This probably is one of the main reasons for its insistence on investing in places that are still active with respect to worship. The state does not want to find itself owner of many places that are costly to maintain and used in a limited and *ad hoc* way. The degree of heritage value proves decisive in this sense.

Debate on Tax Exemptions and Zoning By-Laws

Another critical aspect relates to tax exemptions, as well as regulations related to zoning, under municipal jurisdiction: 'Zoning is the main regulatory instrument for implementing the Master Plan. It determines the future role of different areas of the territory in order to control the use of land and buildings, as well as the implementation, shape and appearance of constructions' (Intercultural Council of Montreal 2009: 8). However, new and minority religious groups escalate tensions when they want to build a place of worship in towns, suburbs or villages. The aforementioned document mentions several examples: unofficial emergence of new places of worship, without municipal permits or adapting the permit with respect to zoning, complaints from nearby residents due to the noise generated during gatherings of communities around buildings of worship, disparities between towns and boroughs in the city of Montreal, with respect to the criteria used to grant a name or a permit, and so on.

Places of worship on the municipal level cause fiscal, political and social issues (Matthew 2012; Gagnon and Germain 2002). Lands that these places occupy, old and new, represent a clearcut monetary loss for municipalities, which cannot collect any tax in line with the Act respecting municipal taxation (R.S.Q., chapter A-19, C.C.Q.).[15] For example, the question arises as to maintaining this beneficial Act, while religious denominations have variable social and community roles, certainly less important than in former times (Germain 2004), with public services having taken over these functions. According to Gauthier (2007), it is important to respect the historical heritage, beyond these immediate functions. And we should add that religious groups are still playing social roles, notably for newly installed immigrants and ethnic communities.

Legislative, cultural and financial challenges intertwine during the debate. How should we manage zoning permits and the new places of worship adopted by communities in a more or less formal manner? After a somewhat wild period of development of new sites, the City of Montreal, which is where the bulk of immigrants to Quebec are concentrated, has successively adopted several Master Plans (Germain et al. 2003). New places of worship often have a multipurpose mission, allowing ethno-religious communities to gather for worship, cultural celebrations and social events. Faced with this multiplication of places, exempt

15 See above the section *The Specificity of Quebec*.

of land tax, there are calls to contest this privilege, in the name of strict secularity (Council for the Status of Women 2011).

The Fate of Churches Without Heritage Status

Among the criteria for the precious classification that ensures financial assistance, as discussed above, we find that of the construction period (pre-1945) and that of the heritage value of the building, determined according to several criteria. There have been various calls to protect certain places beyond this pivotal year – until 1975 for example – but the State of Quebec fears the additional financial costs. The same goes for heritage value, within which community attachment is not taken into consideration. Here I can mention two unfortunate examples in this regard.

The first concerns the Church of Notre-Dame de Fatima. This very original church is part of heritage recently designated the 'white churches of the Saguenay' and was only built in 1964 (outside the CPRQ classification). The two architects who designed it are part of a North American architecture movement that imported modernism via formal expressionism into the construction of white religious buildings, several others of which are present in the region (Morisset, Dieudonné and Noppen 2004). Architect Paul-Marie Côté may have been inspired in his planning of the church by the chapel of the Palace of Dawn (*Palácio da Alvorada*) in Brasilia (Brazil) and the *Maison de la Culture* in Le Havre (France), both designed by Oscar Niemeyer (Bergeron 1987).

However, a decree by the diocese announced the end of its religious use in 2004.[16] Native American tipi-shaped, first it was sold to the *Coopérative de solidarité économique autochtone Kitchisaga* in 2006, which failed in its plans. So, in 2007 it was put up for sale once again. Since then, a private entrepreneur has acquired it and suggested several projects, including the construction of luxury condos and various community buildings for medical use in particular. However, these were all rejected; a motion to remove the municipal heritage status from the church has been filed and should be considered in early 2013. The withdrawal of this status could entail the demolition of the building that many consider a gem of Quebec architecture.[17]

The second example concerns a village church. In 2009, André A. Lafrance chronicled a small village's battle for the survival of its church, which did not enjoy a favourable rating. The village had a rather perturbed past due to various events and the prospect of losing the church seemed unbearable for many residents. The church had been destroyed by fire in 1837 started by British troops who suspected that the villagers were sheltering a cell of patriotic resistants. More recently,

---

16 http://www.evechedechicoutimi.qc.ca/page/paroisse-notre-dame-de-la-paix-jonquiere/ (accessed 17 January 2014).

17 'Church of Notre-Dame-de-Fatima: 125 citizens mobilized.' *Radio-Canada*, 19 December 2012. http://www.radio-canada.ca/regions/saguenay-lac/2012/12/19/002-rencontre-notre-dame-de-fatima-sauvegarde.shtml (accessed 17 January 2014).

many villagers were affected by the expropriation of land experienced by some members of their entourage in neighbouring villages, during the construction of a new airport at Mirabel in the 1970s. Generally speaking, residents have been experiencing pressure to move and relocate, the village is being emptied of its workforce. Several of its institutional pillars have become branches of a larger centre: savings bank, church (the parish was included in a regrouping of parishes whose *fabrique* council only includes a single member from the original parish) and leisure services. Saving the church from degradation, Lafrance (2009) says, has become the unifying project of what remained of the village:

> This identity project did not require them to abandon their differences. On the contrary, it was their individual differences which enabled them to add an original contribution to the community project. The micro-network of town dwellers wanted to protect the architectural "silhouette" of the village where they had chosen to settle. The members of the pastoral micro-network hoped to keep a place of worship at the centre of their daily lives. Those of the agricultural micro-network felt a duty to protect this legacy of their ancestors.

The two examples highlighted recall that the concept of heritage is polysemous and includes criteria other than those of age and artistic value. It is expected that many similar cases will arise in the near future.

Rebuilding a Church Without Heritage Status

One final example illustrates this time the complexity of funding rules regulating the destruction of churches. In Beloeil, a small suburban municipality, there are three churches, only one of which has heritage status. One of them suffered a fire in 2009 and a whole decision-making process ensued (Archambault 2009). It seemed obvious that one could very well deprive oneself of a church, happy to sell the land that had been vacant up to then. But several facts needed to be taken into account.

It turned out that the insurer could pay a sum of 2,300,000 dollars, only if a church reconstruction took place. On the other hand, if there were no reconstruction, the parish *fabrique* lost the land that had been sold a few decades earlier for an amount of 4,000 dollars, provided that its use remained religious. The sons of the seller wanted to recover the land and the adjoining park for a real estate project. The final element of the full picture of circumstances was that close to 20 community-based organizations from the locality had long wished to have premises that enabled them to come together in one place. Although the small town had no need of a church, it was then decided to rebuild it at a cost of 5,500,000 dollars. This was covered by the insurance, as was the mortgage arranged by the *fabrique*, the cost of which will be paid by the town of Beloeil via a rental contract for premises intended for organizations. The building will include a small place of worship, a wing for organizations and another for parish activities. The *fabrique* therefore remains its owner and the town is renting a part of the premises.

Conclusion

From what was said during the very stimulating exchanges at the conference on funding heritage, which has lead to the publication of this book, Quebec may be a point of reference for Europe. Its heritage is certainly less old and not as huge. But it has a very specific historical value. Above all, this province, like other parts of North America, did not hesitate to engage in a process of selecting churches which would have their continued existence assured. For some Europeans, closing a church is an almost sacrilegious gesture. However, it is true that everywhere choices must be made when faced with the large number of places of worship to be maintained, combined with the downsizing of religious officials and members taking care of them. Another aspect is to be emphasized. On both sides of the Atlantic, it has become common to say that, where we are, 'churches are being transformed into luxury condos'. So far, this has been true in a small number of cases that do admittedly enjoy high visibility. The last fiercely debated example is a large building owned by the religious community of Clercs-de-Saint-Viateur, adjacent to a big park. Citizens would have preferred a social/community use, but the building will eventually be transformed into luxury condos (Benessaieh 2011). However, according to reports, several buildings have been sold to other religious groups and today the majority fulfills social and community roles.

Laws governing the protection of heritage are of great importance to ensure the existence of religious heritage which, without state financial aid, finds itself significantly weakened. In this regard, the Government of Quebec has been taking strong action ever since the 1990s, equipped with clear policies and a very influential council. Too little, too late, some would say. It is true to say that this period was preceded by years of gross negligence, the extent of which we will never be able to measure. The climate of the early 2000s was marked by the impression of catching up late, as the state of several items of heritage was already very worrying, especially in the case of archives. In respect of built heritage, the number of decisions crucial to its future increase day by day, in the face of transformations of contemporary religious practices, the fluidity and *ad hoc* nature of which is increasingly taking the place of the stability of ritual attendance.

References

Archambault, H. (2009), 'Un incendie ravage l'église Sainte-Maria-Goretti', *L'œil régional*, 27 June 2009, available at: http://www.hebdosregionaux.ca/monteregie/2009/06/27/un-incendie-ravage-leglise-sainte-maria-goretti (accessed 17 January 2014).

Benessaieh, K. (2011), 'Pétition contre des condos dans l'ancien Institut des sourds et muets', *La Presse*, 17 March 2011, available at: http://www.lapresse.ca/actualites/regional/montreal/201103/17/01-4380206-petition-contre-des-condos-dans-lancien-institut-des-sourds-et-muets.php (accessed 17 January 2014).

Bergeron, C. (1987), *L'architecture des églises du Québec, 1940–1985* (Québec: Les Presses de l'Université Laval).

Bouchard, G. and Taylor, Ch. (2008), *Fonder l'avenir: Le temps de la conciliation: Rapport* (Québec: Commission de consultation sur les pratiques d'accommodement reliées aux différences culturelles).

Bousquet, M.P. and Morissette, A. (2008), 'Inscrire la mémoire semi-nomade dans l'actualité sédentaire. Les églises de Pikogan et de Manawan', *Archives de sciences sociales des religions*, vol. 141, 9–32.

Commission de la culture (2006), *Croire au patrimoine religieux du Québec* (Québec), available at: http://www.ipir.ulaval.ca/pdf/2006_Croire-au-patrimoine-religieux_Commission-Culture.pdf (accessed 18 January 2014).

Conseil du patrimoine religieux du Québec (2003), *Inventaire des lieux de culte du Québec*, Église Sainte-Famille. Fiche no. 2003–16–296.

Conseil du patrimoine religieux du Québec (2012), État du patrimoine religieux, 1, April, available at: http://www.patrimoine-religieux.qc.ca/fichiers/FIC120404170603_2012-04-04_cahier-1_etat-patrimoine-religieux.pdf (accessed 17 January 2014).

Conseil du statut de la femme (Mars 2011), *Avis: Affirmer la laïcité, un pas de plus vers l'égalité réelle entre les femmes et les hommes* (Québec: Gouvernement du Québec).

Conseil interculturel de Montréal (Mai 2009), *Cohabitation urbaine et usages des lieux de culte minoritaires. Dynamisme social dans la gestion municipale.* Avis sur la gestion municipale des lieux de culte minoritaires (Montréal: Ville de Montréal).

Estivalèzes, M. and Lefebvre, S. (eds) (2012), *Le programme d'éthique et culture religieuse: De l'exigeante conciliation entre le soi, l'autre et le nous* (Québec: Les Presses de l'Université Laval).

Fourcade, M.B. (ed.) (2007), *Patrimoine et patrimonialisation: Entre le matériel et l'immatériel* (Québec: Les Presses de l'Université Laval).

Gagnon, J.E. and Germain, A. (2002), 'Espace urbain et religion: Esquisse d'une géographie des lieux de culte minoritaires de la région de Montréal', *Cahiers de Géographie du Québec*, 46: 128, September, 143–63.

Gauthier, R. (2007), 'Un cœur à chœur: La figure du patrimoine ecclésial et les réaménagements d'églises au Québec', in Fourcade, M.B. (ed.), 295–310.

Germain, A. et al. (2003), *Les pratiques municipales de gestion de la diversité à Montréal* (Montréal: Institut national de la recherche scientifique – Urbanisation culture et société), available at: http://im.metropolis.net/GESTION_DIVERSIT__MONTR_AL_FINAL-030616.pdf> (accessed 23 March 2012).

Germain, A. (2004), 'L'aménagement des lieux de culte des minorités ethniques à Montréal: L'Autre, là où on ne l'attendait pas', in Gotman, A. (ed.), 425–44.

Gotman, A. (ed.) (2004), *Ville et hospitalité* (Paris: Maison des sciences de l'homme).

Lafrance, A.A. (2009), 'Le sauvetage d'une église, la survivance d'une communauté', in Lefebvre (ed.), 337–45.

Lefebvre, S. (ed.) (2009), *Le Patrimoine religieux du Québec: Éducation et transmission du sens* (Québec: Les Presses de l'Université Laval).

Lefebvre, S. (2012), 'L'approche québécoise, entre laïcité et sécularité', in Estivalèzes, M. and Lefebvre, S. (eds), 85–110.

Mathieu, S. (March 2012), 'Les impacts du pluralisme religieux sur le cadre bâti en milieu urbain: Le cas de Montréal', *Site Observatoire des religions*, Faculté de théologie et de sciences des religions, Université de Montréal (CRCS, CIPG), 19 pages, available at: http://www.observatoiredesreligions.ca/documents.html (accessed 17 January 2014).

Ministère de la culture (2005), *La protection du patrimoine au Québec: À propos de la loi sur les biens culturels* (Québec: Gouvernement du Québec), available at: http://www.mcc.gouv.qc.ca/fileadmin/documents/publications/mcccf-statut.pdf (accessed 17 January 2014).

Ministère de la Culture. Andréane Beloin (October 2012), *La Loi sur le patrimoine culturel. Guide pratique destiné aux municipalités* (Québec: Gouvernement du Québec), available at: http://www.mcc.gouv.qc.ca/fileadmin/documents/patrimoine/guide-municipalite-vf-19-10-2012.pdf (accessed 17 January 2014).

Morisset, L.K., Dieudonné, P. and Noppen, L. (eds) (2004), *Patrimoines modernes: L'architecture du vingtième siècle à Chicoutimi* (Québec: Presses de l'Université du Québec).

Noppen, L. and Morisset, L.K. (eds) (2005a), *Les églises du Québec: Un patrimoine à réinventer* (Québec: Presses de l'Université du Québec).

Noppen, L. and Morisset L.K. (2005b), 'L'avenir des églises du Québec: Contours et enjeux', in Turgeon, L. (ed.), 73–88.

Proulx, J.P. and Groupe de travail sur la place de la religion à l'école (1999), *Laïcité et religions: Perspective nouvelle pour l'école québécoise* (Québec: Gouvernement du Québec, Ministère de l'éducation).

Radio-Canada (2012), 'Église Notre-Dame-de-Fatima: 125 citoyens se mobilisent', *Radio-Canada*, 19 December 2012, available at: http://www.radio-canada.ca/regions/saguenay-lac/2012/12/19/002-rencontre-notre-dame-de-fatima-sauvegarde.shtml (accessed 17 January 2014).

Turgeon, L. (2005), *Le patrimoine religieux du Québec: Entre le cultuel et le culturel* (Québec: Les Presses de l'Université Laval).

Quebec and Canada Legislation

An Act respecting municipal taxation (R.S.Q., chapter F-2.1)

An Act respecting *fabriques* (CQLR chapter F-1)

Canada Not-for-profit Corporations Act (S.C. 2009, chapter 23)
An Act Respecting Lands of Religious Congregations (CQLR, chapter T-7)
Cultural Heritage Act (R.S.Q., chapter P-9.002), available at: http://www2.publicationsduquebec.gouv.qc.ca/dynamicSearch/telecharge.php?type=2&file=/P_9_002/P9_002.html (accessed 12 April 2014).

Chapter 13

Historical Trajectories, Institutional Particularities: The Funding Regime for Religious Heritage in Turkey

Tuğba Tanyeri-Erdemir

Introduction

The funding regime for religious cultural heritage in Turkey is complicated and can be comprehended only when considered through the historical developments that have brought about the institutional particularities of the system. The institutions of the secular Republic of Turkey that are connected with the maintenance, repair and restoration of cultural heritage are expected to be secular in their organization and operation. However, historical developments related to the management and control of religious diversity in the early decades following the founding of the Turkish Republic have brought about a particular division of authority and responsibility between the Ministry of Culture and Tourism and the Directorate General of Foundations, two major bodies within government for listing cultural property and organizing funds for conservation of heritage. The institutional structure of the Directorate General of Foundations represents a significant continuation of the Ottoman system of administration and therefore is based on religious, that is Sunni-Islamic, ideological underpinnings. This has ramifications in terms of how priorities are designated in relation to the preservation of historic religious heritage.

Turkey has a long history of coexistence and interaction between multiple religious communities and traditions. However, interfaith relations have not always been peaceful and there is also a long history of religious antagonism and conflict. Religious sites have played an important role in the manifestation and escalation of these conflicts (Hayden 2002). As such, historic religious monuments have become loci of interaction, and quite often, contestation between different religions and sects that claim ownership of these monuments. Decisions regarding the use, maintenance and restoration (or destruction) of monuments of religious heritage are inherently tied to the social and political contexts in which they are taken and should not be thought of as independent of other developments taking place in the political sphere.

Definitions and Complications: Religious Cultural Heritage in Turkey

The preservation, maintenance and management of cultural heritage in Turkey has a complicated system, composed of various different institutions and bodies under the control of government, each with a different set of responsibilities and obligations, which may have overlapping areas of control and responsibility (Baraldi et al. 2012). Thus, in order to understand the funding regime of religious cultural heritage, one needs to have a grasp of the related bodies and the various roles that they play in the decision-making mechanisms for funding.

To start with, the concept of religious cultural heritage does not have a single legal definition in Turkey, but is considered to include a vast array of items and monuments. These include both moveable artefacts and immoveable monuments, with tangible and intangible aspects. These are generally to be found in the 'cultural heritage' lists of the Ministry of Culture and Tourism,[1] and the Directorate of Pious Foundations.[2] When a monument is included in one of these lists, the Ministry of Culture is responsible for issuing permissions for conservation and restoration projects, however, funds are not automatically granted. Each list has its own internal logic and the criteria that qualify a monument to be classified on one list or another makes sense only when considered alongside the trajectory of historical developments that brought about the related institutions and how they are formulated to function.

In general terms, immoveable religious heritage includes monuments and sites associated with the functional and conceptual use of a religious community. They can include places of worship, such as mosques, churches, synagogues, temples and burial places of venerated religious people, human-made or natural sites that are deemed sacred by religious communities. Religious paraphernalia, artifacts and items utilized in religious rituals, decorative elements in halls of worship and ritual garbs and costumes may be included among the moveable items of religious heritage, depending on the sacred meaning and artistic value of such objects. The objects and monuments constitute parts of tangible heritage, while the rituals, rites, hymns, sacred performances, music and ritual dances are classified as intangible religious cultural heritage. The entire spectrum of these aspects makes up religious cultural heritage. Ideally, when thinking about funding for the

---

1 'Cultural and Natural Heritage' is defined in Article 3 of the Act 2863 for the Preservation of Cultural and Natural Heritage of 21 July 1983. Act 2863, Article 4 states that when a monument or item of cultural heritage is discovered, it is the property of the state, thus the Turkish state has blanket control over all cultural heritage on its soil. However, Act 2863, Article 5 states that the property of the pious foundations is excluded from this clause because of their special status.

2 Identifying and listing historic property belonging to the pious endowments is the responsibility of the Directorate General of Foundations. The Act 5737, Article 13 includes a statement that non-registered property (both historic and contemporary) is to be registered through the Directorate General.

preservation of religious heritage, all of these aspects should be considered. In reality, though, funding for the preservation of historic monuments is prioritized over other aspects. For the purposes of this chapter, I will focus only on the funding regime for maintenance, conservation and restoration of historic religious buildings in Turkey.

A Complicated Multi-Layered History: Contestations of Dominant and Minority Religions

The territory of the modern Turkish State has a deeply rooted, multi-religious history. Starting with the earliest identified 'temple' from Göbeklitepe dating back to almost 12,000 BC, there are a large number of religious sites belonging to a wide variety of cultures and faiths (Schmidt 2007). This being the case, the control and ownership of religious sites has become a complicated issue, especially in areas in which such sites had changed hands between the adherents of several different religions and/or sects through time.

One of the most vivid examples illustrating religious continuity in Turkey is the Temple of Augustus/Hacıbayram Mosque complex in Ankara. The Temple of Augustus is a still-standing Roman temple which was erected during the reign of Emperor Augustus, possibly on the sacred ground of an earlier religion. After the arrival of Christianity in Anatolia, the temple was converted into a Byzantine basilica (Serin 2009). In the fifteenth century, the temple/church was incorporated into the dervish lodge of Hacı Bayram Veli, a venerated local saint of Ankara. As such, the temple, the mosque and the monumental tomb of Hacı Bayram Veli constitute a physically integrated compound, which has witnessed continuous religious use for almost two millennia. However, institutionally the mosque and the tomb fall under the control of the General Directorate of Pious Foundations and the temple, the wall of which intersects both the mosque and the tomb, under the control of the Ministry of Culture and Tourism. In cases where such sites are used for a long time, even a single site can have conflicting institutional affiliations.

The historical trajectories of religious affairs and contestations have left an imprint on institutional attitudes in the organization of maintenance and care for religious cultural heritage. Among the major considerations are the divisions between religious and sectarian communities within the Ottoman Empire, which were partially inherited by the Republic of Turkey. The Ottoman Empire was a multi-religious imperial construct, which included a sizeable non-Muslim population. The non-Muslims of the Ottoman Empire were composed of a variety of groups, but the most important ones were the Jewish, Greek Orthodox, Armenian Gregorian and Syriac Christian communities. The Muslim population had (and continues to have) sectarian divisions within itself as well. Following the breakdown of the Ottoman Empire and the founding of the Turkish Republic, the number of non-Muslim minorities decreased dramatically. Among the Muslim non-Sunni minorities, the Alevis and the Bektashis were the most important religious minority communities and remain so today.

Each different religious group which was once part of the sociopolitical topography of the Turkish State in the past has left a rich sacred built heritage. This rich heritage, though, comes with a particular history of contestations and at times memories of violence and is potentially a challenge for the ruling authority. In this respect, the ownership of historic religious buildings is often a complicated issue. The particular history of the Turkish State, especially at the juncture of the transformation from a Sunni-Islamic Empire to a secular nation state, has directly affected the policies regarding religious cultural heritage.

In the first decade after the establishment of the Republic of Turkey in 1923, several regulatory acts in the domain of religious minorities were implemented. Two historical junctures of early Turkish Republican history are important in order to conceptualize the underpinnings of the current status of historic religious heritage. The first of these is the enactment of a bilateral compulsory population exchange between Turkey and Greece. The rules regarding this exchange of populations were defined in the Lausanne Treaty of 30 January 1923.[3] Most Muslims residing in Greece were moved to Turkey and the Orthodox Christian population of Turkey, except for those residing in Istanbul, was moved to Greece. This bilateral exchange had ramifications in terms of historic religious heritage on both sides of the Aegean Sea (Hirschon 2003: 3–23; Clark 2006). The religious buildings and halls of worship of the non-Muslim subjects of the Ottoman Empire were left behind after their communities were moved to Greece and, likewise, Ottoman-Muslim monuments were abandoned after the removal of the Muslim population (Hayden et al. 2011; Lowry 2009).

The second historical juncture that had important ramifications for religious heritage was the passing of Act No. 677 on 13 December 1925, which abolished dervish orders and brotherhoods and closed down their lodges and cloisters (Madran 2002: 101). The Sunni and non-Sunni Muslim populations of the Ottoman Empire were organized along sectarian lines, many of which were assembled around various dervish orders and brotherhoods. Through the closing down of the dervish lodges and cloisters, the religious teachings and organizational capacities of the religious orders were debilitated. The material possessions of the orders, including their building complexes and ritual paraphernalia, were confiscated by the state. The dervish lodge complexes were abandoned in 1925. Most of the mosques and *mesjid*s within those lodge complexes were reopened for worship following the passing of Act 2413 on 2 September 1925 (Madran 2002: 101). By contrast, halls

3 'Lausanne Peace Treaty VI. Convention Concerning the Exchange of Greek and Turkish Populations Signed at Lausanne, January 30 1923', Republic of Turkey Ministry of Foreign Affairs, available at: http://www.mfa.gov.tr/lausanne-peace-treaty-vi_-convention-concerning-the-exchange-of-greek-and-turkish-populations-signed-at-lausanne_.en.mfa (accessed 20 January 2014).

of worship of non-Sunni Muslim practices remained closed.[4] Likewise, no action was taken to reopen the tombs of venerated people or Muslim saints located within those complexes. The tombs of saints, *türbe*s, are an important part of both Sunni and non-Sunni ritual visiting practices. Some of them were renovated somewhat arbitrarily, because visits to the tombs continued. A selected few important dervish lodges were reopened as museums (Tanyeri-Erdemir et al. 2010). The graveyards associated with the lodges and cloisters were allocated to local municipalities in 1930 (Municipality Act 1580 and Decree No. 11410 of the Council of Ministers).

These two historical developments that took place during the first decade of the Turkish Republic formed the underpinnings of some of the current practices and problems in the field of religious cultural heritage. As a result of the population exchange and the closing of dervish lodges, a great number of historic religious buildings were abandoned across Turkey. This horizon of abandonment produced a certain level of ambiguity in the ownership of many religious buildings. Consequently, there are ongoing debates and claims relating to several historical sites of religious importance.

Some historic religious sites and monuments are still in religious use today by the communities that initially built them. Others have been converted for the use of a different religion or converted into a different use.[5] Yet some others have either deteriorated into ruins or are slowly suffering destruction by natural elements or damage by humans. Non-Muslim religious architectural heritage in particular suffered serious damage as a result of this complicated set of historical developments. Ownership of some of the abandoned non-Muslim religious buildings has passed onto private citizens, who have inherited them as property along with the land that the property was located on.[6] The owners of these edifices, in many instances, neither had the resources nor the will to properly take care of them. Such buildings were either left to deteriorate or were converted to perform other functions (Ertani 2012). Currently, a great number of non-Muslim religious buildings have taken on non-religious functions ranging from cultural centres to granaries, storehouses and even houses and boutique hotels. There is an ambiguity in the system about what happens to these buildings in terms of maintenance, preservation and restoration practices.

---

4 For instance, the Meydanevi located within the Hacıbektaş Dervish Lodge, one of the most important spaces of worship for believers of the Alevi-Bektaşi faith, was closed and remains so. The mosque located within the perimeters of the same complex, which now operates as a museum, is open for active worship (Tanyeri-Erdemir et al. 2010).

5 See, for instance, Hayden et al. (2011), Kırımtayıf (2001), Lowry (2009).

6 This issue was recently publicly debated in the case of an Armenian monastery complex which is currently owned by a famous editor-in-chief of a Turkish newspaper, *Fatih Altaylı*. The monastery in question, Varaka Vank in Van, was given to the grandfather of Altaylı along with the lands formerly owned by Armenians after 1915. Individuals like Altaylı hold the land deeds to several abandoned churches and monasteries.

As there is always a limited amount of funds available to save such monuments, the relevant departments of the government are responsible for making decisions about prioritizing what to conserve and restore.

Funding Religious Cultural Heritage in Turkey: Major Actors

State centralization and administrative fragmentation are important factors in defining the management of cultural heritage in Turkey (Baraldi et al. 2012: 3). In terms of funding maintenance, conservation, restoration and renovation of historic religious sites, two institutions play the most fundamental role. Those are the Ministry of Culture and Tourism and the Directorate General of Foundations.

The first step required for any monument to be considered for conservation/restoration through state funding is for it to be listed. In the Turkish system there are several overlapping cultural heritage lists. The Ministry of Culture and Tourism,[7] the Directorate General of Foundations[8] and the Turkish Parliament[9] keep independent lists of cultural heritage (Baraldi et al. 2012: 3–5). For the purposes of this chapter, the cultural heritage lists of the Ministry of Culture and Tourism and the Directorate General of Foundations are of primary importance. After a monument is listed, it can qualify for state funding for conservation or restoration projects. However, in some cases, state funding for such projects is partial and can be supplemented through other resources.

Currently, the major source of funding for the maintenance, conservation and restoration costs of religious cultural heritage is the Directorate General of Foundations.[10] The Ministry of Culture and Tourism is responsible for maintaining and then at least partially creating funds for the upkeep of monuments listed in its inventory. Other financial sources are also utilized. In some cases, local governments provide funds for restoration projects on historic religious buildings. Sometimes corporations, NGOs, private individuals and families may partially or fully sponsor conservation or restoration projects. Non-Muslim minority communities, in most cases, raise funds for the maintenance of their own religious

7 The immoveable cultural and natural heritage that is deemed important for preservation is defined in the Act 2863, Articles 3 and 6 of the Act for the Preservation of Cultural and Natural Property.

8 Act 5737, Articles 28 and 29 states that it is the responsibility of the Directorate General of Foundations to identify, list, maintain, conserve and restore the immoveable heritage of the pious endowments, both in Turkey and abroad.

9 The cultural property of the Ottoman Palaces are listed in the inventory of the Turkish Parliament. Act 2863, Article 10 states that for the conservation and restoration of the cultural and natural heritage under the control of the Turkish Parliament, the Parliament is to be aided by the Ministry of Culture and Tourism in technical matters.

10 Act 5737, Article 40 states that the income generated from the pious endowments can be used in the maintenance, conservation and restoration of immoveable cultural property belonging to the foundations, both in Turkey and abroad.

sites and buildings, most of which are listed under the General Directorate of Foundations.

The Ministry of Culture and Tourism

The Ministry of Culture and Tourism in Turkey is responsible for the control and maintenance of the majority of archaeological sites, museums and collections (Baraldi et al. 2012: 6–9). In general terms, the responsibilities of the Ministry are concentrated around ancient remains. All archaeological sites, excavations and museums are under the control of the Ministry of Culture and Tourism. From a religious heritage perspective, the Ministry has some monuments of religious importance in its heritage list. In addition, there are some monuments that have a status that overlaps the Ministry and the Directorate General of Foundations.

The Ministry of Culture and Tourism is the general body that oversees conservation, restoration and renovation projects at ancient and historic sites, including religious buildings. The Ministry has 12 geographically designated architectural planning and monument directorates within its administration (Baraldi et al. 2012: 3). Thirty-four Regional Conservation Councils, which are responsible for overseeing the conservation projects of immoveable heritage, operate under the Ministry. The primary duty of these regional councils is to check and approve restoration projects to be conducted on listed heritage property (Act 2863, Article 51). The Act on the Conservation of Cultural and Natural Property (Act 2863) makes a distinction and places the financial responsibility for maintenance and restoration of mosques that are used for active worship under the Directorate General of Foundations.

Religious heritage has deep roots in Turkey. The ancient remnants of religious sites from the earliest civilizations to medieval remains are listed with the Ministry of Culture and Tourism. These encompass a wide spectrum of monuments, from the earliest pre-Neolithic temple at Göbeklitepe, to the ancient temples of the Hittite or Roman Empires, to the Christian cave monasteries of Cappadocia. Ensuring the protection of these ancient buildings for posterity is the responsibility of the Ministry. The Ministry has funds allocated for conservation projects. However, it encourages and sometimes enforces archaeological excavations to secure funds for the conservation of the remains they unearth. Thus, domestic and international archaeological research projects may establish budgets for restoration projects under their control using a variety of sources. Most of Byzantine religious heritage falls into this category and is classified by the Ministry of Culture and Tourism.

There is yet another important category of monuments that falls partially under the responsibility of the Ministry of Culture. These are the historic religious buildings that were turned into museums. The prime example of these is the Hagia Sophia in Istanbul, which was turned into a museum in 1934 (Öztürk 1995: 500–501). Others, such as the Mevlana Museum, which is located in the former dervish lodge of the Mevlevi order, and the Hacıbektaş Museum, which is the former dervish lodge of the Bektaşi order, were later reopened as museums (Madran

2002, 123; Tanyeri et al. 2010). These buildings are listed by the Directorate General of Foundations, but are designated to be used for a specified purpose by the Ministry of Culture. As such, these buildings have a status that overlaps the Ministry of Culture and Tourism and the Directorate General of Foundations.

The allocation of funding for the conservation and restoration costs of these religious monuments currently serving as museums is complicated. In the case of Hagia Sophia of Istanbul, there was a discussion in the 1930s regarding which government body should be responsible for funding the renovation project to turn this edifice into a museum (Madran 2002: 124). Because of the ambiguous status of these buildings, such tasks are open for discussion and negotiation. In general terms though, the Ministry of Culture is solely responsible for the daily tasks and maintenance of those museums. Costs of staff and maintenance are covered by the Ministry of Culture. The ticket revenue from these museums goes into the state budget, which is a collective pool. The money collected from the ticket revenue is not earmarked to be used for the particular museum from which the revenue comes, but rather is collected and redistributed by the Ministry. For major restoration and renovation projects, the Directorate of Pious Endowments is the major decision-making body for such projects. Even though, during the time that the building is leased to the Ministry of Culture and Tourism, the costs of major restoration projects may be covered by the Ministry of Culture or the Ministry it may be necessary to find the resources to undertake those projects. The funding for maintenance, conservation, restoration and renovation of those buildings may come from multiple sources.

Some of these sites have an ambivalent legal status. The 'Museum' status of two 'museumified' sacred buildings has recently been scrutinized and is the focus of recent debates in Turkey. The Hagia Sophia of İznik (Nicaea) in northwestern Turkey and the Hagia Sophia of Trabzon on the Black Sea coast were both Byzantine churches that were converted into mosques after the Ottoman conquests of Nicaea and Trabzon. Both mosques were parts of pious endowments and they are listed in the directory of Directorate General of Foundations. Both of these buildings operated as museums, but they were not officially leased by the Directorate to the Ministry at the time that they were turned into museums. The Hagia Sophia of Nicaea was reopened for religious use as a mosque after a major restoration project funded by the General Directorate of Pious Foundations, in 2011. The General Directorate published an official statement to the effect that they were planning to reopen the Hagia Sophia in Trabzon as a mosque in December 2012 (Finkel 2013); and the Hagia Sophia of Trabzon opened for Islamic worship on 5 July 2013 (*The Economist* 27 July 2013; Zaman 2013). The debate which initiated these developments is anticipated to continue.[11] There is an ongoing demand on changing the museum status of the Hagia Sophia of Constantinople to mosque among some conservative circles in Turkey.

11 Tanyeri-Erdemir, T. (17 May 2013), 'A Tale of Three Hagia Sophias: Conversion, Museumification, Contestation', paper delivered at Cambridge University, UK.

The Directorate General of Foundations

The Directorate General of Foundations, *Vakıflar Genel Müdürlüğü*, is the most important body responsible for management, maintenance, conservation and restoration projects for religious sites. This institution illustrates a remarkable continuity from the Ottoman system into the modern Turkish Republic.

The *waqf/vakıf* institution has its historical roots in the Islamic world. In its broadest definition, a pious endowment, or a *vakıf* is an 'institution, whereby a privately owned property, corpus, is endowed for a charitable purpose in perpetuity and the revenue generated is spent for this purpose' (Çizakça 2000: 1). As such, under Ottoman law, a pious endowment was a legal person, which functioned within the Ottoman legal system. The defining feature of the Ottoman endowments was the fact that they were charitable institutions endowed for the general well-being of society, with a pious purpose (Öztürk 1995: 22). Depending on their specific purpose, the pious endowments could fulfill a large range of functions, including education, health services or providing services related to urban infrastructure, like public baths, fountains, travellers' inns and so on, in addition to building mosques. The *vakıf* institutions were initiated by endowments of different sorts, given by families, religious sects, brotherhoods and communities. When they were being founded, the endowments were defined by a deed of trust (*vakfiye*) which specified the purpose and functions of that particular institution (Öztürk 1995: 19–48). The deed of trust was drawn up by the trustees initiating the endowment.

The religious brotherhoods and orders were traditionally organized around pious endowments. Each brotherhood would have its own endowment, the functions of which were defined by the deed of trust. The dervish lodges and cloisters, along with other revenue generating lands and edifices, were organized around pious endowments. As such, the pious endowments of religious brotherhoods and orders included a variety of religious buildings, like mosques, *medresahs* (religious schools), *türbes* (monumental tombs of saints) and cemeteries.

The economic system organized through the Pious Foundations of the Ottoman State was partially adopted by the Turkish Republic and has left an imprint on the management of religious heritage. The Pious Foundations are important in understanding the system of funding for religious heritage in Turkey for two reasons. The first is that a large number of historic religious buildings are listed under the Directorate General of Foundations, because they were parts of endowments in the Ottoman Empire. A second reason is the fact that the Directorate General of Foundations is the major source that organizes funding for renovation and restoration of these edifices.

The current inventory of the Directorate General of Foundations lists 19,184 antiquities. This inventory includes a large variety of monuments, buildings and works of art. The Pious Foundations were essentially revenue-generating institutions and were endowed by families or communities; some were at the core of Islamic brotherhoods and non-Muslim communities. The current inventory of historic monuments under the control of the Directorate General of Foundations is composed of all the buildings that were owned by the pious endowments in the Ottoman system. Thus, the structures listed with the Directorate of Pious Endowments include a myriad of different types. These may, for instance, include buildings of urban infrastructure such as bridges, fountains, public baths, institutions offering services such as hospitals, religious schools, orphanages and so on. *Vakıf*s also included buildings and monuments related to religious use and practice: mosques, *mescid*s (smaller prayer halls), *türbes* (tombs of saints) and dervish lodge complexes, as well as churches and synagogues of the non-Muslim communities.

The *vakıf*s originally functioned as large financial estates established around religious communities, both Muslim and non-Muslim, of different sects and brotherhoods. These estates possessed large inventories of buildings. Some of these were religious buildings, but these inventories also included buildings with an infrastructure and urban function, such as bathhouses, caravanserais, bridges and so on. It is evident from the written records from the nineteenth century that the *vakıfs* were financially responsible for maintenance and renovation of the historic buildings under their control (Madran 2002: 9).

The Directorate General of Foundations, as an institution, illustrates both a remarkable continuity and a significant break from the Ottoman administrative system. The Directorate is a semi-autonomous body under the government, which receives funding from the state and generates further revenue from its endowments. The Directorate General of Foundations was established as an institution in its current form in 1935 (Act 2762), although, from 1924 onwards, it was one of the primary funding institutions for religious heritage (Madran 2002: 105). The historical pious endowments of the Ottoman Empire were collected under this Directorate following the foundation of the Turkish Republic. The 'Regulations of Pious Foundations' was established in 17 July 1936 through Decree no. 2/5042 of the Council of Ministers. The protection and conservation clauses in this decree appointed the Directorate General of Foundations as the responsible institution. It also authorized the Directorate to create a full inventory of all property belonging to the historical endowments. The property belonging to the historical Ottoman endowments was taken over by the state and the directorate became the sole institution responsible for the property formerly owned by those institutions. In 1938, a specific branch dealing with building and conservation programmes was established under the Directorate (Act 3461). Currently, the Directorate of Pious Foundations is the main state institution that both controls and funds management, restoration and renovation of historic monuments listed under its directory.[12] The Directorate can generate revenue through the currently functioning endowments

12 The Directorate has a separate department responsible for creating an inventory and arranging and controlling the regular maintenance of heritage of the pious foundations. This is the Department of Works of Art and Construction. The duties of this department are defined in Act 5737, Article 53, and includes making architectural surveys of monuments, organizing conservation and restoration projects.

and the majority of the funds allocated to conservation and restoration projects come from that budget.

One of the major changes in the legal formulation of the Directorate General of Foundations was the addition of clauses to include the property of non-Muslim communities under the Directorate in 1936. This development allowed non-Muslim communities to establish Pious Foundations and declare their religious property (including churches, synagogues, schools for pupils and schools for clergy). This should not be regarded as an entirely novel development. From the nineteenth century onwards, there were already several precedents of non-Muslim communities establishing endowments (Öztürk 1995: 337). However, those endowments had a limited area of function and were closely monitored. The legal framework organized in 1936 allowed non-Muslim communities to establish endowments to claim their rights as stated in the Lausanne Treaty (Section III, Article 40). The terms used for endowments established by the non-Muslim minority in Turkey are *Cemaat Vakıfları* (Community Foundations) or *Azınlık Vakıfları* (Minority Foundations) (Hatemi 2012: 149–52). The Minority Foundations were required to submit a list of their properties (including religious buildings) to the General Directorate of Pious Foundations in 1936 (Vingas 2012: 49). The Lausanne Treaty includes a clause guaranteeing the ownership and right to control religious property belonging to those non-Muslim communities that stayed in Turkey after the compulsory exchange of populations between Greece and Turkey in 1924. Though there are problems with actually exercising those rights granted by the Lausanne treaty to the non-Muslim minorities of the Turkish Republic (particularly in the area of schools for clergy), these communities own and control their religious buildings and are allowed subsidies for the daily running and maintenance of those edifices (such as free electricity and water), but these subsidies do not include any funds for conservation and restoration. As such, funding the maintenance, conservation and restoration of non-Muslim historic religious buildings of Community Foundations depends primarily on the communities that control those monuments.

The non-Muslim heritage that was abandoned after the population exchange – and was not claimed by the relevant non-Muslim minorities in 1936 – has an ambivalent status. Non-Muslim religious heritage which is not listed with the General Directorate of Pious Foundations is not qualified to receive funds through the Directorate and religious communities may increase their efforts to ensure the protection of their historic religious heritage. The recent developments in Bursa can be used as an example to illustrate this point. The Greek-Orthodox community recently purchased two former Byzantine churches in the Mudanya district of Bursa through funds that they raised themselves, which were under private ownership and were in a dilapidated state. The churches were put up for sale by their owners, as is allowed within the legal framework of such historic religious edifices. The Greek-Orthodox community is currently gathering funds for restoration projects for those buildings, and stated that they plan to reopen these monuments both for worship as well as cultural activities.[13]

Conclusion

The historical developments that took place during the transition from the Ottoman Empire to the Republic of Turkey in the 1920s have defined the institutional framework relating to the preservation of religious heritage. The Lausanne Treaty of 1923 defined the right of ownership of religious buildings of remaining Christian minorities in Turkey. However, the disappearance of Christian populations of Anatolia in the earlier part of the twentieth century has left many churches without practicing communities. The closing down of dervish lodges and cloisters in 1925, likewise, left many historic religious buildings without practicing communities. The current complexity of the system stems from this historical set of events, which eventually caused a rupture between religious buildings and practicing populations. This historical particularity has ramifications in terms of conservation of religious historic heritage.

Two institutions play the most important role in providing the funding for preserving religious cultural heritage in Turkey. These are the Directorate General of Foundations and the Ministry of Culture and Tourism. These two institutions have partially overlapping roles and responsibilities. The Directorate General of Foundations is the most important body of government for the funding of religious cultural heritage in Turkey. However, the priority of the Directorate is preserving the heritage of the pious foundations, 'Vakıf Mirası'. In the historically multi-layered, multi-religious and multi-cultural Turkish context, this prioritization is problematic, and creates an inherent inequality between the Muslim and non-Muslim heritage on the one hand; and Sunni and non Sunni heritage on the other.

References

Baraldi, S.B., Shoup, D. and Zan, L. (2013), 'Understanding cultural heritage in Turkey: institutional context and organizational Issues', *International Journal of Heritage Studies*, vol. 19, 728–48.

Benli, D., Günel, G., Kurtoğlu, M. and Başkaya, H. (eds) (2012), *Balkanlarda Osmanlı Vakıfları ve Eserleri Uluslararası Sempozyumu* (Ankara: Vakıflar Genel Müdürlüğü Yayınları).

Clark, B. (2006), *Twice a Stranger: How Mass Expulsion Forged Modern Greece and Turkey* (Cambridge, MA: Harvard University Press).

13 'Dünyanın en eski 3. Kilisesi hem ibatede hem ziyaraete açılacak', *Bursa 24 Online Haber*, available at: http://bursa24.com.tr/dunyanin-en-eski-3-kilisesi-hem-ibadete-hem-ziyarete-acilacak.html (accessed 20 January 2014).

Çizakça, M. (2000), *A History of Philanthropic Foundations: The Islamic World From the Seventh Century to the Present* (İstanbul: Boğaziçi University Press).
Ecevitoğlu, P., İrat, A.M. and Yalçınkaya, A. (eds) (2010), *Hacı Bektaş Veli: Güneşte Zerresinden, Deryada Katresinden* (Ankara: Dipnot Yayınları).
The Economist (27 July 2013), 'Erasing the Christian past, a fine Byzantine Church in Turkey has been converted into a mosque'.
Ertani, E. (28 September 2012), 'Fatih Altaylı'ya ait oldugu ortaya çıkan Yedi Kilise ve diğer özel mülke ait kiliseler o kaçınılmaz soruyu sorduruyor: Hani bu kiliselerin ilk sahibi?', *Agos*, 5.
Finkel, A. (2013), 'Mosque conversion raises alarm, Christian art in Byzantine church-turned-museum is at risk after controversial court ruling', *The Art Newspaper*, 245, 15–16.
Hatemi, K. (2012), 'Yunanistan ve Türkiye'de Azınlık Vakıfları' in Benli, D., Günel, G., Kurtoğlu, M. and Başkaya, H. (eds), 149–52.
Hayden, R.M. (2002), 'Antagonistic tolerance: Competitive sharing of religious sites in South Asia and the Balkans', *Current Anthropology*, 43:2, 205–31.
Hayden, R.M., Sözer H., Tanyeri-Erdemir, T. and Erdemir, A. (2011), 'The Byzantine mosque at Trilye: A processual analysis of dominance, sharing, transformation and tolerance', *History and Anthropology*, 22:1, 1–17.
Hirshon, R. (ed.) (2003), *Crossing the Aegean, An Appraisal of the 1923 Compulsory Population Exchange Between Greece and Turkey* (New York: Berghahn Books).
Hirschon, R. (2003), 'Introduction: Background and overview' in Hirshon, R. (ed.), 3–23.
Kırımtayıf, S. (2001), *Converted Byzantine Churches in Istanbul, their Transformation into Mosques and Masjids* (İstanbul: Ege Yayınları).
Lowry, H. (2009), *In the Footsteps of the Ottomans: A Search for Sacred Spaces and Architectural Monuments in Northern Greece* (İstanbul: Bahçeşehir University Press).
Madran, E. (2002), *Tanzimat'tan Cumhuriyet'e Kültür Varlıklarının Korunmasına İlişkin Tutumlar ve Düzenlemeler: 1800-1950* (Ankara: Orta Doğu Teknik Üniversitesi Mimarlık Fakültesi).
Öztürk, N. (1995), *Türk Yenileşme Tarihi Çerçevesinde Vakıf Müessesesi* (Ankara: Türkiye Diyanet Vakfı Yayınları).
Schmidt, K. (2007), *Taş Çağı Avcılarının Gizemli Kutsal Alanı Göbeklitepe, En Eski Tapınağı Yapanlar* (İstanbul: Arkeoloji ve Sanat Yayınları).
Serin, U. (2009), 'Ankara bizantina e la trasformazione del tempio di Augusto e della dea Roma: ideologia o pragmatismo?', in *La Parola del Passato*, 64:367, 271–312.
Stovel, H. (2005), 'Introduction' in Stovel, H., Stanley-Price, N. and Killick, R. (eds), 1–11.
Stovel, H., Stanley-Price, N. and Killick, R. (eds) (2005), *Conservation of Living Religious Heritage, Papers from the ICCROM 2003 Forum on Living Religious Heritage: Conserving the Sacred* (Rome: ICCROM Conservation Studies).

Tanyeri-Erdemir, T., Harmanşah, R. and Hayden, R.M. (2010), 'Serçesme'den Hacıbektaş Müzesi'ne: Kültür Mirası Olan Bir Mekanda Ritüel ve Kurumsal Pratikler', in Ecevitoğlu, P., İrat, A.M. and Yalçınkaya, A. (eds), 437–43.
Vingas, P.L. (2012), 'Osmanlı'dan Günümüze Cemaat Vakıfları: Cemaatlerin Yeni Yönetim Anlayışında Vakıfları Rolü ve Geleceği' in Benli, D., Günel, G., Kurtoğlu, M. and Başkaya, H. (eds), 47–50.
Zaman, A. (2013) 'Another Byzantine church becomes mosque in Turkey', *Al-Monitor*, 7 August 2013.

Conclusion

Anne Fornerod

The purpose of these concluding words is not to comprehensively describe each national context but, rather, to emphasize the main emerging trends. Current domestic funding schemes can be compared bearing in mind two major points:

1. diversity from one country to another (whether this arises from the system of relations between state and religions is precisely one question to be answered);
2. the essential connection between funding and the overall framework in which heritage is considered, including elements like conservation policy, legal procedures or tourism development (Committee on Culture and Education 2000).

An overview of the funding schemes in the countries under survey here reveals that they all possess a system of public funding for heritage, which expressly or *de facto* covers religious monuments. However, this statement does not reflect the whole picture. Mapping out the situation would constitute a preliminary step, before drawing conclusions about the influence that relations between state and religions have over the funding of religious heritage on the one hand and over the impact of secularization in this area on the other hand.

Mapping out the Funding of Religious Heritage

A decision to list a building imposes additional constraints on the owner's shoulders, justified by the cultural value of the property. Yet restoration and maintenance work on monuments require huge budgets, which are not easily matched by the heritage authorities in charge. As stated by way of introduction, the first aim of this volume is to achieve a mapping of the funding made available for religious heritage for two main reasons. On the one hand, limitations on public resources make it necessary to rely on private means. In countries having a tradition of public financial commitments to cultural heritage, this introduces new challenges – a need to vary and identify alternative resources, thus creating a certain complexity. On the other hand, in the knowledge that religious heritage is composed of buildings likely to be publicly funded as places of worship, the question arises of how both sources of funding – cultural and religious – are combined. This leads to a diversification of resources through combining public and private resources, supported by fiscal incentives.

Public Funding for Religious Heritage

Although public funding for religious heritage often seems insufficient with regards to actual needs, it should necessarily be considered, not only because it reflects public authorities' involvement in a field deemed to be in the general interest.

Direct public funding

In *all* countries under survey, albeit to a very variable extent, religious heritage is funded through *direct* public aid. It should be specified at once that a great majority of countries grant aid on cultural grounds, provided that the places of worship are listed.[1] Denmark (*Folkekirke*) and the United Kingdom should be considered apart here, as funding is not mainly and narrowly linked to cultural heritage policies. In both countries, religious buildings belonging to the main historical church (the Evangelical-Lutheran Church or *Folkekirke* on the one hand, the Church of England and the Church of Scotland on the other) are subject to a specific legal and funding framework which leaves them outside the mainstream regime of cultural heritage. As regards the United Kingdom, valuable church buildings are publicly funded as places of worship in the first instance, although this funding obviously 'tends to be concentrated on the largest and most important buildings from a heritage point of view' (Cranmer).

Public support takes on various forms, ranging from direct state and local authority subsidies through specific religious heritage-oriented programmes (Estonia, France, Spain and the United Kingdom), to non-pecuniary measures like free expertise (Danish religious communities outside *Folkekirken*).

In addition, in order to achieve a comprehensive view, it should be emphasized that these culturally-based aids add to direct or indirect funding aimed at places of worship. This support for places of worship overwhelmingly takes the form of tax exonerations on property.[2]

Indirect public support

It remains that the most widespread form of public support consists of indirect financial contributions for the preservation of religious heritage, mainly through

1 However, this listing does not systematically ensure the related funding. See for example, the case of the Turkish non-Muslim minorities, which have to 'raise funds for the maintenance of their own religious sites and buildings, most of which are listed under the General Directorate of Foundations' (Taniery-Erdemir).

2 The situation of Danish *Folkekirke* at first sight stands apart in that state support for *Folkekirke* is used for religious leaders' salaries and not for places of worship. However, it could be argued that public funds allocated to personnel allow the church to use its revenue to fund the maintenance of places of worship.

tax measures. These measures are above all aimed at supporting the upkeep of non-publicly owned monuments. They range from tax deductibility on donations to tax exemption for restoration works through lower VAT rates. Opportunities for tax deduction apply to individuals and to non-profit organizations, which can offset a percentage of the gift or donation against income tax or benefit from tax deductibility on gifts.

This study of indirect public support cannot be considered without dealing with private funding for religious heritage in that most of these measures are aimed at fostering private financial support.

Private Funding for Religious Heritage

Private funding encompasses religious denominations and individuals, as well as companies or associations that take care of monuments. Indeed 'private trusts and associations are playing an increasingly important role in the conservation of religious heritage' (Haynes 2008: 17). Domestic funding schemes variously combine public and private resources and offer varying tradition and experience in matters of trust and association involvement. For example, in Estonia, 'private donors or trusts have had only a minor role in funding certain church restorations, mainly due to the absence of tradition of private donors for restoration work' (Ringvee). Moreover, legislation has been passed that fosters patronage (France, Spain).

Religious heritage largely funded by public means is not spared from the need to resort to private resources, as the French case shows. Due to a lack of resources and the impossibility of bearing the costs, several local referenda have taken place in small rural *communes* in order to decide whether the municipally-owned main place of worship should be destroyed or preserved. In Paris, a recent, meaningful initiative consisted in the creation in early 2014 of a private foundation 'The Future of Heritage in Paris' (*Avenir du patrimoine à Paris*), tasked with raising private funds to complement municipal grant aid.[3]

In addition, several countries offer examples of public-private bodies specifically targeted at religious heritage (Spain, Quebec, the United Kingdom).[4]

In conclusion, if attempting to roughly position the various funding schemes onto a scale starting from mainly, if not exclusively, public funding and ending with almost exclusively private funding, the countries selected would be ordered as follows: Estonia, Turkey for Muslim monuments, France, Italy and Spain, Quebec, the Netherlands, the United Kingdom and Denmark, Turkish non-Muslim monuments. Then the question arises of whether this is influenced by the relationship between states and religions.

---

3 Information available on the Foundation's website: http://www.fondationavenirpatrimoineparis.fr/ (accessed 2 March 2014).

4 The French Heritage Foundation follows the same purpose and structure, but targeted specifically at *non-listed* buildings.

The Influence of the State-Religion Relationship on Funding Religious Heritage

Although we feel familiar with religious heritage, sometimes in our daily lives the question remains of the specificity of these valuable buildings within the general debate on funding heritage. Does special treatment of the buildings derive from their status as religious assets? Here, do the domestic specificities of state-religion relations prevail while implementing heritage legislation? If so, to what extent do these systems favour the protection of religious heritage? The exact influence of state-religion relations is nevertheless hard to identify when religious heritage is concerned, mainly due to the fact that heritage-making legislation and state-religion relations are both intrinsically shaped by history and identity, with various consequences.

State–Religion Relations and Heritage Legislation: The Common Weight of History

As a first consequence of such a weight of history, it seems fruitless to search for the influence of 'categories' of state–church relations: they prove to be a limited tool when drawing relevant conclusions about the issue at hand.[5] Scholarly works have shown how difficult it is to characterize domestic systems of relations between the state – but also local public authorities – and religious communities.[6] Although here and there one can observe common features and comparable situations among the constituents of these categories, there are common points between countries belonging to different 'categories'. These differences show how much state-religion relationships are definitely shaped by history. It is of common knowledge that 'the diversity of the civil ecclesiastical law systems in the European Union mirrors the diversity of the national cultures and identities' (Robbers 2005: 577). Hence, the focus should rather be on national contexts considered individually.

Secondly, it proves difficult to clearly connect differences between the various national schemes pertaining to the funding of religious heritage to the mere historical legacy and/or to the specificities of state-religion relationships. The legal framework applicable to state-religion relations and the heritage approach can hardly be considered separately. One observes an unavoidable intertwinement. This is due to the essential purpose of heritage legislation, which precisely aims to protect the tracks of history – and culture – as embodied by public and private valuable goods. Religious assets which today form a prominent part of cultural heritage have for decades been subject to specific legislation in national contexts. Managing religious heritage means managing the legacy of the past in the area of state-religion relationships, including tensions which have

5 Although it constitutes a convenient tool from a methodological point of view, as the structure of this volume shows.

6 See, among others, Robbers (2005: 578 *et seq.*).

not altogether dissipated. Turkey is a striking illustration of this. More precisely, both France and the Netherlands have a regime of separation between church and state. However, the historical circumstances of the early implementation of the French 1905 Act introduced a specific regime of – public – property for numerous Catholic buildings, thus critically influencing the funding regime and creating a gap between French and Dutch systems. As regards the United Kingdom and Denmark – somewhat hastily included within the category of national or established church – the management of religious heritage here results in very different issues and solutions. When further drawing the comparison, it looks as if Denmark has not yet been touched by the redundancy of church buildings, while the United Kingdom has long since adopted funding mechanisms in order to face up to this issue (Haynes 2008: 4).

As another illustration, it cannot be denied that heritage ownership plays a direct role in funding conservation. Hence, although one could at first sight consider ownership by religious communities as a distinctive feature of the state-religion system – in the sense of the place assigned to religious communities – the fact that the latter have to fund maintenance and restoration of their listed buildings reflects rather the implementation of the heritage funding framework, which consists in the owner ensuring the upkeep of buildings. This is more broadly the implementation of the core principle of cultural heritage legislation which aims at limiting the exercise of ownership rights in the name of the cultural interest of certain outstanding properties.

Seeking to isolate what results from the state–church relationship and what results from heritage legislation would very soon prove to be in vain. However, by introducing the financial parameter, two elements emerge which reflect a certain influence of state–church relations and the status of religious assets.

Where State-Religion Relationships Stand Out

Two points should be considered here. The first and most tangible influence of the religious status endowed by systems of state-religion relationships over support for listed religious assets lies in the additional funding allowed by such a status. In financial terms, it means that countries offer a kind of support to places of worship, directly through subsidies or indirectly through tax incentives.

In this regard, it is argued here and there that funding religious heritage still amounts to funding the religious communities which own these buildings and their assets (Belgium, Netherlands, Estonia). The main response to such an objection lies first in the inevitable statement that European heritage is largely made up of religious assets belonging to religious groups for obvious objective, historical reasons. The high proportion of religious buildings within cultural heritage is incontestably a legacy of history and very often accounts for their funding as such. However, this gives rise to various analyses. In the Spanish and Italian cases, it looks like the overwhelming share of Catholic religious heritage (due to the role of the Catholic Church in national history) makes public support generally unquestionable. In both countries, the Catholic Church *de facto* absorbs almost all the funding from a system designed for it. A brief overview shows how a clear distinction between funding heritage and places of worship proves to be quite theoretical, although the funding appears to be much more targeted at buildings as elements of cultural heritage. In addition, phrasing the problem in these terms does not reflect the real challenges. Without ignoring criticisms about the funding of *religious* heritage, the issue and urgency rather stem from the worrying situation of thousands of church buildings considered foremost as heritage.

The second point worth emphasizing here is the role played by religious groups' representatives in the management of religious heritage and notably its funding. To varying degrees, they represent unavoidable spokespersons of public authorities, at local or national levels. In this regard, the Italian system shows how religious heritage is fully subject to the existing framework of state–church relationships. Like in Italy, Spain's public and religious authorities resort to classical instruments of state–church relationships to manage religious heritage. In both countries, the implementation of legal frameworks pertaining to state–church relationships undeniably benefits the protection of religious heritage.

Resources from the funds granted to places of worship – and hence their legitimacy – is marginally contested, perhaps reflecting a certain consensus about the need to ensure the material conservation of this heritage. Yet, funding places of worship might draw its legitimacy from their being used for activities other than religious practice, particularly as they provide venues for cultural events. In the latter case, there would be a shift in the legitimacy of the funding as well. Above all, it shows how much the question of use is central, in that it notably reveals the change in perception of religious heritage that has occurred over recent decades and raises the question of the secularization of religious assets under the influence of their heritagization.

Funding Religious Heritage and Secularization

The purpose of this section is to assess – still within the limitations of a comparative study – the degree of secularization of religious heritage through the question of its funding. A general survey shows that the level of funding of religious heritage has not witnessed a real decrease. Without denying widespread concern about the lack of financial resources, the question arises of a possible distinction, as far as religious heritage is concerned, between that which is due to heritagization and that which is rather the consequence of a general context of secularization. In general, heritagization of religious assets is likely to amount in itself to a form of secularization in that it obeys a non-religious logic. However, it cannot be definitely and systematically mistaken for the secularization process, which has its own forms of expression. A dynamic intertwinement ensues with several consequences, such as a new balance between all the stakeholders and questions about the most suitable way(s) of funding to accompany an increase in culturally-oriented funding.

Heritagization and Secularization of Religious Heritage

In essence, and however variously managed according to the country, listing religious immovable and movable goods generates a new and additional approach to their meaning, which is not of a religious nature, but cultural. In many countries, religious assets become heritage according to criteria related in the first instance to history or culture.[7] The reference to the religious character of goods likely to be listed in national legislation amounts to an acknowledgment of the legacy constituted by such outstanding religious assets to architecture and history. The implementation of such legislation very often covers, *de facto*, a considerable number of religious immovable and movable goods.[8] These heritage–related legal frameworks imply a selection among religious buildings, first according to cultural criteria, combined with religious significance or, secondly and most importantly, a religious community's subsequent needs or liturgical requirements.[9] This might lead to the omission of a certain number of places of worship which sometimes become redundant, as shown by, for example, the large nineteenth century churches, which suffer from 'negative perceptions of their heritage value in comparison with older buildings' (Haynes 2008: 4).

Alongside this structural heritagization of religious heritage, it is possible to hypothesize a secularization, whose most visible and tangible impact on the funding of religious heritage is mainly indirect. Indeed, the secularization process that European societies have been undergoing for decades does not in itself entail a significant decrease in public funding on religious or cultural grounds. However, the decrease in the number of faithful and in church attendance has a double impact. First, this signifies the end of – or at least a severe reduction to – the conservation process resulting from the regular use of church buildings. Secondly, the reduced resources of religious communities – notably due to less income from church members – has put the former in a difficult situation when

7 The legislation occasionally does not exclude consideration for the religious nature of the goods: see, among others, the Spanish Act 42/1994 of 30 December 1994 on Tax, Administrative and Social Actions, DT 1, which provides that 'the movable items declared to be of cultural interest and those included in the general inventory possessed by religious entities can only be sold or donated or the property transferred to public entities or other religious entities. Private owners or companies cannot acquire them' (Garcimartin).

8 In Denmark and the United Kingdom, valuable church buildings belonging to the main church are subject to specific legal provisions, outside the legislation on historic monuments. In a way, the Italian system is comparable in that the recognition of the cultural interest of – Catholic – religious goods is regulated apart through an agreement between the Department of Cultural Heritage and the Italian Episcopal Conference (Ferrari).

9 On the variety of criteria of the relevant legal protection, see the detailed analysis provided in Tsivolas (2014: 95 *et seq.*).

it comes to complying with the legal framework for heritage maintenance and restoration, which mainly relies on owners. In this regard, one might also observe a disconnection between the religious approach to the building and its cultural dimension. It is the case when church authorities put an end to the religious use and decide to sell the building: the listing and its effects remain.

All this goes hand in hand with a new balance between different interests and conceptions of religious heritage by the various stakeholders, ranging from cultural state and local authorities to religious groups and including visitors, heritage associations and the setting up of various bodies, more or less closely connected with public authorities.

A New Balance Among Stakeholders

With regard to the top-down approach which characterized the nineteenth century conception of heritage shaping and management, today one observes a particularly diversified range of stakeholders. This is also the result of the democratization process that religious heritage has undergone. The religious nature of heritage gives rise to specific adaptations.

Specific bodies for religious heritage management and funding

Managing the upkeep and enhancement of cultural religious heritage is likely to influence the nature of the relations between public – cultural – authorities and religious groups in this specific area: both camps find themselves dealing with the same premises, but with different purposes. Institutional adaptations vary from one country to another with, on the one hand, the increasing involvement of organizations taking care of monuments and, on the other hand, the setting up of specific mixed bodies which bring together public authorities and representatives of one or several religious groups (Estonia, Spain, France[10] and Quebec).[11] A wide array of structures is observable, ranging from small and modest local associations to public-private bodies. Whilst the former focus on locally-driven projects, the latter have a larger scope and appear to be connected with public authorities. Their intervention opens up funding, in the knowledge that their creation is often precisely aimed at raising funds (France, the Netherlands,[12] the United Kingdom and Turkey for non-Muslim minorities). The Dutch context offers an example of how the involvement of organizations caring for monuments contributes to a sort of secularization of religious heritage. When it comes to benefiting from grant aid for maintenance, 'a more prominent position is given to professional organizations for the preservation of monuments, on the condition that they own

10 It should be noted that the former French Religious Heritage Committee (*Comité du patrimoine cultuel*) had no competence in grant-aid matters but was more an advisory council.

11 The idea of such a structure was supported in the Netherlands in the late 1980s.

12 See the Dutch cultural ANBI system in Chapter 11.

at least 20 monuments (Articles 30–35 and 30-2 *SIM 2012*). [...] This means that a local parish, owning one (or even a handful of) church building(s) will be in a less favourable position when the applications for subsidy exceed the upper limit' (Overbeeke).[13] Another example is to be found in the French system, which offers the possibility for the faithful to intervene via support funds in order to contribute partly or wholly to the costs of repair works (Prélot). This was decided by the courts in the early 1930s for religious purposes. However, this mechanism tends nowadays to be replaced by the creation of local associations that take care of monuments.

The intertwinement between heritagization and secularization gives rise to a complex institutional landscape, in which it is tempting to search for a reflection of the domestic traditions relating to religious issues. Indeed, the question is whether the general framework provided by state–religion relationships facilitates such coordination between the various stakeholders. Religious communities can hardly be considered private owners of ordinary historical monuments. If only because of the numerical importance of their valuable property, their structure and organization call for organization and coordination with public authorities entrusted with cultural heritage policies. In this regard, the existing domestic systems of state–church relationships, together with the religious context, are likely to weigh on the debate, perhaps more than the private ownership of listed religious buildings. Hence, the question arises of whether the general framework provided by state–religion relationship systems facilitates such coordination between the various stakeholders. As regards Italy and Spain, management and funding mechanisms obviously rely on the existing framework, which is mainly characterized by the passing of agreements between state and local authorities and several religious groups.

One should note the role played by individuals in this area, who are competing with or even replacing the faithful in their intention to preserve religious heritage.

Faithful v. heirs

The heritagization of religious goods – as for other cultural assets in general – takes on a modern form which goes beyond the listing as historic monuments and the related measures of maintenance and conservation. Cultural heritage cannot any longer be considered separately from enhancement. One has entered the area of the 'heirs', namely the public, who is now used to having access to 'its' heritage. Alongside this democratization of access, the contemporary approach to cultural heritage drives a sort of democratization of management, in that the listing decided upon by public authorities takes place within a context of a desired societal appropriation of cultural heritage. This evolution towards a more inclusive and

13 As the author precises: 'However, denominational communities can also act as a professional organization for the preservation of monuments. This means, however, a change in the community structure for those denominations where church buildings are, in principle, owned by the local parish or congregation.'

democratic approach towards cultural heritage implies perhaps revisiting heritage management policies and their level of implementation in the sense of their more favourable reception by local communities.[14] In this regard, decreasing church attendance for religious practices is likely to weaken the position of churches, which argue that the fate of the buildings closely depends on their ownership and their entitlement to take decisions on their own. This debate is in some way illustrated by the statement made by the Dutch scholar Koen Raats: 'The fundamental question is if a church building is private property of a select group with a specific confession, or a building with a societal value' (Raats 2012: 97).[15]

The requirements of religious heritage management – and a lack of funds – have brought about a partial reshaping of the financial framework. The democratization that goes hand in hand with secularization of religious heritage takes on several forms. The spreading phenomenon of crowdfunding[16] illustrates this tendency and reflects the appropriation of heritage beyond the circle of public authorities and heritage bodies. This popular dimension – in the noble sense of the term – singularly echoes remarks made regarding the adoption of the FARO Convention within the Council of Europe and according to which: 'Heritage atrophies in the absence of public involvement and public support. This is why heritage processes must move beyond the preoccupations of the experts in government ministries and the managers of public institutions, and include the different public who inhabit our cities, towns and villages' (Palmer 2009: 8).

In this regard, the impact of secularization on religious heritage should however be put in perspective. Indeed, belonging to cultural heritage results in the fulfillment of criteria defined by public – cultural – authorities vested with the responsibility of selecting which movable and immovable goods reflect local or national history and identity. Hence, the same authorities have still less the necessary resources to ensure conservation of selected goods. The increasing role played by private bodies and associations looking after monuments is likely to call into question the limits of officially or administratively defined cultural heritage in that they have an even greater capacity to raise the related funds. This is all the more true for religious heritage, which more than any other category of heritage shapes the landscape and is familiar to inhabitants leaving in the surroundings. The size of religious patrimony logically prevents cultural authorities from listing all goods, leaving a number of places of worship and their assets outside the regime and funding of protected monuments. Private trusts and, more often, associations will mobilize precisely – but not exclusively – to support those buildings that do not benefit from state support on cultural grounds. This is particularly true for small associations created for locally-driven projects and focusing on one single church building under threat. In this regard, the increasing role of private actors in granting

14 On this issue, see Ashworth and Larkham (2013: 2).

15 See the comparable debate which took place in Quebec in Lefebvre, Chapter 12 of this volume.

16 See Onnée and Renault (2013).

funds for cultural heritage calls into question the process of heritage selection and heritagization in general. Besides competent public authorities' implementation of legal criteria, private stakeholders – like associations – have decided to focus on other monuments which are valuable from their own perspective by funding their conservation. Alongside ways to raise funds, which clearly shows the emergence of non-religious stakeholders, there arises the question of the secularization of religious heritage when dealing with its use.

Is There a Future in Funding Religious Heritage?

This fairly provocative question can be explained by deeming that, as seen above, religious heritage, like cultural heritage in general, cannot be considered separately from the question of its use. In this regard, it appears that funding religious heritage comes down to two separate challenges, depending on whether it is still used for worship or not.

The twofold influence of secularization

History provides many examples of changes in use of places of worship (see, among others, Estonia, Denmark, the Netherlands and Turkey), be it only as the result of a change to the national religion. Modernity and the pressure on traditional usage of places of worship that it brings with it cannot be reduced to the perspective of an eventual absence of religion. One thinks here, for example, of Christian places of worship being transformed into mosques or Muslim places of prayer. However, the contemporary secularized context amounts to an in-depth evolution, with seemingly no going back, that is possibly leading to an abandonment of even the religious purpose of the building. Except perhaps for Turkey, all the countries studied in this volume face the same situation: financial crisis and severe decline in church attendance, resulting in an increasing number of deserted or redundant places of worship to maintain. The solution to this equation varies from one country to another. It should be noted at the outset that several countries' regulations establish a connection between funding and the use of listed places of worship, but without necessarily requiring it to be *religious* (Denmark, the United Kingdom,[17] the Netherlands,[18] Italy and Quebec[19]). It is either in relation to 'classical' cultural

---

17 In the United Kingdom, 'it is a specific requirement of the Heritage Lottery Fund's scheme of Repair Grants for Places of Worship that a recipient place of worship must subsequently be kept open for at least forty days outside normal service times' (Cranmer).

18 As regards the Netherlands, 'since 2013, grants for maintenance are only available if the owner, the religious community, provides a "Declaration of permanent use" (for six years) (Article 8-2, h, *SIM 2012*). This permanent use does not have to be a religious use' (Overbeeke).

19 It is worth noting that, under a change that came into effect in February 2014, the requirement of religious usage was suppressed and replaced by accessibility to the public as a criterion to apply for funding before the Quebec Council for Religious Heritage. The

uses, such as tourism, or in the prospect of supporting a re-allocation of redundant buildings (the Netherlands, the United Kingdom). The underlying intention is that usage means better material conservation.

The secularization process proves here to be tangible in that it might amount to the disappearance of religious use. Hence, the first challenge lies in the redundancy of an increasing number of church buildings. The second relates to churches that are still in use, but whose owner – public or private – can no longer face and afford the conservation and maintenance costs. In both situations, fundraising through non-religious usages and radical alterations is more and more frequent, but variously regulated according to the country.

Funding redundant religious buildings

Nearly all European countries must deal with a comparable combination of declining church attendance and decreasing public resources to satisfactorily maintain a common heritage, but each provides varying responses. In financial terms, religious owners might logically see in redundant church buildings heavy financial burdens, once the original use has disappeared.

The issue of reusing redundant, yet valuable, church buildings raises several specific questions. It deals first with the feasibility of projects to transform them, all places of worship being not suitable or easily convertible to other uses. Over a century ago, two statements illustrated the durability of the debate. During the parliamentary discussion preceding the passing of the French 1905 Act, MP Victor Augagneur argued that Catholic real estate was composed of so many places of worship belonging to public authorities and that it was of very low value. According to him, 'churches are usable for the purpose of worship only. One wanted to install museums in some of them: the most beautiful are Gothic churches, in which the lack of light will forbid forever the installation of any museum'.[20] Then, one can read in a Council of Europe report on *Financing the architectural heritage* that, while thinking about the selection of projects and activities eligible for financial assistance 'specific types of building can be given priority, such as religious or cultural buildings that are unlikely to have a beneficial economic use'.[21]

Once again, one observes national diversity. For example, an English body created years ago was even named accordingly, before changing its designation: the Churches Conservation Trust was formerly the Redundant Churches Fund. The Netherlands possesses a specific funding scheme aimed at supporting the re-allocation process. The Belgian context should be mentioned as well. The question of redundant church buildings is not regulated by law there, but has started to appear in courts: the financial parameter is likely to take precedence over the

press release announcing the change is available at: http://www.patrimoine-religieux.qc.ca/fichiers/FIC140214114350_2014_02_14_cprq_communique_budget_2013_2015.pdf (accessed 28 February 2014).

20 See Chapter 2 of this volume.

21 Pickard (2009: 79).

religious interest. No country has yet provided a global scheme dealing precisely with this issue. It will in any case require the involvement of religious authorities, not only because they are very often still the owners, but also because of the meaning of this heritage.

While undeniably providing a way to preserve buildings' architectural and historical qualities, reallocating former places of worship leads to more theoretical and symbolical questions: how should one deal with the meaning of such a change? Although more and more places of worship are no longer in use, and while only their valuable dimension as monuments remains, symbolically overcoming the hurdle does not always prove easy. Not all religious traditions easily accept such a fate for 'their' buildings. Moreover, the local population often feels attached to these buildings which it sees as places of family and personal memories. Sometimes, and although the change is agreed upon by religious authorities, opposition surprisingly comes from groups such as heritage associations, which fear that a planned transformation will not respect the heritage qualities of the monument. The change in use is not always welcomed positively and deserves global reflection.

The somewhat alarming and striking issue of the redundancy of church buildings should not, however, obscure the situation of religious heritage which is still in use for religious purpose and still represents the major part of heritage to be managed.

Funding 'living' religious heritage

The challenge lies here in fundraising through non-religious use(s), while religious practices still take place in the church building, against a backdrop of a declining religious community and its insufficient resources. In the case of religious heritage still used for religious purposes, income sources from cultural fundraising prove to be of minor – in some cases even insignificant – importance (Denmark, Estonia, France, Italy, Spain, the Netherlands) and/or to be more difficult to establish and exploit. Moreover, depending on how attractive religious monuments are to tourists, these resources are quite unevenly distributed among monuments, often being focused on major buildings like cathedrals.[22] The religious use can be legally protected and accordingly constitutes, if not an obstacle, at least a decisive factor, when the need arises to combine it with other uses likely to be sources of income (France, Italy, Spain). A more pragmatic approach combines religious and cultural uses by either alternating in time between both or by renting out premises that belong to the monument, which then become regularly available for non-religious events. Beyond their financial aspect, the advantage of such alternative uses stems from their influence over conservation: the more the building is open and frequented, the less it is subject to theft and vandalism and natural degradation.

22 On this topic, see the Recommendation 1484 (2000) adopted by the Parliamentary Assembly of the Council of Europe on 'Management of cathedrals and other major religious buildings in use'.

A religious, heritage or ... funding issue?

The role of religious authorities is critical in this debate in that not all religious traditions adopt the same position towards non-religious uses of church buildings. The challenge could lie precisely in the need to raise awareness of religious heritage value among religious groups. Faced with the challenge of less frequented buildings, religious authorities are more than ever being encouraged to take part and be involved in reflecting on how to best manage such assets in the future. It could be argued that it does not fall within the priority missions of churches to tackle heritage issues. It remains that they will increasingly face such a dilemma of taking a stand: the current trend lies in non-religious solutions to financial difficulties. This awareness-raising could be entrusted to public authorities, thus illustrating the part they – still – have to play, in that their role would evolve in its nature from financial to more managerial.[23] The secularization process results in an accentuated heritagization of religious heritage, which calls for a diversification of resources for its maintenance and conservation, but above all for coordination among stakeholders.

Finally, and without denying the financial difficulties and their influence on the conservation of religious heritage, it also proves that better protection and promotion of heritage is not entirely a matter of funding. The financial parameter combines with several other different elements ranging from the local/state, public/private level of heritage management to the understanding of religious heritage by religious groups themselves.

References

Ashworth, G. and Larkham, P. (eds) (2013), *Building a New Heritage* (London and New York: Routledge).

Committee on Culture and Education, Council of Europe (2000), *Cathedrals and other major religious buildings in Europe*, 27 September, document no. 8826.

Haynes, N. (2008), *Research report on church-state relationships in selected European countries*, Commissioned by the Historic Environment Advisory Council for Scotland (HEACS), available at: http://www.heacs.org.uk/documents/2009/church-state-relationships.pdf (accessed 3 March 2014).

Markiewicz, Ph. (2013), 'Églises: chefs-d'œuvre en péril?', *Arts sacrés*, 25, 24–61.

Onnée, S. and Renault, S. (2013), 'Le financement participatif: atouts, risques et conditions de succès', *Gestion*, 3: 38, 54–65.

23 Although sounding anecdotal, the example of the French *département* of the Orne is significant in this regard: while the local authorities could not afford to pay for the complete restoration of a church, it was decided, in connection with the Heritage Foundation and a local association, to start the programme of work with the restoration of a remarkable painting, so as to launch a synergy and attract donations. See Markiewicz (2013: 47).

Pickard, R. (2009), *Funding the Architectural Heritage: A Guide to Policies and Examples* (Strasbourg: Council of Europe Publishing).
Robbers, G. (ed.) (2005), *State and Church in the European Union* (Baden-Baden: Nomos).
Robbers, G. (2005), 'State and Church in the European Union', in Robbers, G. (ed.), 577–89.
Tsivolas, Th. (2014), *Law and Religious Cultural Heritage in Europe* (Springer).

Index

For Product Safety Concerns and Information please contact our EU representative GPSR@taylorandfrancis.com Taylor & Francis Verlag GmbH, Kaufingerstraße 24, 80331 München, Germany

Batch number: 10725973

Printed by Printforce, the Netherlands